F. R. Allchin, M.A., Ph.D., F.S.A., has been a lecturer in Indian studies at Cambridge University since 1959, and is a fellow of Churchill College. He was born in London in 1923 and served in India during the war. He has carried out several periods of field work in India, Pakistan and Afghanistan: in 1952 he excavated a neolithic settlement at Piklihal, now in Mysore; he excavated a neolithic cattle-pen at Utnur in Andhra Pradesh in 1957; and in 1963 he jointly led the Cambridge–Peshawar excavations at Shaikhan Dheri, Charsada. From 1954 to 1959 he was lecturer in Indian archaeology at the School of Oriental and African Studies in London. He is also the author of *Piklihal Excavations* (1960), *Utnur Excavations* (1961) and *Neolithic Cattle Keepers of South India* (1963). He has translated two volumes of Hindi seventeenth-century devotional poetry by Tulsi Das, *Kavitavali* (1964) and *The Petition to Ram* (1966).

Bridget Allchin, M.A., Ph.D., was born in Oxford in 1927 and educated in Great Britain. She read archaeology and anthropology at the University of Cape Town, was for some time a research student at the Institute of Archaeology, London, and is a fellow of University College, Cambridge. She has taught for the extra-mural departments of the Universities of London and Cambridge, and has travelled widely in India, Pakistan and Afghanistan. Her principal research and independent field work has been upon the Stone Age of India and Pakistan, and she has worked with her husband in excavations in both these countries. Bridget Allchin is the author of *The Stone Tipped Arrow* (1966), and of numerous papers on the earlier prehistory of the Indian sub-continent and other tropical regions of the Old World.

Bridget and Raymond Allchin were married in 1951 and have two children.

THE BIRTH OF
INDIAN CIVILIZATION

India and Pakistan before 500 B.C.

BRIDGET AND RAYMOND
ALLCHIN

PENGUIN BOOKS
BALTIMORE · MARYLAND

Penguin Books Ltd, Harmondsworth, Middlesex, England
Penguin Books Inc., 7110 Ambassador Road, Baltimore, Maryland 21207, U.S.A.
Penguin Books Australia Ltd, Ringwood, Victoria, Australia

—

First published 1968

—

Copyright © Bridget and Raymond Allchin, 1968

—

Made and printed in Great Britain
by Richard Clay (The Chaucer Press) Ltd,
Bungay, Suffolk
Set in Monotype Imprint

CONTENTS

6   *Contents*

LIST OF PLATES

LIST OF FIGURES

PREFACE

THIS book is a joint production and the authors claim joint responsibility for its contents throughout, both for anything that may be regarded as an original contribution and for any mistakes it may contain. The book seeks to present a digest of the results of a great body of research, much of it barely completed, as far as possible in terms of the data themselves as the authors see them. Within these confines we have necessarily had to exclude much discussion of the views of other scholars where they differ from our own, or where there are matters of wider controversy. We believe that the references for each chapter are fairly comprehensive and those who wish to discover such views may best do so by referring to the original publications. Indian prehistory and protohistory are still a relatively new field of study and inevitably some parts are more developed than others. This uneven development is inescapably reflected in the book as a whole: there are still so many gaps to be filled and questions to be answered. As a result some chapters can be presented in a more digested form than others. The recent spate of radiocarbon datings makes it possible to place some periods in a more or less independent framework, while for others even the sequence remains largely hypothetical, or at best circumstantial. One of the most vital gaps of this kind, which we hope may shortly be filled, is the absence of carbon datings for later Stone Age industries. This means that it is extremely difficult to assess the relationship between the first settled communities in any region and groups responsible for the Late Stone Age industries, whom we assume to have lived by hunting and collecting, with the possible addition of pastoralism, or even shifting agriculture.

In collecting the material for this book we are indebted to a great many people and institutions. First, there are all those whose published works we have used, or who have supplied us with as yet unpublished information, or who have in discussion contributed to the formation of our ideas. Second, there are those individuals and bodies who have assisted us in various ways, particularly in supplying illustrative material and in permitting us to use illustrations of which they hold the copyright. We are indebted to many individuals: to Sir Mortimer Wheeler for help and advice over many years; to officers of the Archaeological Survey of India for their continuous help and collaboration at every level from discussion of their recent discoveries to practical arrangements which enabled us to visit so many sites throughout the country. Among them we would like to thank particularly B. B. Lal, M. N. Deshpande, B. K. Thapar, S. R. Rao, R. V. Joshi, K. D. Banerji, J. P. Joshi, I. K. Sharma, K. S. Ramachandran, R. Gupta, and many more besides. We are likewise indebted to Harunur Rashid of the Pakistan Archaeological Department. We gratefully acknowledge the help and collaboration of Professor H. D. Sankalia and his colleagues of the Deccan College, Poona; D. P. Agrawal of the Tata Institute of Fundamental Research; Professor M. Seshadri of Mysore University; Dr T. C. Sharma of Gauhati University; Mr Farid Khan of Peshawar University; Professor W. Fairservis of Washington University; Dr George Dales of Pennsylvania University; M. J.-M. Casal of the French Mission Archéologique de l'Indus; Miss Beatrice de Cardi of the Council for British Archaeology; Mr J. Kinnier-Wilson of Cambridge University, and Mr A. C. Pal. We also gratefully acknowledge the kindness and help of Shri S. P. Gupta of the National Museum, New Delhi. A special acknowledgement is due to Dr Nagaraja Rao of the Karnatak University, who has not only contributed unpublished research material of his own, but has also read the manuscript and made many valuable suggestions. The book owes a great deal to the active participation and criticism of all our students in Cambridge during the time it was being written and particularly to Dr S. Settar and Mr B. Chattopadhyaya for their assistance in making the index.

Perhaps our greatest debt in all respects is to the Archaeological Survey of India. They have supplied us with many of our photographs and allowed us to reproduce numerous drawings from their publications. We are also indebted to the Archaeological Department of Pakistan. Among other bodies who have helped us are: the Archaeological Departments of the State Governments of Andhra Pradesh, Rajasthan and

Bihar; the Indian National Museum, New Delhi; National Museum of Pakistan, Karachi; the British Museum; the Musée Guimet, Paris; Government Museum, Madras; Museum of Archaeology and Ethnology, Cambridge; the University Museum, Pennsylvania; the Deccan College, Poona; University of Peshawar; Délégation Archéologique Française en Afghanistan; and the Mission Archéologique de l'Indus. Thames and Hudson have been kind enough to supply us with previously published photographs and drawings from their archives. For permission to use illustrations previously published we are grateful to the editors of the *Journal of the Royal Anthropological Institute; Man; Bulletin of the Institute of Archaeology*, London; *Bulletin of the School of Oriental and African Studies*, London; and *Antiquity*.

Finally we gratefully acknowledge a Leverhulme research award which contributed to a visit to India and Pakistan for the purpose of collecting materials for this book.

CHAPTER I

INTRODUCTION

THE civilization of India – that is to say of the area now comprising the modern states of India, Pakistan, Ceylon and Nepal – presents to the outside observer – be he casual or serious – a number of perplexing contrasts and problems. For example, there is on the one hand a sense of overriding unity throughout the whole sweep of her history, and on the other there is a baffling degree of local and regional variation. The conception of the unity and therefore the distinctness of Indian civilization has long been recognized by outsiders, and has become a commonplace . in European thought; indeed it is implicit in the stereotypes which have been handed down since the times of Alexander the Great. The past century and a half have witnessed a remarkable rediscovery of ancient India, and it is now possible to examine such concepts in the light of the evidence afforded not only by modern observation of all kinds, but also by history and archaeology: our purpose in writing this book is to examine the archaeological evidence for the prehistoric period.

The rediscovery of ancient India was in origin almost entirely European, indeed to a large extent British. It began from the early days of European exploration and colonization, and reached its first coherent form in the programme of research laid before the Asiatic Society of Bengal by Sir William Jones in the last decades of the eighteenth century. Not surprisingly the earliest attention was centred upon Sanskrit and its ancient literature, and upon the reading of the largely forgotten scripts. To James Prinsep goes the credit for reading the earliest of these, the Brahmi script of the time of Asoka, and for the inception of the study of Indian numismatics. From such researches it became possible for Christian Lassen, in 1847, to publish the first edition of his *Indische Alterthumskunde* (*Indian Antiquity*), attempting to bring together whatever information had been thus far gleaned about Indian history and civilization.

During the first decades of the nineteenth century the record-ing of monuments had begun, and these records led up to James Fergusson's successive studies of Indian architecture. The discovery and publication of accounts of prehistoric re-mains also began in the first decades of the nineteenth century. Among the first to receive attention were the megalithic graves of the peninsula, stray hoards of bronze weapons from the Ganges–Jamuna Doab, and the ash-mounds of Mysore. The first recorded find of stone implements was in 1842, when a certain Dr Primrose discovered a 'bagful' of stone knives and arrow-heads during the clearing of his garden in the Raichur district, but it was eleven years later that John Evans published the first account of worked flints discovered on the Narbada river near Jabalpur.

The second half of the nineteenth century witnessed notable advances. In 1861 Major General Alexander Cunningham, at the age of forty-seven, retired from the army to become the first Surveyor General of the Archaeological Survey. During the next two decades his unflagging energy led him to explore hundreds of sites throughout North India from the frontiers of Afghanistan to Bengal. Among those which he discovered was the city of Harappa, and he published a plate of illustra-tions of stone blades and a typical seal inscribed in the un-known Harappan script. He visited site after site, recording plans of ancient cities, monuments of all kinds, inscriptions and other noteworthy discoveries, and he produced apart from the voluminous reports of his tours a number of special volumes on ancient geography, numismatics, etc. The work of Cunningham was largely in the field of historic archaeology, but the foundations he laid contributed to the later develop-ment of the Archaeological Survey of India.

In prehistory two other names stand out from this time. The first is Colonel Meadows Taylor who during the fifties carried out and published a number of outstanding excavations of megalithic graves in Hyderabad. The excellence of his excava-tion technique was perhaps outstanding in any country at that date. The other is the geologist Robert Bruce Foote, who has rightly been called the father of Indian prehistory. During the sixties, seventies and eighties he worked unceasingly in the

field, and wherever his geological duties took him, he discovered archaeological treasure in the shape of Stone Age
remains. In 1949 it was still true to say that almost every important prehistoric site in peninsular India owed its discovery
to him. During the past decade Indian archaeologists have
celebrated the centenaries of two great events: the foundation
of the Archaeological Survey, and the discovery by Bruce
Foote in 1863 of the first Indian Palaeolithic artifact from
lateritic deposits near Madras.

We pass rapidly over the next decades. In 1901 the Archaeological Survey was reconstituted under the direction of Sir
John Marshall, as a many-sided Government Department,
equally concerned (in Curzon's striking words) 'to dig and to
discover, to classify, reproduce and describe, and to cherish
and conserve'. Marshall instituted a new series of Annual
Reports, and an impressive series of excavations of historical
sites, culminating in his work at Sarnath, Taxila and Sanchi.
He filled the museums with the sculptures and other antiquities he discovered, and organized the first consistent work
of conservation of the principal monuments of all parts of the
country. Without doubt he may be said to have achieved
Curzon's aims, but he did so with one notable exception, for
apart from the excavations of Mohenjo-daro, Harappa and
Chanhu-daro, during the years preceding 1945 the Archaeological Survey almost totally neglected exploration and research
in prehistory and protohistory. What work was accomplished
in this field was largely done by outsiders and amateurs.
During this time however great advances were made in our
knowledge of the Early Historic period and of Indian art and
architecture. The excavations of the Indus valley cities are
monuments of large-scale work, and anyone reading this book
will realize how much we still owe to Sir John Marshall and
his collaborators, but the Indus cities stood in isolation until
1945, and a great hiatus intervened between them and the
civilization of the Ganges valley from the third century B.C.
onwards. Moreover, in spite or perhaps because of their
enormous scale, the excavations lacked precision, and to a large
extent were undertaken without the framing of clear-cut
objectives. Hence when they failed to answer such outstanding

questions as those of chronology or sequence, it was all too
often because such problems had not been clearly posed at the
outset of the work.

Two events of the 1930s stand out in terms of prehistoric
research: in 1930 Mr M. C. Burkitt of Cambridge University
published an account of the collections of a magistrate, L. A.
Cammiade, from the Krishna basin, and in 1935 Professors
H. De Terra and T. T. Paterson led the Yale–Cambridge
Expedition to study the glacial sequence of Kashmir and the
Punjab and to relate their findings to the prehistoric industries
of the Punjab, the Narbada and Madras. One other development of Sir John Marshall's term of office deserves mention:
it witnessed the first appointments of Indians to positions
of responsibility in the Survey. Notable among those thus
appointed were R. D. Banerji, to whom goes the honour of the
first discovery of Mohenjo-daro, Pandit M. S. Vats, the excavator of Harappa and Mohenjo-daro, Daya Ram Sahni, the
first Indian to become Director General of Archaeology, and
N. G. Majumdar, the first excavator of Amri. Another man
who contributed greatly to our knowledge of Indian prehistory
during these decades was Sir Aurel Stein, whose continuing
expeditions led him to Baluchistan and eastern Iran, the
Punjab and the North West Frontier Province, no less than to
the more remote regions of central Asia.

The last years of British rule in India coincided with a
revolution in her archaeology, produced by the dynamic personality of Sir Mortimer Wheeler. The results of this revolution are still being experienced. Basically the most important
innovations introduced by Wheeler were the reorganization of
the excavations branch, and his insistence that research was
henceforward to be linked with intelligent planning. In a
stirring address delivered to the Anthropology and Archaeology
section of the Indian Science Congress in 1946, he set out
the need for organized and coordinated planning, and for the
selection of clear-cut objectives for research. He also envisaged
the need to bring in scientific and specialized techniques to
broaden the scope of India's archaeology. He set about training
a body of younger field archaeologists to execute the work. By
and large the achievement of this new planning has been the

extension, period by period and region by region, of our knowledge of the entire prehistoric culture sequence of the subcontinent, and there can be no argument as to where the credit for initiating this campaign lies.

Another symptom of the new approach to India's past was the publication in 1950 of Professor Stuart Piggott's *Prehistoric India*. Here an archaeologist set out to produce a critical survey of the whole range of Indian prehistory, in terms of the actual Indian evidence, but in the light of archaeological methods current in western Europe. If the resulting volume is compared with Panchanan Mitra's pioneering book of the same name, published a quarter of a century earlier, the fundamental reorientation which it involved will become clear. Less than twenty years have passed since Piggott's *Prehistoric India* first appeared. It remains a notable milestone in its field, still unsurpassed in its treatment of the prehistory of Baluchistan especially. During the intervening years the picture of the whole subcontinent has changed out of all recognition, and whole regions which were then almost blank have now come into clearer focus. This indeed is the main reason for the present work, which does not aim to supplant, but rather to extend the scope of the former.

The partition of India and Pakistan in 1947 and the independence of Ceylon found the three countries in a very different state, so far as archaeology was concerned. Since that time little research has been done on any aspect of prehistory in Ceylon excepting the work of Dr P. E. P. Deraniyagala. The old Archaeological Survey of India was divided into two parts. The newly formed Pakistan Archaeological Department has carried out excavations at Mohenjo-daro and Kot Diji, as well as a number of historical sites, and in recent years has begun to publish a journal, *Pakistan Archaeology*. In the same period a number of American, French, Italian and British teams have worked in Pakistan and made useful contributions. Peshawar University has lately inaugurated Pakistan's first teaching department of archaeology, which has already been responsible for a number of important researches in the former North West Frontier Province. In India the Archaeological Survey has carried out a most impressive series of excavations and other research activities in almost every State, including excavations at such sites as Lothal, Kalibangan and Hastinapur, and has published two series of reports in *Ancient India* and *Indian Archaeology — a Review*. Several of the Indian State governments also have Archaeological Departments of their own. Further, many universities have appointed archaeologists and some, foremost among them the Deccan College, Poona, have large, well-equipped teaching departments of archaeology, and many published excavations to their credit. The Archaeological Survey of India has also set up a School of Archaeology in Delhi. For the coordination of the work of all these diverse bodies and growing numbers of active fieldworkers, the Indian Archaeological Survey has instituted a Central Advisory Board whose annual meetings coincide with a symposium on the results of the preceding year. This body has already shown its usefulness in checking the progress of research programmes and directing attention to current problems. Archaeology in the Indian subcontinent formerly suffered particularly from the paucity of historical chronology or dating points, and the development of the radiocarbon dating technique has therefore been of peculiar importance. The establishment of a radiocarbon-dating laboratory in the Tata Institute of Fundamental Research in Bombay, and the periodical list of dates which the laboratory produces, are therefore among the prime factors enabling us in 1966 to reach a more definite chronological framework for the prehistory of South Asia.

As a result of the growing tempo of discovery, there is an obvious need for books which provide a general picture of Indian prehistoric cultures. The difficulty in writing a book of this kind, which aims to give both a general, overall picture, and also some account of the factual basis from which it is derived, is one of selection and compression. The writer must try to stand back sufficiently far to be able to see the whole wood, but not so far that he cannot distinguish the individual trees. To achieve its aim, such a book must never remain too long in the airy realms of interpretation, important as they may be, but must for ever come back to earth to examine a stone flake, a potsherd or a section of stratified soil. Another difficulty is to keep pace with the current rate of discoveries. The ultimate object of archaeological research must be to reconstruct as fully as possible the cultural development of the past. But this cultural interpretation only becomes possible as and when a sufficient volume of information is available to establish chronological and sequential relationships between sites and regions. The prehistory of India and Pakistan is still at a stage where this is only partly possible: for some areas and cultures a reasonably complete picture can be obtained, but for others we have almost no evidence, or no more than a sketchy outline of the culture sequence which we cannot as yet interpret in human terms. The comparative novelty of this new pattern of research in the Indian subcontinent means moreover that the problems with which we shall be dealing are still at an early stage, and that some of the refinements of technique and interpretation long familiar in western Asia, Europe or America are scarcely appropriate as yet. We do not mean to cast doubt on the value of such new techniques, but rather to point to the need for keeping their importance in perspective at the present stage of research. The plan which we have adopted in this situation, therefore, is to divide the book into two parts. The first (Chapters 2 to 8) gives an outline of the culture sequence of the subcontinent, as far as it is known, region by region. In the second part (Chapters 9 to 12) we attempt to give an account of certain aspects of ancient cultures in so far as the present archaeological record permits.

In the first part of the book, our method is broadly as follows. The size and diversity of the subcontinent makes it necessary to establish the basic geographical regions. As our knowledge advances it becomes increasingly clear that each region is distinct, and that only by first establishing the cultural history of each can inter-regional relationships be understood. Some grasp of the physical and human geography of the subcontinent is thus an essential prerequisite for any understanding of its archaeological past, and the basic division of our material is therefore given in terms of geographical regions. The recognition of the importance of the regional framework was first suggested by F. J. Richards, but was only worked out on a continental basis by the late Professor

Subbarao, who used it with increasing success in the two editions of his *Personality of India* (1956 and 1958). His untimely death robbed India of one of her most promising younger archaeologists.

So many excavations have been made, in many regions, that it is now possible – at least for the Neolithic and later periods – to base the regional sequences entirely upon them. Here, too, one is struck by the enormous advances that have been made since Piggott wrote. We have, as far as possible, relied upon excavations throughout, and only been forced to fall back upon other methods of establishing sequences when this sort of evidence is not yet available. Again, to establish a chronological framework, Piggott had to rely upon cross-datings often over very great distances to the sites of Mesopotamia or Iran, which were often themselves imprecisely dated by similar means. We have been able to employ the new fund of radiocarbon dates from both India and Pakistan to provide an absolute chronology, and thus to have a scale of dating undreamt of twenty years ago. It goes without saying that runs of dates from single sites are more likely to give accurate information than unique dates. We have unashamedly ignored dates which stand out of such runs as out of place, and also dates or even runs of dates which give consistently meaningless results: happily such dates are not common, and in some instances they seem to reflect the unreliability of the excavation rather than the fallibility of the method. The dates we have used have all been published, either in the annual volumes of *Radiocarbon*, or in the preliminary notes of the radiocarbon laboratory at the Tata Institute. We have found, in common with others, that for our purposes, for determination of later prehistoric dates, the calculation according to the half-life of radiocarbon of 5730 ± 40 years gives better results than the previously used half-life of 5568 ± 30 years. We have thus used the former throughout. Also we have in general not quoted the ± principle of error, but only the central date. The principle of error and the calculation according to both half-lives are however listed in the select list on pages 333–8. It follows that we have needed to place relatively less reliance upon cross-datings to establish chronology, and we have mainly used comparisons of this kind over only relatively short distances and within single cultural regions, where they may be employed with reasonable confidence. We have, however, also indicated certain of the more remote cross-datings when they appear relevant or of interest. In the several comparative sequence charts we have indicated divisions between periods with a firm line when they are related to radiocarbon datings, and with a dotted line in other cases.

In recent years there has been a certain amount of discussion of the terms which may most fittingly be used for the prehistory of India and Pakistan. Although it may be argued that such discussion becomes all too soon mere verbalism, we have been faced with a number of difficult choices, and hence we wish to explain the terms we have adopted. *Protohistoric* has often been used in two main senses: either to describe the Harappan civilization for which written records are available, even though not yet deciphered, or to describe the mainly post-Harappan cultures and periods about which certain inferences may be made on the basis of texts handed down orally, or only written at a much later date. We admit the value of both these usages, but we have not altogether followed them. We have treated the *Historic* period as beginning only when written documents or records of an historical character become available in any region: strictly this is to say that it begins in many regions with the edicts of Asoka in the third century B.C., but there is a body of near-historical material in for example the early Buddhist scriptures, for parts of north India from the time of the Buddha (*c.* 500 B.C.), and the Historic period may be extended back in such areas to about that time. We have called all cultures which precede the Historic period *Prehistoric*. This does not imply any disrespect for their levels of cultural achievement, but simply that they demand our attention as archaeologists rather than as historians. When, as happens in the Punjab, the Ganges–Jamuna Doab, and even the Central Ganges region, there is a growing certainty of the archaeological cultures to which the Rigveda or later Vedic literature originally belonged, we accept the relevance of the term *Protohistoric*.

With regard to the Stone Age, agreement was reached at the

Congress of Asian Archaeology in New Delhi in 1961 that in the existing state of knowledge the most satisfactory terms were *Early*, *Middle* and *Late Stone Age*. These were used to refer to the three major groups of stone industries recognized in the Indian subcontinent: the hand-axe industries; the flake industries which corresponds in very general terms to the Levallois–Mousterian industries of Europe and western Asia; and the various microlith-using hunting cultures. The last group corresponds, again very generally, to the Mesolithic of Europe and the Mediterranean. Thus in India there is no major phase corresponding to the Upper Palaeolithic blade and burin industries of Europe and western Asia. In this respect the main industrial groupings seen in India resemble those of sub-Saharan Africa: conversely one might say that, seen from a south Asian standpoint, the blade and burin industries are a specialized feature of temperate Europe and western Asia at the end of the Ice Age. This does not of course preclude the possibility that occasional blade and burin industries may be found in India, contemporary with the later flake industries, as they have been in East Africa and the Caspian region. The value of the terminology agreed in 1961 is that it rightly stresses in broad terms the threefold sequence of stone industries: this is of greater importance than the actual terms used. The terms Early and Middle Palaeolithic and Mesolithic, although they have often been used, and are readily understandable in our context, none the less carry strong European overtones, which can be misleading in themselves, and moreover carry the verbal implication that Upper Palaeolithic industries should follow those of the Middle Palaeolithic as a major cultural phase.

There has also been extensive discussion of the way in which the terms *Neolithic* and *Chalcolithic* are to be used in south Asia. In our view they largely overlap and therefore we have frequently used them in combination. However, the present data suggest that in Baluchistan, the southern Deccan and perhaps also Kashmir, at any rate, there is a period during which settled life, animal husbandry, and some form of cultivation, depended solely upon the use of stone, and these may thus be said to constitute primary Neolithic phases.

Equally there is a subsequent phase, beginning in Baluchistan and spreading through the subcontinent, in which copper and at a surprisingly early date, bronze, augment stone. This we may call Chalcolithic. In the south for instance the quantities of metal are very often small and stone still predominates, and it is a moot point – and not of very serious significance – whether we describe such cultures as Neolithic or Chalcolithic.

The quantity, importance and technological significance of bronze has never been on anything like the scale seen in the Bronze Age of Europe and many parts of Asia, and therefore we have rarely used this term. The terms Harappan, pre-Harappan and post-Harappan are used in two related senses, more narrowly for the culture of the Indus civilization and for that which preceded or succeeded it, and chronologically to designate periods corresponding to these over a wider area. Iron Age is used basically as a technological term and in no way coincides or conflicts with the boundaries between history and prehistory.

CHAPTER 2

GEOGRAPHICAL AND HUMAN
BACKGROUND

BOTH the fundamental unity and the internal diversity of Indian culture accurately reflect her geographical situation. India is unique and distinct from other great cultural entities of the world in the same sense that Europe or China are unique and distinct. In all cases the frontiers between spheres of influence created by such major centres shift from time to time, and tend to be continually blurred. India's cultural frontiers have proved to be remarkably constant and closely defined, partly no doubt because her physical frontiers are correspondingly clearly marked. To the south, south-east and south-west she is effectively contained by wide expanses of ocean which, although they have sometimes facilitated trade, have always tended to isolate her culturally. To the north-west, north and north-east, massive mountain ranges, including many of the highest mountains in the world, divide her dramatically from the rest of Asia. Not only have they always prevented the easy passage of traders and travellers and acted as barriers to human contact generally, but they also screen India from the arctic winds and air currents of central Asia. As a result the climate of almost the entire subcontinent, even where it lies technically outside the tropics, is hot and dependent upon a monsoon cycle of seasonal rainfall, which is chiefly precipitated during the hotter months of the year. These northern mountains therefore form not only cultural frontiers but also a series of major climatic frontiers. Within the subcontinent itself almost every type of tropical or near-tropical climate can be found, ranging from the arid expanses of the Thar desert to the dense forests of the Eastern and Western Ghats.

The Indian subcontinent is comparable in size to western Europe, but it is more decisively isolated from the rest of the world and not quite so clearly divided within. Throughout it is still predominantly agricultural and the density of its rural population is very great; it is comparable only to that of China or Java. The population of India and Pakistan together in 1951 (1951 census) was reckoned to be 433 million and is by now considerably greater. The actual density ranges from six persons per square mile in Baluchistan to well over a thousand in Kerala, on the south-west coast, where it sometimes rises over small areas to anything between two and four thousand. In the past the pendulum has swung from more or less complete continental unity to the local autonomy of regions or groups of regions. Within India separate nationalities have never developed with the same intensity as they have within Europe, but on the other hand overall unity and centralization have not been as strong as they have in China.

Over a large part of India all traces of the original vegetation cover have been lost, due to anything up to several millennia of human activity, and one can only speculate as to what this cover may formerly have been. But the soils and the topography vary widely, and this, together with variations of climate and especially of rainfall, creates a number of different regions each with a distinct character of its own. Such regional and local character is partly natural and partly man-made as it must be in a densely populated country. In some cases the dominant features of a region are natural, such as high mountains, or extremes of climate: in others they are the result of human interference, the whole aspect of the landscape being created by a system of irrigation, or by the allocation of large areas to the cultivation of certain crops. For instance paddy fields, meticulously levelled, terraced and irrigated, and changing colour from the dark brown of wet earth to the vivid green of young rice, and then to pale gold as the crop ripens, form almost the entire landscape of some of the most fertile parts of India, such as Bengal or the Tamil plain. Tea estates have transformed the hillsides of large areas of Assam and Ceylon. The vale of Peshawar, although it is surrounded by spectacular ranges of mountains, of which one is always aware, presents an almost totally man-made landscape of villages, cultivated fields, irrigation channels, gardens and plantations across the whole extent of its alluvial floor. Virtually the only uncultivated areas are graveyards, and ancient settlements marked by mounds of mud-brick and other debris. Today the wide plains of the Punjab and the Ganges valley and the Deccan plateau also derive their character from patterns of human settlement and agriculture, as indeed they must have done for a very long time past. Only in the foothills of the Himalayas, and in other major mountain ranges, in the deserts, in parts of the Eastern and Western Ghats, and in the wilder regions of Central India does some natural vegetation survive; and only in such places do natural features contribute directly to the character of a region or a locality.

The structure of the subcontinent as a whole is the basis from which all regional distinctions spring. It depends upon the interrelationship of the peninsula, a stable and extremely ancient land-mass, with the young folded mountains which form the northern frontiers. These mountains are considered by many authorities to be still in process of active formation, and weathering and erosion are certainly taking place at great speed. As a result the mountain zone is far from stable and vast quantities of alluvium are continually being carried down into the plains. These plains have formed in two great river basins, that of the Indus and that of the Ganges, one flowing to the south-west and the other to the east. Both are potentially extremely fertile, and both are subject to flooding and to periodic changes in the course of their rivers. The Indus basin also appears to have been subject to minor tectonic movements even in recent historic times; and the Ganges trough is thought to be still sinking as a result of the upward thrust of the Himalayas.

The great block of Archean rocks which are the skeleton of peninsular India and Ceylon have also undergone certain disturbances, on a lesser scale, from time to time, but for the most part the peninsula shows every sign of stability. Mature, graded rivers flow across it, and much of its plateau surface consists of ancient peneplains. Central India, the northern edge of the block, is an area of hills and broken country, which divides the two great riverine plains from the plateau to the south and also partially divides them from each other. It consists of deep valleys and ranges of steep hills and escarpments, running generally from east to west, which are wild and inaccessible but of no great height. The plateau itself slopes gently from west to east; on the west it ends abruptly with the escarpment of the Western Ghats, which falls away to the narrow coastal plain and the sea. On the east the Eastern Ghats consist of a rather irregular series of ranges of hills which separate the plateau from the somewhat wider eastern coastal plain. The Nilgiris, the Cardamom Hills and the island of Ceylon are all outlying blocks of the same Archean rocks, which form the main body of peninsular India.

From one point of view the young folded mountains of the north-west, north and north-east may be said to form a single major zone, but the variation in rainfall, from the west, where it is very low – parts of Baluchistan receive less than ten inches per year – to the east, where it is as high as 120 inches and more in Nepal and Assam, is so great that this alone divides it into a number of minor zones. It could also be divided into a series of narrow bands running roughly east–west according to the height and nature of the mountains. Due to successive phases of folding and uplift of the Himalayas the whole region is extremely complicated geologically. Rivers which were formerly part of one system have been captured, and now form part of a completely different system. Over large areas the entire drainage pattern has been changed or even completely reversed since tertiary times. The instability of the mountain zones in recent geological times also means that each valley tends to have unique features. This is often caused by the local formation of a barrier, due to landslides or tectonic movements, and its subsequent breaking down, followed by down-cutting and the regrading of the course of the river. In human terms such mountainous country lends itself to the development of many small distinct communities, each valley being a micro-region, both in geographical and in human terms, whose inhabitants form a largely self-contained economic and cultural entity (Figure 1).

For our purposes it would be pointless to try to enumerate different regions according to any of these systems: it is sufficient to divide the northern mountains into three major regions, western, central and eastern. The eastern mountain region consists of those mountains which lie to the east of the

Brahmaputra, and along the summit of which runs the frontier between India and Burma. They are the first of a series of ranges which run from north to south and extend from Assam to south China. They are divided by a corresponding series of deep river valleys and covered for the most part with thick forest. Much of the area has a high rainfall, and the

Figure 1. Map of the cultural regions of India and Pakistan

population is concentrated in the valleys. Although India has obviously been subject to a certain amount of influence from Southeast Asia and south China both in prehistoric and in historic times, the routes through the eastern mountains are difficult, as the Burma campaign during the last war showed, and few major conquests or movements of people into India appear to have taken place from this direction.

The central Himalayan region, which extends from Bhutan to Chitral, differs from the mountains of both the east and the west because behind it lies the great tableland of Tibet, cold, inhospitable and thinly populated. Trade contacts have long been kept up between India and Tibet but no major formative influences can be said to have come into India across this formidable frontier. In Bhutan and eastern Nepal the rainfall is as high and the forests as thick as in the eastern mountain region, but by the time one has travelled a thousand miles north-westward to Swat and Chitral the rainfall is much lower. The valley floors are fertile and intensely cultivated with the aid of irrigation from the perennial snow-fed rivers, and their sides are covered with small bushy plants and grasses, and occasional groups of trees which often extend to the tops of the mountain ridges.

Following the mountains south-westwards from here into the former North West Frontier Province (the ancient Gand-hara), their slopes soon become almost completely bare. In this, the western mountain region, the valley floors are still irrigated and cultivated wherever possible, but they look like oases in a rocky desert. The mountains which enclose them are stark and bare and their slopes often consist of nothing but rock and scree. The desert conditions become more intense as one moves south-west into Baluchistan. But along these valleys and over the passes in these inhospitable mountains run the routes to central Asia and China on the one hand and to Persia and the west on the other. They have been trade routes throughout historic times and long before, and this is the way that invaders have many times poured into India. With trade and military conquest, great numbers of people and all kinds of external influences have also come. From the archaeologist's point of view, therefore, the western mountain region is by far the most interesting and most important part of the mountain zone.

Among the great routes from Iran into the plains of India we may notice the Gomal pass leading down from northern Baluchistan, the Bolan pass leading down from the fertile region of Kandahar (the ancient Arachosia) and the Quetta valley, the Kurram river and the Khyber pass leading from Kabul to the north, and the routes of southern Baluchistan through the valleys of such rivers as the Kej and the Dasht. The passes from the western mountains come down into the great plains of the Indus basin, and these in turn fall naturally into two regions or provinces, Sind and the Punjab. Sind consists of the lower Indus valley and the delta. It is contained between the mountains of Baluchistan on the north-west and the Thar desert on the south-east. The rainfall is low, as in Baluchistan, but the alluvial soil is potentially fertile. The Indus barrage at Sukkur (more correctly Sakhar), below the confluence of the major tributaries of the Indus, was completed in 1932 and provides perennial irrigation over a very wide area. When the canal system is fully complete it is estimated that it will irrigate five and a half million acres. Sind on the whole is a highly productive province, producing a considerable surplus of rice and wheat, but it is subject to extremes of temperature, and to the inroads of dust and sand from its desert surroundings. The Punjab, literally 'the land of the five rivers', has a rather different character. The five rivers, the main tributaries of the Indus, flow across a vast alluvial plain from their sources in the Himalayas, carrying water both from the melting snows and from the monsoon rains. Like Sind, the southern Punjab is contained between the western mountains and the desert, and the northern Punjab abuts upon the foothills of the main Himalayan ranges. On the east the plains of the central Punjab merge almost imperceptibly into those of the Upper Ganges basin. Thus the central Punjab has often served as a highway between the Kabul valley, one of the most important means of entry into India from the north-west, and the even more fertile plains of the Ganges–Jamuna Doab (literally 'two rivers'). Irrigation has added greatly to the agricultural wealth of the Punjab in recent centuries.

With the exception of the northern Punjab, which enjoys a higher rainfall than the rest of the Indus plains, the greater part of both Sind and the Punjab had a population density of less than a hundred to the square mile in the 1941 census. Due to irrigation, this has been increasing steadily, in spite of the devastation and the great loss of human life caused by the partition of India and Pakistan in 1947. This is the region

which produced the Harappan culture during the third millennium B.C. Its two major cities of this period, Harappa and
Mohenjo-daro, are of no mean dimensions, and this shows that
the surrounding country must even then have produced enough
food to support their inhabitants not only in a good year, but
even in a bad one. It has been suggested that this was made
possible by a slightly higher rainfall than today, but even if
this were so, it seems unlikely that it was ever possible to
support such large communities without some system of
irrigation, either by simple inundation, or by some other
method, whose traces are still undiscovered. Lambrick has
recently pointed out that the population of one of these ancient
cities was probably not more than 35,000, equivalent to that
of a town the size of Shikarpur a century ago. Irrigation by
simple inundation, in climatic conditions like those of today,
could have supported such a population, given an effective
system of organization.

The climate of the Ganges basin is decidedly more humid
than that of the Indus, and the rainfall increases steadily as
one moves from west to east, rising from about 20 inches per
annum in the Indo-Gangetic divide to well over 80 inches in
Bengal. Today this is one of the most heavily populated rural
areas in the world. The population is over 1,000 to the square
mile in places and rarely less than 500. The Ganges plains fall
into three regions. In the west is the Doab of the Ganges and
Jamuna rivers, extending from Delhi to Allahabad and corresponding approximately to the state of Uttar Pradesh. The
Central region corresponds approximately to the state of Bihar
with part of eastern Uttar Pradesh. These two regions lie
between the Himalayas on the north and the Central Indian
hills on the south. The Eastern region consists of the Ganges–
Brahmaputra delta and its hinterland – Bengal. The first two
regions have supported city life and been centres of the trade
and culture of north India since the time of the Buddha (sixth
century B.C.) and probably considerably earlier. Evidence for
the extension of the Harappan culture into the western Ganges
basin is only now beginning to emerge. Archaeological finds
however do suggest that settlement and city life began in the
western and central regions and later spread to Bengal. This

is what one would expect, as the low-lying plains of Bengal with their high rainfall must originally have consisted of forests and marshes, which would have needed a considerable labour force, equipped with effective tools, to bring them under cultivation. The fertility of the alluvial soil, which now supports such a large population, must have made these areas more difficult to clear in the first place. The situation is probably analogous to that found in many parts of Europe where heavier and richer soils could not be, or were not, utilized until well into the Iron Age. Today the density of the population of the Ganges valley and the close proximity of villages to one another is almost oppressive, and already by the fifth century the poet Kālidās spoke of villages as 'a cock's flight' apart.

Passing from the plains up the first escarpment of the Vindhya hills one moves into a different world. Central India consists of a wide, flattened triangle of hilly country. The hills are nowhere very high, but they are steep and broken, with many escarpments and intersected by precipitous valleys. The ranges of hills tend to run in an east–west direction, except for the north-western extension of Central India, where the Aravalli hills run from south-west to north-east. These and certain other features are the result of earlier movements than those that formed the Himalayas, but some features are thought to be due to the secondary effects of the earlier phases of Himalayan folding. Due to its inaccessibility, and also to the relatively low fertility of much of its soil, Central India has been until very recently, and to a considerable extent still is, the resort of people who represent ancient ethnic elements in the Indian population, and also preserve archaic ways of life. These communities usually include certain later elements also, for in times of stress people from the more sought-after plains have found refuge with the 'tribal' people of the hills and have generally been absorbed by them. The hill tribes have also been subject to influences from adjoining regions from which traders and officials have come, and to which they go out as labourers. The Bhils of western Central India, for example, reflect the influence of several more advanced regions. The north-western Bhil groups, whose land adjoins Rajasthan, reflect its influence in their dress and in many other details of everyday life, while those farther south reflect the dress and customs of their Marathi neighbours.

Central India is crossed by a number of routes, which link the more advanced regions surrounding it. Along these routes are settlement sites and small enclaves of village agriculture, many of which, like Tripuri on the Narbada near Jabalpur, go back to Chalcolithic times. The Malwa plateau lies in the angle between the Aravalli hills and those of Central India proper. Today part of the plateau is included in the state of Rajasthan. Settlements of the Chalcolithic period have been found widely distributed there, and it must be regarded as a separate subregion. Its position also means that it must have played an important part in the interrelationship of the Harappan culture with the Chalcolithic cultures of other regions, both to the south and east. On the east the Chattisgarh plain is another minor region contained within the forest belt of Central India. It consists of the fertile basin of the upper Mahanadi. The plain, which is surrounded by broken forest country, is almost entirely covered with paddy fields. It has a rainfall of 55 inches per annum, augmented by canal and well irrigation, and until the Maratha conquests in the eighteenth century it was an independent Gond kingdom.

Gujarat, lying at the western end of the Central Indian belt of hills, is another region of ancient settlement, and is rich in sites of every period from the Harappan onwards. It has always had considerable agricultural wealth, and today this is augmented by textile and other industries. It is centred upon the Gulf of Cambay, and consists of a low-lying plain which is enriched by the alluvium brought down from the hills of Central India by four great rivers, the Sabarmati, the Mahi, the Narbada (ancient Narmada) and the Tapti (correctly Tapi), together with the two peninsulas of Cutch (Kacch) and Kathiawar. Unlike the rivers which rise in the Himalayas, and carry a great deal of water derived from the melting snow in spring as well as that of the summer rains, the rivers of Central India and the peninsula carry only the water of the monsoon rains. But, as the rainfall in Gujarat ranges from 20 inches to over 60 per annum, perennial irrigation is not vital as it is in

Sind and southern Punjab. The climate of Gujarat is humid and hot for most of the year. In the past the plain of Gujarat has formed a land corridor between the Indus basin and the peninsula, and as a result of its sheltered position on the Gulf of Cambay it has always had a number of ports through which both coastal and external trade have passed. In recent times most of the external trade has gone to Bombay.

Orissa, at the extreme eastern end of the Central Indian hills, includes the coastal plains to the south-west of the Ganges delta, and the delta of the Mahanadi together with their hinterland which extends back into the hills of Central India and the eastern Deccan, as far south along the coast as Mahendragiri, a rocky outcrop which juts out towards the sea and forms the boundary with Andhra Pradesh. The rainfall is almost as high as that of Bengal, and almost as reliable. Rice is grown everywhere on the coastal plain, and a certain amount of canal irrigation is used, but with the high rainfall this is not as important in a normal year as it is farther south. Isolated from the outside world between the hills of Central India and the sea, and with bad communications with both Bengal and the south until the building of the railway along the east coast in the last century, Orissa has remained in some ways socially and economically backward. The chief city, Puri, is a great centre of pilgrimage, and Orissan culture and folk art have a strong individual character of their own. From some points of view the Chattisgarh plain which we have already mentioned might be included as part of the same region as Orissa, but its history and its general character remain distinct, and it seems better regarded therefore as a separate minor region within Central India.

Peninsular India consists of the central plateau and the surrounding coastal plains as we have already described. The plateau is a very old land surface sloping gently from west to east, with mature graded rivers following this trend, in contrast to Central India where the rivers flow to both west and east. The coastal plains are broader on the east and in the extreme south, and at their narrowest from Bombay to Palghat, along the west coast. The plateau falls into three major regions which roughly correspond to the present states of Maharashtra,

Andhra and Mysore (Karnataka). Maharashtra consists of the Deccan proper, which means the north-western third of the plateau where the Archean granites and gneisses are masked by spreads of later basaltic lava known as Deccan trap. Today the corresponding section of the western coastal plain is included as part of the state of Maharashtra, for although it is totally different ecologically it is too small to form a separate political unit, and it also provides Maharashtra with ports, making the whole a more viable economic and administrative unit. Indeed this has been the situation for some time past, and the ties between upland Maharashtra and its seaboard are very close. The Deccan plateau has sufficient rainfall to make possible a certain amount of dry cultivation (i.e. without irrigation), and crops are also grown with the aid of well or 'lift' irrigation. Today, rice, wheat, millet, pulses and cotton are grown in Maharashtra, cotton being one of its major exports.

South of Maharashtra is Mysore, otherwise known as Karnataka. Here the granites are no longer covered by lava rocks, except in small areas, and where intrusive trap dykes appear and cut through them in long narrow bands which sometimes extend for many miles. The countryside has a stark appearance; ranges of rocky hills, or isolated outcrops of granite rise from the plains, which, except where they are irrigated on a fairly large scale, are bare and dusty for much of the year. Local irrigation here is from surface drainage tanks made by building bunds or dams across the shallow valleys, often between two granite hills. The northern part of the region has the lowest rainfall in peninsular India, but it becomes better watered and altogether more hospitable towards the south. The territory of the former independent state of Mysore is outstanding in India for the care that has been lavished on the countryside and on the villages, and its silks, produced and woven in numerous small factories, are justly famous. An appropriate section of the Western Ghats and the western coastal plain are included with the plateau in Mysore state, as in Maharashtra, although Mysore has no port equivalent to Bombay. The principal harbour on this stretch of coast is Goa, which until recently was a Portuguese possession. Goa has never developed greatly as a port, having been outstripped by Bombay, which occupies a focal situation for both sea trade and land trade both with the peninsula and with western India, and also via several long established routes with the Gangetic plains. Mysore has a long tradition of gold-mining which goes back at least to the beginning of the Christian era, and is still carried on.

The eastern third of the plateau again is predominantly a granite region, but it has a somewhat higher rainfall than any of the western parts, and therefore has not the forbidding aspect of North Mysore. This part of the plateau, together with a stretch of the Eastern Ghats, and the eastern coastal plain, from the borders of Orissa in the north to Madras in the south, including the fertile soil of the combined Krishna–Godavari delta, all form one major cultural and linguistic unit. This is the Telegu language area which corresponds more or less exactly to the State of Andhra Pradesh. Andhra Pradesh, like Central India, includes a number of subregions, particularly in the Eastern Ghats and other hilly tracts, each with its own character. In the wilder parts of Andhra also a number of tribal groups are found, such as the Chenchu of the lower Godavari hills, some of whom still live only by hunting and gathering. The rainfall of coastal Andhra is considerably lower than that of Orissa, but it has two brief wet seasons. As a result there is a much greater dependence upon irrigation both from tanks and from canals which lead water off from the main rivers. Rice, millet and pulses are all grown in Andhra.

In the extreme south the plateau breaks down into isolated blocks of hills, the chief of which are the Nilgiri and the Cardamom hills, which still partially divide the eastern and western coastal plains. The eastern coastal plain, which widens out towards the south, forms, together with its immediate hinterland, a separate lowland region, known as the Tamil plain or the Tamilnad. This corresponds approximately with the modern state of Madras. Here the climate, methods of irrigation, and crops resemble those of the most fertile and developed parts of coastal Andhra. The western coastal plain also widens out to form a separate region which has much in common with the Tamilnad. It is often known as Malabar, and it now forms the state of Kerala. Both Madras and Kerala are extremely heavily populated like the Ganges plains. Their fertile soil, with the aid of irrigation of various types, produces several crops per year. Both are primarily rice-producing, but grow considerable amounts of millets, pulses and other crops in addition. Kerala also produces pepper and spices, which have been exported to the West since Roman times.

Geologically Ceylon is an extension of the Deccan plateau, like the Nilgiris or the Cardamom hills. It is divided from India by twenty miles or so of shallow sea, and for some purposes it can be regarded as the end of the Indian peninsula; the end of a long cul-de-sac into which population and cultural influences have poured from time to time from a general northerly or north-westerly direction. Its position in the Indian Ocean has made it a natural staging post on the sea routes between Europe and the Arab world on the one hand, and the Far East and Australia on the other. Since the fifteenth century it has benefited increasingly from its position, but before that time also it must have been subject to more external influences of all kinds than India. This and its situation as an island have caused Ceylon to develop along somewhat different lines from India. Its aboriginal population, now represented by the Vedda tribes of the south-east, closely resembles that of peninsular India, and indeed the name Veddoid is often taken to describe the Indian aboriginal population as a whole. To them were added in or after the fifth century B.C. a considerable body of population from north India, whose descendants, the Sinhalese, are mainly Buddhists. They live in the southern parts of the island and form one of the major sections of Ceylon's population today. The other major part, the Tamils, most of whom are Hindus, inhabit the more northerly part of the island, which is both lower-lying and drier than the south. The Ceylon Tamils have much in common with those of the Tamilnad, and some have come to Ceylon within living memory, but the majority have been there for an indefinite length of time, and there is no record of when the first Tamilian settlers arrived. In all probability Tamil settlement of northern Ceylon has been taking place for many centuries. East–west trade has brought many other communities to Ceylon, Arab, Portuguese, Dutch, and British, to name only a few, and all these have added to the peculiar blend of the cosmopolitan and the parochial which constitutes her personality. The climate and agriculture of northern Ceylon are much like those of the Tamilnad. Tea and coffee are grown in the mountains of the south, which have a very high rainfall, and some minerals are mined in the central part of the island. There are also parts of the centre of the island which are rich in gem stones.

The people of each of the regions of India have their own character, which is as clearly marked and as constant as that of the country in which they live. Naturally their character derives largely from the country, and from their mode of life in it, which has developed over the course of time as they discovered ways of making their living from the resources it offered. Many features of such regional cultures, therefore, are clearly related to practical day to day needs, and to the materials locally available. Other features have no apparent relationship to local conditions. Some may have an historical explanation, but many are simply the result of local taste and tradition long established and often actively fostered. Anyone who travels about in India will quickly become aware of these cultural differences, many of which have great force and vitality, and which leave one in no doubt when one has passed a regional frontier. Not only are there changes in the countryside, but the dress and bearing of the people is different, and frequently also their language, for many but by no means all geographical and cultural frontiers correspond with linguistic frontiers. It is no exaggeration to say that the variations in manners and taste between any two major cultural blocks in India are as marked as those between any two major European countries.

From the point of view of the archaeologist the different regions of India have a twofold interest. Firstly many of their distinctive features are capable of being traced back in time, and the development and differentiation of regional cultures is the very stuff of archaeology. Secondly certain regions have advanced far more rapidly than others, and the more backward often preserve many features which elsewhere belong only to a distant past. For example, city life and a system of fairly intensive agriculture have been established in the Ganges valley certainly for almost three millennia, and perhaps for somewhat longer. Yet in the adjacent hills and forests of Central India communities can still be found who live by primitive methods of shifting agriculture, augmented by hunting, and by gathering the natural products of the forests, such as honey, fruits, and various edible leaves and roots. Until the beginning of this century there were also communities who lived only by hunting and gathering, and small groups may be found who still do so, although the majority of such people now add to their livelihood by occasional labour and by selling forest products such as honey, or baskets and other things which they make. There are also communities such as the Bhils and Gonds who practise relatively advanced forms of agriculture, using ploughs, wheeled carts and draught oxen, and sometimes also irrigating their land, but who are yet outside the main body of Indian village life and peasant agriculture. All such communities are loosely known as tribal peoples. Many formerly independent groups of this kind can be seen in the process of being absorbed into the Indian village structure.

For the vast majority of the population of India the village is the mainspring of life. In the past it has supplied all the basic essentials of life for its inhabitants, and to a large extent it still does so. India's economy is primarily based upon agriculture: the subsistence agriculture of the peasant farmer within the structure of the village. The basic foods, rice, wheat, millets and pulses, are produced in varying quantities in different parts of India, and in many areas cotton is also produced for clothing and export. Textiles and spices have been India's chief exports since Roman times, and possibly also since Harappan times. Other things such as jute, tea and coffee, to mention only a few, have been added to these. The mining and export of gold and gem stones have also played a part, which it is not easy to estimate. Peasant agriculture, however, has always been the basis. It has provided the continuity and strength of Indian society in times of war and political stress, because any or every village can be entirely self-sufficient for long periods, but its very self-sufficiency has also been its weakness in times of famine, when poor distribution and lack of social mobility, which both arise from the self-sufficient nature of village life, have proved almost insurmountable obstacles in dealing with the situation. Today industrialization is only beginning to make some impression on the Indian economy. The effects of cities and the wider economic life implicit in their presence, and of centralized government and taxation, have long been felt, but next to the family the village is the most important factor in the life of the individual. Reduced to its simplest form the village could be said to consist of farmers and craftsmen, naturally dependent upon one another: in fact it has a highly complex structure into which it can absorb outsiders at various levels.

Indian society constantly overwhelms western observers by its complexity. Not only are there communities at every stage of development from long-established cities to virtually independent groups of hunters, living within a relatively short distance of one another, but within the cities and even within the villages there are numerous groups and communities of people who are wholly or partly self-contained. We have already mentioned hunting tribes who have resorted to selling forest produce, or labouring for more advanced people. This is usually the combined result of agriculturalists encroaching upon their hunting grounds, and of their natural desire to buy food and cloth from village traders. Many of these tribal people make attractive mats and baskets and other objects, for which they find a market in towns and villages, and some have established themselves upon the outskirts of larger settlements, where they live largely by labour and by their crafts. Such people are accepted in a sense by the rest of the community, but no one will intermarry with them or eat with them, and they will marry only among themselves and with their tribal relatives. The acceptance of the group as part of a larger community, but not of the individual with any degree of intimacy, runs very deep through Indian society. Self-contained groups and hereditary specialists of many kinds are met with everywhere and each is assigned a position in the caste hierarchy of their locality, and ultimately in the India-

wide network of castes. There are groups of people who
specialize in almost every possible trade and occupation:
potters, blacksmiths, goldsmiths, quarrymen, labourers,
ballad-singers, acrobats, merchants of various kinds, and
money-lenders. There are people who specialize in carrying
goods from place to place, barbers, washermen, midwives,
prostitutes – the list is endless. Even in traditional society
however, one group may carry out several occupations which
may or may not be closely related. The great majority of the
population, of course, are farmers.

The caste system, first described in the *Purusha Sūkta* of the
Rigveda, probably around 1000 B.C., divides society into four
major groups, *Brāhman, Kshatriya, Vaishya* and *Śūdra*. This
division still holds good today. The *Brāhmans* or priestly
caste are the highest, and were the traditional custodians of
religious, legal and customary knowledge, who knew the
scriptures by heart, and officiated on all occasions such as
weddings, name-giving ceremonies, and so on. Today some
village *Brāhmans* still continue in this role, and some are the
hereditary custodians of temples, but many have moved with
the times and occupy all sorts of professional and administrative positions; one might almost say they form a large part of
the intelligentsia of India. The *Kshatriyas* are the traditional
warrior caste, to which many landowners belong, and they
too have moved into a variety of occupations. *Vaishyas* include
the majority of 'respectable' traders and artisans, and many
peasant farmers. *Śūdras* include a few groups who are regarded
as unclean, such as sweepers or village road-cleaners, and
leather-workers, together with outcasts or people who for
various reasons are regarded as falling right outside the normal
structure of society, like many of the tribal groups we have
already mentioned. Within each of these major groups there
are endless sub-groups and castes, each self-contained, and
each occupying a special place in the caste hierarchy, with the
reservation that the precise position occupied by the same
group or caste in different regions may be somewhat different,
according to their economic position, and the esteem in which
they are held locally.

Upon this ancient and immensely intricate structure came

the impact of Western technology and the industrial revolution. The caste system, which had already been challenged by the Buddhists, by certain Hindu reformist sects, and by the Muslim invasions of the twelfth and fourteenth centuries, had subsequently tended to harden, perhaps as a reaction. Many indigenous people although converted to Islam have continued to marry and eat only with other converts of their own caste. Muslims as a whole form a recognized group, or more accurately a series of groups, within Indian society. In both respects converts to Christianity have tended to follow the same course. This elaborate structure seems to have fossilized further under the policy of religious toleration of British India. Already since independence (1947) considerable inroads have been made upon the caste system, both by legislation, and perhaps more effectively by the increasing effects of industrialization and modern city life, under which it tends to crumble. How and why this system arose and why it has survived so tenaciously for three millennia, are fascinating problems, but for the moment they lie largely in the realms of speculation, and consequently they are definitely outside the scope of this book.

Throughout historic times India has been subject to periodic invasions. Although many of the invaders have made successful military conquests, they have nearly always subsequently been effectively absorbed into Indian society. The great majority of such invasions have come from the west or north-west, via one of the major passes from Persia or Central Asia. Through this way passed the armies of Cyrus and Darius to annex Sind and Gandhāra, of Alexander the Great, of the Bactrian Greeks, the *Śakas* (a branch of the Scythians), the *Pahlavas* (or Parthians), the *Kushāns* (related to the Central Asian Yueh-chi), the Hephthalites and the Huns. From the eighth century began a series of Muslim invasions. That of the Moghuls in the sixteenth century was the latest of its kind. In prehistoric times also a long series of invaders appears to have entered India from the same direction. These people have been of many different origins, with the result that in India today there may be found an almost infinite variety of physical types. The majority of tribal people, and indeed the basic substratum of the population as a whole, belong to the type

known as Proto-Australoid or Veddoid. These people resemble
the Australian aborigines, except that they are considerably
smaller. They are short and slender, with dark brown skin,
dark brown or black wavy hair and large dark eyes. They are
long-headed, and have a fairly pronounced eyebrow ridge
and corresponding depression of the root of the nose. The
nose itself is often broad, and the lips fairly full, and there is a
tendency to prognathism or protrusion of the jaws. People
possessing some or all of these features are found at all levels
of Indian society, but in general as one moves up the social and
economic scale other types and features predominate.

In the east, among the Munda-speaking tribes of eastern
Central India, in Assam, and to varying degrees throughout
Bengal, Orissa and Andhra – in fact over much of eastern
India – a completely different type is found, at times mixed
with Proto-Australoid elements and at times distinct. This is
short-headed, with somewhat slanting eyes and a wide range
of skin colouring, ranging from light yellowish brown to black.
These are all features which suggest connexions with the
peoples of Southeast Asia, but as to what these connexions are
and when they came into being we have as yet few indications,
and little or no concrete evidence. In Maharashtra, northern
Mysore, and much of Madras another type is common among
the village people, tall, dark and round-headed with a squarish
face and small features, and often potentially very powerfully
built. In southern Mysore and parts of Madras this type is
not so common, and many small dark people with longer,
more pointed faces are to be seen. There is a suggestion of a
Negrito element among the tribal people of the Western
Ghats, but this does not form a significant element even in the
population of this region, let alone of India as a whole.
Throughout India there are many people belonging to the
range of types commonly grouped together as Mediterranean,
and in south India such people are found in every walk of life
and particularly in the upper strata of society. There is a
general tendency for skin colouring to be darker in south
India than in the north, but there are many exceptions to
this, and in certain communities in the south there are many
fair-skinned people, and vice versa.

In western and north-western India, in addition to the ubiquitous Mediterranean and Proto-Australoid types, there are a great many fair-skinned, short-headed people, often with rather pronounced features and robust in build, who are quite distinct from the short-headed peoples of Bengal and eastern India. These people seem to be closer to the Caucasoid than to the Mediterranean range of physical types. In parts of the Punjab and Gujarat they appear to be the dominant type, while elsewhere they seem to be outnumbered by more lightly built and longer-headed Mediterranean types, or as in parts of Rajasthan and Sind, by tall dark people like those of Maharashtra and north Mysore. In Central India the Proto-Australoid types are predominant, with various admixtures from adjoining regions. The Ganges valley seems to have been a melting pot of all physical types, representatives of any one of which can be found there in significant numbers, but there is a distinct, if gradual change from the east, where the Bengali or eastern type predominates, to the west, where this type is almost entirely absent, and if any one type is dominant it is the Mediterranean. The extent to which Tibetan physical elements have been incorporated into the population of Northern India appears to be almost negligible.

Since records began the population of the subcontinent has spoken languages belonging to four separate families. The people of the Himalayan fringe, from Ladakh to Assam, speak languages of the Tibeto-Burman branch of the great Sino-Tibetan family. In our context these are mainly tribal languages. In eastern Central India another group of tribal peoples, including the Santal, Juang and Oraon, speak Munda languages which are generally assigned to the Mon–Khmer family of Southeast Asia. The two remaining families are of much greater importance in terms of modern population and of Indian history. In the south of the peninsula and the northern half of Ceylon are spoken the four great Dravidian languages, *Tamil*, *Telegu*, *Kannada* or *Malayalam*. These, together with a group of tribal languages in Central India (particularly *Gondi*), constitute almost the entire representatives of the Dravidian family. Its affinities outside India are not yet agreed, but it is sometimes claimed to be related to the Finno-

Ugrian family. A single small pocket of Dravidian-speaking pastoral people is also found in north Baluchistan, speaking the *Brahui* language. Across the whole of the north and west of India and both West and East Pakistan the population speak languages of the Indo-Iranian branch of the Indo-European family. These were divided by Sir George Grierson into two bands: an inner, probably the development of a slightly later branch, comprising *Hindi* and its dialects, and an outer band – therefore a development of a slightly earlier branch – comprising *Bengali*, *Oriya* and *Bihari* in the east, *Marathi* in the south, and *Panjabi*, *Sindi* and *Gujarati* in the west. *Pashtu* and the languages of the Kaffir tribes of the North-West Frontier region constitute a separate Dardic division of the Indo-Iranian branch. The oldest Indian literature in an Indo-European language is the Rigveda (second half of the second millennium B.C.), and the oldest in a Dravidian language is found in the anthologies of 'Sangam' poems in Tamil of the last centuries B.C.–A.D.

CHAPTER 3

THE EARLY AND MIDDLE STONE AGE

THE whole of the Indian subcontinent is rich in archaeological sites. The remains of cities, temples and settlements of every age abound, and pottery, stone tools or minor antiquities can frequently be found lying upon any stretch of bare ground, or in the newly turned soil of cultivated fields. By contrast most of northern Europe and northern Asia seem something of an archaeological desert. In many of the drier parts of India, as in the drier parts of Africa and western Asia, objects of considerable antiquity are often found lying on the surface of the ground, or immediately below it. This is due to the general tendency to erosion which prevents their being submerged by the top-soil. In temperate or equatorial zones where rainfall is distributed more evenly throughout the year the growth of plants and the formation of soil submerges small objects within a few months or years, and structures also become submerged in the course of time. In climates with a marked seasonal rainfall this is not the general rule, and although many antiquities are submerged by the formation of soil or the accumulation of alluvial silt, many also remain exposed, or are re-exposed by cultivation, erosion and the general instability of the soil cover. Stone Age sites, therefore, are both numerous and obvious in much of the Indian subcontinent, as indeed are the monuments and other remains of later periods. It is not surprising therefore that tools of the Early Stone Age were found and recognized in India only shortly after they had received official recognition in Europe.

It is now clear that the pre-Neolithic cultures of India fall into three major groups which in general follow one another sequentially throughout the subcontinent, and for which the terms Early, Middle and Late Stone Age are frequently used. The three groups represent a continuous process of development, subject at times to a greater or lesser degree of external influence; the lines which divide them are therefore arbitrary, but there can be no doubt that the basic differences between them are real enough. There are also marked regional differences within these groups which we shall try to indicate as we go on, and it is highly probable that certain regions lagged behind others as they do today, so that in terms of absolute time there may have been considerable cultural overlap in the subcontinent as a whole: in some regions new techniques and tools and ways of life would be adopted, while in others old ways would continue for longer or shorter periods of time.

Bearing in mind these reservations, the three main divisions of the Stone Age can be briefly described as follows. The Early Stone Age group, about which we have as yet very little cultural information beyond that to be gained from the stone tools themselves, includes hand-axe industries which generally parallel those of western Asia, Europe and Africa, but with certain differences and exceptions which we shall consider. The principal tools are the hand-axe and the cleaver, core tools of discoidal and elliptical outline made in a similar manner to the hand-axes, chopping tools of various types, and flakes. The Middle Stone Age industries, which appear to have developed from those of the Early Stone Age, are all based upon flakes. Collectively they have a character which distinguishes them from flake industries elsewhere in the world, but they include a whole range of regional variants. The principal tools are now scrapers of several kinds, made on flakes, together with other flake tools and cores. We still have very little general cultural information, as tools of this period have only rarely been found in caves in the Indian subcontinent, and almost never with the kind of occupation deposit which indicates regular habitation. The one exception to this is Sanghao Cave in West Pakistan, where a series of flake industries have been found in massive occupation deposits. But this is in a region which is marginal in terms of India proper, and forms a transition zone between India and Central Asia. The industries of the Late Stone Age show clear signs both of continuity from those which preceded them, and of important external influences. The characteristic tools of the period are microliths. Regional variation is even more marked than previously, and now at last, in addition to the stone tools, there is a considerable body of

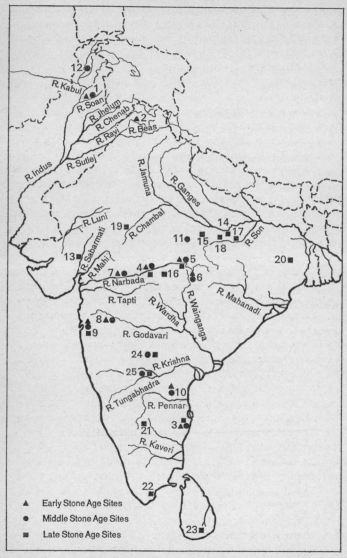

Figure 2. Map of Stone Age sites

cultural information provided by occupied caves and rock shelters, rock paintings, ethnographic survivals and so on. Assemblages of tools of all the main groups have been found very widely in India. Indeed in all regions except the central and eastern mountains and the alluvial plains of the Ganges numerous finds of each group have been recorded briefly in the pages of *Indian Archaeology* or elsewhere, and a number of sites have been more intensively studied. Recently there have been references to finds from the Ganges plains also, either in river gravels, or upon isolated outcrops of rock, but these short notices need confirmation and more detailed publication in order to make them available for discussion. In Pakistan there are few records of Stone Age sites of any kind outside the Punjab, apart from one or two isolated examples.

The problem for the prehistorian in India has never been lack of material; there have always been plenty of collections to study, and more can readily be found in almost every part of the country. The difficulty in studying all the pre-Neolithic cultures has been to find means of dating them, even in relative terms, and of relating them to one another and to the more advanced cultures of the subcontinent. In Kashmir and parts of the north-central mountain region there is evidence of periods of increasing and decreasing glacial activity during the later part of the Pleistocene which may be related to similar events in Europe and other parts of the world. This was demonstrated by the work of de Terra and Paterson during the

KEY TO FIG. 2

1. Soan Valley	13. Langhnaj
2. Beas Valley	14. Barkaccha
3. Attirampakkam and Gudiyam Cave	15. Sidhpur
4. Adamgarh	16. Jambudip and Dorothy Deep rock shelters
5. Jabalpur area - Bhera Ghat, Barasimla, etc.	17. Lekhania
6. Wainganga River sites	18. Morhana Pahar
7. Maheshwar	19. Modi rock shelter
8. Nevasa	20. Birbhanpur
9. Bombay area -Khandivli, etc,	21. Jalahalli
10. Gundla-Brahmeshwaram	22. Teri sites
11. Pandav Falls	23. Bandarawela
12. Sanghao	24. Kondapur
	25. Krishna Bridge

1930s. Their findings indicate the pattern of events during the later part of the Pleistocene, but the region as a whole was also subject to considerable tectonic movements at this period, and was generally unstable, so that the history of each valley and subregion is likely to have differed to a considerable extent. Differences might be caused by local uplift, resulting in the formation of a barrier across a valley with the subsequent ponding back of the river and accumulation of silts; or by river capture; or by the breaking down of a barrier, followed by down-cutting and the formation of terraces. These events may not seriously alter the geological picture of a region as a whole, but they make the work of the archaeologist who is trying to relate the remains of early man to the succession of events in the geological record extremely complicated. Consequently, although de Terra and Paterson succeeded in demonstrating a general development in the stone industries associated with terraces formed during the latter part of the Pleistocene in the river valleys they studied, the successive stages of this development are never very clearly demarcated.

Peninsular and Central India are outside the direct effects of the glacial and interglacial phases noticed in Kashmir and the north-eastern Punjab. The river valleys show clear indications of climatic fluctuations during the later part of the Pleistocene, and some attempt has been made by de Terra and Paterson, and by others, to correlate these with glacial and interglacial phases farther north. Once again the relationship can only be a very general one, as the whole question of climatic change in tropical zones during the Pleistocene is controversial; furthermore, attempts to equate the river terraces of the north-east Punjab with those of the Narbada and other Indian rivers have depended upon comparisons of the tools they contain, and therefore do not provide the kind of independent register which the archaeologist requires. The rivers of Central and peninsular India do however provide a consistent pattern of phases of erosion and aggradation. This pattern begins with the deposition of gravels, usually upon an old eroded land surface or upon bed-rock. These gravels are almost invariably cemented, and continue upwards into a thick deposit of silt, sometimes containing further occasional small deposits of gravel within it, which may be as much as 100 feet or more in depth. Then follows another period of erosion, and disconformably upon the eroded surface a second gravel deposit is found, sometimes less firmly cemented than the first. This in turn gives way to silt, similar to the first. In places the pattern is repeated a third time with a less massive and uncemented gravel followed by silt which grades into the topsoil. This of course is an 'ideal' sequence. In the field all phases are rarely if ever found at one spot on any river, and the sequence has to be worked out by systematic study of the river valley. The exception to this pattern is the river Luni in western Rajasthan, which has laid down deposits of a somewhat different nature during later Pleistocene and recent times. This is not unexpected, as it flows through an area which is a desert today, and which even if conditions were somewhat different in the past must have had a considerably drier climate than the rest of India. Correspondingly the stone industries of the Luni valley and western Rajputana show certain differences from those of other parts of India. The more general pattern has been noticed from the river valleys of Gujarat in the west, right across Central India to Orissa on the east, and in the valleys of a number of the major rivers of the peninsula. Although the pattern is clear its meaning is not. The causes of erosion and deposition have been frequently discussed, and there is no doubt that they must have some relationship to the worldwide pattern of changes of climate and sea level which took place during Pleistocene times. Therefore when this relationship can be defined it should be possible to work out how these phases of erosion and aggradation in India relate to glacial and interglacial phases in other parts of the world.

Studies have now been made of a number of Indian rivers. The reports of these studies, with the exception of that on the Luni river mentioned above, suggest a consistent pattern of periods of erosion and aggradation, but it must be remembered that parts of these regions, especially coastal Gujarat, have been subject to tectonic disturbances in recent times, and therefore the sequence seen on any particular stretch of river may not fully equate in time with those seen elsewhere, as it may be influenced by factors of purely local significance. The effects of these disturbances are not so dramatic as in the Himalayan region, but they are sufficiently marked to be reflected in deposits laid down by the river. The stable region of peninsular India can be expected to give more reliable results which could perhaps be used as a control against which to assess sequences observed in the less stable regions. Work on the Godavari and its tributaries such as that done by Sankalia at Nevasa (1956), and by R. V. Joshi and others on various stretches of this river and its tributaries, and surveys carried out farther south have already made valuable advances in this direction. As pointed out by Vishnu Mittre and R. V. Joshi at a seminar held in Poona in 1964, it is to be hoped that surveys of ancient shore-lines on the east coast, now in progress, may in due course enable these to be related to the river terraces and stratified deposits of the eastward-flowing rivers of the peninsula. This will provide a framework to which other events and local sequences can be linked. Further, the analysis of pollens found in ancient soils, which is now beginning in India, should make it possible in course of time to get some idea of the climatic conditions in which these soils were formed, and so of the climatic pattern in India in early human times.

The cemented gravels referable to the beginning of each phase of aggradation very frequently contain considerable numbers of stone tools. Those associated with the first phase invariably belong to Early Stone Age industries, while those from the gravels of the second phase sometimes include a few of Early Stone Age types, but the great majority belong to the Middle Stone Age group of flake industries. Tools in the gravels of the third cycle of aggradation, where these are found, also belong to the Middle Stone Age complex, but to a very much more advanced stage of its development. The last point is demonstrated by the reduced size of both cores and flakes, and by a corresponding refinement of technique and variety of forms. Industries of the Late Stone Age are found in and immediately below the top-soil. Naturally, where subdivisions of any of the gravels occur, tools which they contain are of the greatest interest, as they provide evidence of sequential development within the first two major subdivisions. Tools of all phases are also frequently found on the surface where they have either lain exposed since their makers left them, or been covered for a.time by soil, sand or silt, and then re-exposed. Some surface sites clearly belong to a fairly limited period, while others were continually or repeatedly exploited at several different periods. In both cases they can yield valuable evidence: factory sites provide one of the principal means for reconstructing the processes by which stone tools were made.

THE EARLY STONE AGE

There are clear indications that the hand-axe industries developed along lines comparable to those seen in Europe. This was shown in the south by Cammiade and Burkitt (1936), and in the north by de Terra and Paterson. The latter demonstrated that tools from succeeding terraces of the Soan river, a tributary of the Indus in West Pakistan, ranged from crude, heavy hand-axes and chopping tools made on pebbles in the upper terraces, to small finely worked hand-axes, cleavers, discoidal cores, flakes and chopping tools in the lower. The youngest industry they describe, the Late Soan, is a flake industry, which parallels the flake industries of the Middle Stone Age group found elsewhere in India. There is a high proportion of chopping tools, not only in the earliest Soan assemblages where they might be expected, but also in the more advanced phases of these industries. Indeed in all phases except the Late Soan they are a predominant type. Reliable statistics are not available for whole assemblages, but in certain of them chopping tools amount to more than half the finished tools, and in others very much more. According to de Terra and Paterson they show a progressive development comparable to that seen in the hand-axes and other core tools. A similar situation was reported by B. B. Lal (1956) from the valley of the Beas river, another tributary of the Indus, on the Indian side of the frontier. The Early Stone Age industries of south India are often termed Madrasian, because hand-axes and other tools were first found at Attirampakkam near Madras in 1863. The chief difference between the Soan and Madrasian industries is in the proportion of chopping tools in relation to other forms, as we have already mentioned. Early Stone Age industries have now been found so widely that it has become clear that no very precise line of demarcation can be drawn between the two groups, but, as B. B. Lal has shown, the proportion of chopping tools decreases rapidly as one moves south-west, south or south-east from the Punjab into other parts of India.

The site of Attirampakkam has been discussed by many authorities. The deposits cut through by a small stream, the Budida Manu Vanka, yielded a sequence of hand-axes, flake tools and finally, on the surface, microliths. Formerly the hand-axes and flake tools were thought to come from deposits brought down by the stream itself, but recent work by R. V. Joshi, K. D. Banerjea and others has shown the tool-bearing deposits to be widespread over an area many miles in extent. Excavations near the river bank at Attirampakkam revealed the following sequence, starting from the surface on and immediately below which microliths were found. Below the surface soil was a sterile layer of brown silt; then detrital lateritic gravel containing a flake industry; below that again decomposing shale, the surface of which had become clayey, and which contained hand-axes, cleavers and other tools of an Early Stone Age industry of Acheulian type. The excavators consider that these tools perhaps originally lay on the surface of the shale, and then sank into it as it became softer. Elsewhere in the same countryside hand-axes and other Early Stone Age tools are found in profusion among spreads of boulders and large pebbles on the modern ground surface. Tools which are spread over ancient or modern land surfaces in this way may have been moved by various agencies some distance from the places where their owners left them, and the soils on which they first lay may have been slowly eroded away from beneath them, so that they now lie on very different surfaces; but they cannot have formed part of the load carried by a river in flood as tools contained in ancient river gravels must have done. At Gudiyam cave, a few miles distant, a small excavation showed a corresponding sequence of Early, Middle and Late Stone

Age tools, but they were very few in number, and other evidence of occupation was almost entirely absent, suggesting that the cave was not regularly inhabited. Today it contains the shrine of a local mother goddess. How these finds in the Madras coastal region can be interpreted remains to be seen. The problem of relating them to material from the river gravels must depend, like so many others, upon working out the relationship of ancient shore-lines to the river terraces and deposits in the subcontinent as a whole. These tools do however provide corroborative evidence for the sequences seen in river valleys.

Another site from which a sequence of Early and Middle Stone Age assemblages has been obtained is Adamgarh Hill in the Narbada valley, excavated by R. V. Joshi in 1964. This is an isolated low hill, free from direct river action. The hill is composed of sandstones, quartzites and shales, and partly covered by a derived laterite crust, which in turn is covered by fine gravel, and then by sands and red clay. The clay contains fragments of rock, some of which also overlie it, and Early Stone Age tools make their appearance among these rock fragments. The assemblage near the bottom includes hand-axes, chopping tools, ovates and a few cleavers. Higher up the proportion of hand-axes and chopping tools decreases, and cleavers become more numerous, varied and finely made. In the upper part there is a marked change to flake tools, including scrapers and pointed flakes. These phases approximately parallel the development of Acheulian and post-Acheulian industries in the west, as the excavator points out. More important perhaps in the Indian context, the sequence bridges the gap typologically between the Early Stone Age and early Middle Stone Age assemblages found in the two cemented gravels of the Narbada nearby, and in many other parts of India. Further assemblages which bridge this gap are reported from the alluvial deposits of the upper and middle Narbada, where hand-axes and flakes said to be comparable to Abbevillian and Clactonian types were found in the gravels of the first aggradation phase, and more evolved hand-axes and cleavers were in clay deposits immediately overlying them (Sen and Ghosh, 1963). The lower gravels (A) of the Wainganga river, a tributary of the Godavari, were found to contain an industry which can be assigned to a late phase of the Early Stone Age on typological grounds, and exhibits many late-Acheulian features.

At present we can offer no explanation for the difference between the Early Stone Age industries of the north-eastern Punjab and those of other regions of India so far explored, and it can only be put on record as a factual observation. The adjacent regions of the former North West Frontier Province, and the south-westerly parts of both the Pakistani and the Indian Punjab are all unexplored from this point of view; so are the foothills of the central mountain region to the east, and the Ganges plains themselves. The affinities of the Soan industries with their high proportion of chopping tools therefore are still problematic: they may be related to the so called chopper-chopping tool industries of eastern Asia as suggested by Hallam J. Movius, or they may be a local phenomenon.

The majority of Early Stone Age tools found in all parts of the subcontinent are made of quartzite. Sometimes quartzite pebbles were used, particularly for making the earlier and cruder hand-axes, and for making chopping tools at all periods (Figure 3, Nos. 1, 2 and 6). The other source of quartzite was outcrops of rock and boulders. Factory sites where both pebbles and boulders of various sizes had clearly provided the raw material have been seen by the present writers on the terraces of the Soan valley in West Pakistan, and also recorded by other archaeologists in various parts of India. In order to make tools large flakes or pieces of quartzite had been removed from the parent rock. It was not always clear whether this had been done by striking the rock with another stone – an operation which would require great strength – or by fire-setting, that is lighting a fire against the rock and so causing large pieces to break away from the main body. Perhaps both methods were used. Some tools, usually cleavers, can be seen to have been made from flakes which had been struck off larger blocks of raw material (Figure 3, No. 4). But in the

Figure 3. Early Stone Age tools

1–4, Soan valley, Punjab: 1 and 2, chopping tools; 3, hand-axe; 4, cleaver 5–8, Attirampakkam, Madras: 5, discoidal core; 6, chopping tool; 7, hand-axe; 8, cleaver.

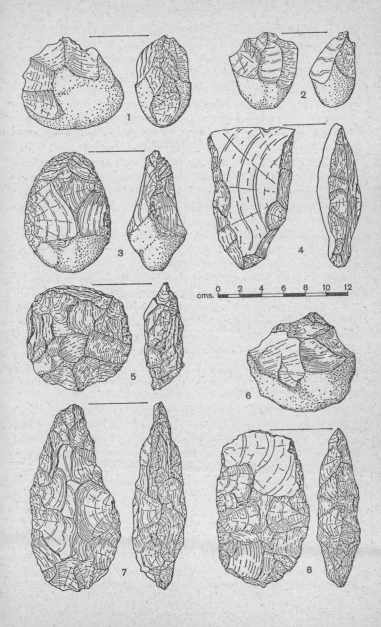

cms. 0 2 4 6 8 10 12

case of many tools all traces of a primary flake surface or a bulb of percussion, if they were ever there, have been lost in the removal of further flakes, in the process of giving the tool its final form. A collection of Early Stone Age tools from a surface site at Kibbanhalli, situated on a quartzite ridge in Mysore, illustrates this point. This includes cleavers made on large flakes, and hand-axes and other tools also of quartzite, but flaked all over, so that all traces of a primary flake surface have disappeared (Figure 3, Nos. 7 and 8). Quartzite is the material from which Early Stone Age tools in river gravels and other geologically stratified deposits are most commonly made, although tools of other materials, such as vein quartz, volcanic rocks, and various types of crypto-crystalline silica are sometimes found.

Large quartzite flakes lend themselves to the production of cleavers more readily than pebbles or nodules of rock, and it seems probable therefore that the increasing numbers of cleavers in later phases of the Early Stone Age may be related to a change in the source of supply. Other core tools, more or less elliptical or circular in outline, and made by the same flaking techniques as the hand-axes and cleavers, are found in almost every Early Stone Age assemblage (Figure 3, No. 5). These generally show signs of use around the edge, but this is often concentrated in one or two areas. There is little doubt therefore that these tools were used for chopping and cutting, and also perhaps for digging and scraping hides. In most large collections they grade imperceptibly into the hand-axe forms, and sometimes also into the cleavers. In the later stages of the Early Stone Age, as for example in collections made from the lower gravels of the Wainganga river in eastern Maharashtra, they also grade into the 'tortoise' cores from which flakes were struck for use as tools. In this capacity they continue as a basic and essential part of the succeeding flake industries of the Middle Stone Age.

Flakes, first mainly as by-products of the manufacture of core tools, and later as the main objective of the tool makers, are an intrinsic part of the hand-axe industries in India, as indeed they are elsewhere in the world. Some collectors have overlooked them, but they are there with other tools at factory sites and in river gravels to be found by anyone who looks for them. Many flakes show signs of use, and the practice of striking flakes from specially prepared cores and using them as a basis for making the more delicate tools, had already begun in the later phases of the Early Stone Age. This can be seen in the Wainganga (A) assemblage mentioned above, and that from Velaungudi in Trichinopoly District in the extreme south, and among the tools from the upper levels of the deposit containing the hand-axe industry at Adamgarh.

As in corresponding periods in other parts of the world, the methods of flaking used to produce the tools become steadily more refined throughout the Early Stone Age. At the beginning a flake was knocked off by a blow with another stone, leaving a markedly concave flake scar with a pronounced bulb of percussion. Gradually the maker's control over his material increases, and by using a more delicate hammer, probably a piece of hard wood or bone, in the later stages of making a tool, shallower and more regular flakes are taken off. By dint of these and other means, including step-flaking (Figure 3, No. 3), it was possible to produce a small, light, regularly shaped hand-axe, thin in section and with a straight-cutting edge. Small, shapely hand-axes are present among the assemblage of tools from Velaungudi just mentioned, and they were also found by de Terra and Paterson at Chauntra in the Punjab, but in both cases unfortunately the provenance of the tools is rather vague. The association of similar tools with a flake industry in the Luni river valley in the Rajputana desert also deserves closer investigation. The assemblage from the Wainganga (Λ) gravels is better documented than any of these sites, but is said to have included no hand-axes. A tool of this kind must have taken considerable time and skill to produce, and alongside it will be found a great many less perfectly made, but none the less effective tools. Chopping tools, cores, flakes, and many objects that can only be described as utilized pieces of stone, will generally be found in profusion at a site which yields a few finely made hand-axes or cleavers. This is demonstrated by collections from factory sites, and also from the earlier cemented gravels of most of the major rivers, including those we have mentioned.

During the Early Stone Age man does not seem to have lived regularly in caves anywhere in the subcontinent. A considerable number of caves and rock shelters have been examined and excavated. At some, such as Gudiyam, or the rock shelters on Adamgarh hill, occasional tools of the Early or Middle Stone Age probably indicate casual visits from time to time during these periods. There is as yet no evidence of continuous occupation, and some caves such as Billasurgam in the Kurnool District of Andhra Pradesh, excavated by H. B. Foote, son of the famous prehistorian – though rich in faunal remains – show no evidence of human presence until much later times. As a result stratified river gravels, gravel or boulder spreads, and occasional factory sites are the only sources of information. It is to be hoped that Early Stone Age living or camping places from which something may be learnt about the people of that time may be found in India in due course. It would also be of great interest to know what Early Stone Age industries there are in the south-western Punjab and Sind, for now that tools of this period have been found in the Rajputana desert there is every reason to expect to find them in the corresponding desert region on the other side of the Indo-Pakistan frontier. As we have already suggested, the former North West Frontier Province of Pakistan and the northern edge of the Ganges plains, which are still *terra incognita* from the Stone Age point of view, deserve investigation, and might throw light upon the relationship of the Soan industries to the chopper-chopping tool complex of eastern Asia.

THE MIDDLE STONE AGE

The industries of the Middle Stone Age for long proved difficult to isolate. Flake industries were recognized in stratified deposits by Todd at Khandivli near Bombay in 1938; by Cammiade and Burkitt in their classification of tools from south-eastern India in 1930; and again by de Terra and Paterson on both the Soan and the Narbada in 1939. Both Todd and de Terra associated them correctly with deposits of the second phase of aggradation. But it was left to the post-independence archaeologists, Indian and European, to describe them and to work out their relationship to the other major industrial groups. A great deal of work still remains to be done on both these questions, but the sequential position of the flake industries as a whole is clear and, as we have already seen, there are a number of sites at which transitional assemblages, or a continuous sequence in terms of statigraphy and typology from Early to Middle Stone Age have been found. The tools from the gravels of the second cycle of aggradation at Hoshangabad, Nevasa or Bhera Ghat or in the Damoh area, for example, which are all representative of Central and peninsular India as far as we know it, are largely made on flakes struck from prepared cores. A small proportion of these show prepared striking platforms.

The materials from which the Middle Stone Age tools were made are chiefly crypto-crystalline silica of various kinds such as agate and jasper, or chalcedony, which have a smoother and more regular concoidal fracture than the somewhat granular quartzites favoured in Early Stone Age times. Most frequently the material appears to have been obtained in the form of river pebbles. These would derive from nodules of silica formed in the volcanic trap rocks which are found in so much of Central India and the more northerly parts of the peninsula. Pebbles of the same kind are also found in river gravels outside the main trap regions, and here again they were sometimes utilized. When quartzites were employed in Middle Stone Age industries, as at Gundla-Brahmesvaram, a site described and illustrated by Cammiade and Burkitt (1930), they were always fine grained, and probably carefully chosen.

The flakes vary considerably in shape, including round, rectangular and pointed forms, and long parallel-sided blade-flakes (Figure 5, No. 3). All show fairly pronounced bulbs of percussion, where these have not been removed, indicating that they were probably struck off the parent core with a hammer made of wood or a small pebble. Elongated oval pebbles, battered at one or both ends, are found at Middle and Late Stone Age factory sites in many parts of India and suggest that this was the means used. But some archaeologists consider that flakes of this kind could only be obtained by using a wooden hammer. With these flakes are found cores of the well-known 'tortoise' type (Figure 4, Nos. 1, 2 and 4); and cores of another type, made by removing one or two flakes from a suitable pebble to provide a striking platform, from which thick but sometimes approximately parallel-sided blade-flakes are then struck off (Figure 4, No. 14). A certain number of cores of both kinds show signs of subsequent use as chopping tools, which indeed the second type closely resemble. Occasional hand-axes are found in the upper gravels, in association with the flake tools and cores, and these are invariably small, and usually rolled. In such a context it is difficult to prove that they are derived from earlier deposits, as all tools must be rolled to some extent if they have been incorporated in a river gravel. However, an occasional hand-axe found at a Middle Stone Age factory site, as for example at Pandav Falls in Central India (Figure 4, No. 6), strengthens the case for those in the gravels belonging to the Middle Stone Age complex. As we have already pointed out, small hand-axes form an integral part of the Middle Stone Age assemblage in the gravels of the Luni river in western Rajputana.

With the exception of these small hand-axes, bifacially worked points are seldom if ever found in Indian Middle Stone Age industries. Pointed flakes, generally more or less leaf-shaped, and sometimes with fairly steep retouch or regular use marks along one or both edges, occur fairly commonly in collections from many parts of India, and also in the Late Soan industries of the Punjab (Figure 6, No. 1). Unfortunately no industries of this period have been recorded in any other part of West Pakistan, with the exception of Sanghao, which we shall discuss below. Pointed flakes of the kind we have described could have been used either as knives or as missile points. A feature noticed in many regions, including Rajputana in the west, and Orissa in the east, as well as in the centre and south, is a pointed flake with a bulb of percussion which is considerably 'off centre'. Large borers or awls, worked with steep retouch on thick flakes are also characteristic of the earlier Middle Stone Age industries in Central and peninsular India in particular (Figure 5, No. 6). Frequently they form part of a composite tool consisting of a 'beak' or borer point and two hollow scrapers (Figure 4, No. 15). Burins are rare

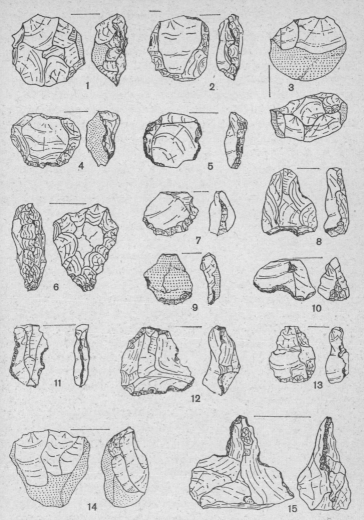

Figure 4. Middle Stone Age tools from Central and peninsular India.
1:3

1, prepared core; 2 and 4, prepared cores from which flakes have been struck;
6, hand-axe; 3, chopping tool; 5 and 7–13 scrapers made of flakes; 14, utilized core;
15, beaked tool. 1, 3, 12 and 13, North Mysore; 2, 5, 8, 9, 10 and 14, gravel II, Bhera
Ghat; 4, 6 and 7, Pandav Falls factory site, Central India; 11 and 15, Adilabad high-
lands, Andhra Pradesh.

and of a simple undifferentiated kind at this stage, although in certain of the later Middle Stone Age industries they are rather more common (Figure 5, No. 5).

There is a wide variety of scrapers, as we have already pointed out, and they are undoubtedly the characteristic tool of this whole group of Middle Stone Age industries. Concave, convex or straight scraper edges have been worked, generally with steep retouch, on round, square or pointed flakes either

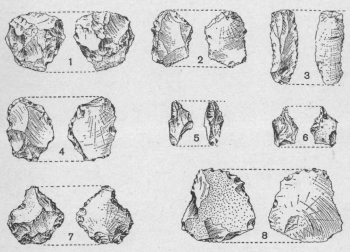

Figure 5. Middle Stone Age tools from gravel II, Nevasa, Deccan. 1:3

1, core; 2–4, 7 and 8, flakes; 5, burin; 6, borer.

with or without prepared striking platforms. Scrapers are sometimes also found worked on the long edges of blade-flakes. A form characteristic of the middle Narbada, and also found in the south, has the scraper edge worked on the distal end of a thick squarish flake, and has been frequently re-edged until a considerable proportion of the flake has been worked away (Figure 4, Nos. 8, 10, 12 and 13). It has been suggested that all these features are the characteristics of a woodland industry, in which scrapers were used to make various tools from hard tropical woods. The absence of developed types of stone points suitable for missile points certainly suggests that these, if they were used, were made from other substances, presumably wood or perhaps bone. In Southeast Asia today arrow-heads and knives are made from bamboo. The latter serve for general cutting purposes, even when metal is available. It seems quite possible therefore that during Middle Stone Age times the same was true of much of tropical India.

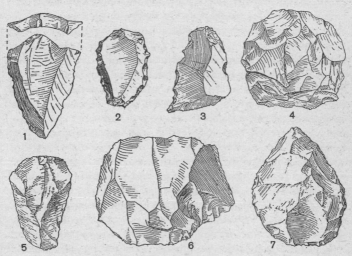

Figure 6. Middle Stone Age tools from the Punjab.
1:3 (approx)

1–4, Late Soan A: 1–3, flakes; 4, prepared core. 5 and 6, Late Soan B: 5, flake; 6, prepared core. 7, hand-axe from Chauntra.

On the very frontiers of the Indian subcontinent an industry has recently come to light to which these generalizations do not altogether apply, and which deserves our attention for a number of reasons. This is at Sanghao Cave, in tribal territory adjoining the former North West Frontier Province in West Pakistan. It was discovered and excavated by A. H. Dani, Head of the Department of Archaeology in Peshawar University. The preliminary excavation report (1964) does a great deal less than justice to this unique site and also to what was from many points of view a competent excavation. The mountain valley in which the cave is situated is steep and narrow, but opens out towards the south-west. It thus provides almost ideal living conditions in a region of extreme climate, being high enough to escape excessive heat in summer, and also sheltered from the cold winds of winter. A trench approximately 50 feet long by 10 feet wide was cut from the talus slope outside to the back of the cave. This exposed some 10 feet of occupation deposit, rich in bones, charcoal and stone tools. Unfortunately the bones and charcoal, which would almost certainly have given a great deal of information about the life of the occupants, climate conditions, etc., and provided material for radiocarbon dating, were not kept. Four periods of occupation can be distinguished, the first three of which grade into one another apparently without any break in continuity. Throughout these the tools are made entirely of quartz, of which there is a prominent outcrop, not much more than 100 yards from the cave. Quartz always tends to fracture irregularly on account of its crystalline structure, and it is therefore a difficult material to work. For the same reason it is difficult to recognize tools made of quartz, as their outlines tend to be broken by its irregular fracture. At Sanghao it must have been used because it was readily at hand. The industry of period I in particular testifies to a remarkable degree of control over this awkward material.

In the absence of any comprehensive published classification or enumeration of the tools from the excavation – which must run into some thousands – we shall endeavour to give some account of the industry in general terms, on the basis of the material which the excavators retained, and which the present writers were fortunate in having an opportunity to study in 1963. Throughout the tools were made from flakes struck from prepared cores, generally round, oval or elliptical in outline, and comparable to those with which we are already familiar in flake industries of the Indian Middle Stone Age. Some cores have had a major flake struck from one surface, and a number of them show signs of having been used for chopping and hacking. The final flakes struck from these carefully prepared cores can be distinguished from those struck off in the process of core preparation by their greater regularity both of outline and section, and by a more acute angle between striking platform and flake surface. No flakes with prepared striking platforms were recorded, and only a few with any regular secondary work. There are a small number of hollow scrapers, but scrapers of every other kind, and trimmed or reworked points are remarkable by their absence.

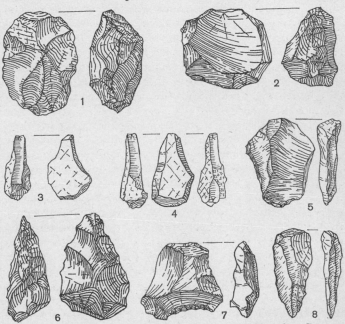

Figure 7. Middle Stone Age tools from period I, Sanghao Cave, West Pakistan. 1:2

1 and 2, cores; 3 and 4, burins; 5, 7 and 8, flakes; 6, hand-axe.

One small hand-axe was recorded (Figure 7, No. 6). Cores and flakes of triangular outline are seen in small numbers, and parallel-sided blade-flakes are more numerous. The bulbs of percussion on these blade-flakes are pronounced as in the Indian Middle Stone Age industries, suggesting direct percussion with a fairly robust hammer. Conical or cylindrical cores from which such blade-flakes might have been produced were not among the tools preserved, and nor were cores of the kind from which blade-flakes appear to have been struck in Middle Stone Age industries in India. There were however certain pieces of quartz from each of which one or two blade-flakes of this kind appeared to have been struck, using the natural angularity of the material in place of preparation of the core. One of the most interesting features of the industry is the burins, of which there are a considerable number (Figure 7, Nos. 3 and 4). They are made from convenient fragments of tabular quartz, frequently using one of its natural facets as a striking platform. Many show signs of heavy use on the burin edge. A number of naturally pointed flakes appear to have been used for piercing and boring, and a few fragments or flakes have been carefully worked to a point and can be classi-fied as awls.

In period II there is a slight decline in the number of the tools and also in their size and in the quality of the quartz. In period III this decline is more marked, but the actual quantity of tools and quartz debris increases. Burins continue, though reduced in size; blade-flakes disappear, but a few fine micro-lithic blades and blade cores make their appearance. The latter call to mind the microlithic industries of Central and penin-sular India. The industry in the lower levels at Sanghao has some obvious affinities both with the Late Soan of the Punjab and thence with the Middle Stone Age of the Indian sub-continent generally, and also with the Levallois–Mousterian industries of central and western Asia. Probably the nearest site at which an industry of this kind has been found is Teshik-Tash, in a similar situation on a tributary of the Oxus in Soviet Tadjikistan. Sanghao gives some indication of the potential archaeological wealth of West Pakistan. The answers to many problems concerning the relationship of the cultures of South Asia to those of West and Central Asia will have to be found there.

The North West Frontier Province, as its name implies, is on the edge of the region with which this book is dealing. Until a full report of the 1962–3 excavation at Sanghao is pub-lished, and until some further work has been done both there and in surrounding regions this industry cannot be accurately related to the Stone Age sequence of the Indian subcontinent as a whole. Within the political confines of India the earlier phases of the Middle Stone Age are amply represented by assemblages of tools from the gravels of the second aggradation phase on most of the major rivers – nearly all in fact that have so far been investigated. The industry of each region at this period can be seen to have a distinctive character of its own, due partly to the raw materials, and partly to differences in handling them. The time will shortly come when it is possible to make a systematic analysis of these differences, but at the moment this would not be possible. One cannot help noticing an apparent similarity between the Middle Stone Age assemblage from western Rajputana and the Late Soan of the Punjab. This is highly suggestive. Both have a somewhat 'Mousterian' character, exemplified by the small hand-axes found on the Luni river and at Chauntra, by the prepared cores from which flakes were struck off, and by the flakes themselves. In these respects they contrast particularly with the earlier Middle Stone Age industries from both gravels and factory sites in Central India and Maharashtra, which demonstrate the essentially Indian characteristics outlined earlier. If Sanghao is representative of a fairly widespread industry, as a site yielding such a large quantity and depth of occupation material may reasonably be expected to be, then this in turn will form another regional variant. What Sind and Baluchistan on the one hand, and the eastern Himalayan foothills on the other, may contain remains to be seen.

Over much of the Indian subcontinent the earlier Middle Stone Age industries are fairly well represented by material from stratified gravels, as we have already pointed out, but for the later Middle Stone Age we have no such reservoir of material. Certain assemblages, such as that from the upper (B) gravels of the Wainganga, appear on both typological and stratigraphical grounds to represent a fairly late phase in the Middle Stone Age series. This collection is said to contain 'a fairly large number of flake-blades or blades, burins, and several tanged and shouldered points'. The first appear to be blade-flakes of the Middle Stone Age type already described, somewhat refined and reduced in size. The burins are of particular interest as they appear to be worked on thick flakes and fragments of chert – which is the predominant raw material here. They are simple and unspecialized, but in each case one or more burin spalls have been removed to produce a burin edge. The present writers are of the opinion that burins of this kind are present in many Middle Stone Age assemblages, although they have not always been recognized or recorded. The tanged points are thick, more or less pointed flakes roughly worked to a tang at the bulbar end. It seems reasonable to suppose that this was done for the purpose of hafting; but it seems unlikely that these tools can have served as missile points, and more probable that they were used as knives and scrapers. A brief description by de Terra and Paterson of an assemblage of tools from the basal gravels and sands of the new alluvium (third aggradation phase) at Hoshangabad on the Narbada indicates a similar character, but unfortunately it is not illustrated. Larger assemblages briefly described and illustrated by D. Sen and A. K. Ghosh (1962) from factory sites near Jabalpur also appear to belong to a late phase of the Middle Stone Age and to continue into Late Stone Age times. The same can be said of industries found by K. R. U. Todd in the vicinity of Bombay, and there are other examples from various parts of Central and peninsular India. Farther south the flake industries from two factory sites, one on the bank of the river Krishna, and the other overlooking a small stream near Kondapur about forty miles west of the city of Hyderabad, are even more highly developed. Both cores and flakes are further reduced in size, and the tools include large, thick lunates made both on flakes struck from small 'tortoise' cores, and on small versions of typical Middle Stone Age blade-flakes. In each case a Late Stone Age factory site, yielding microlithic blade cores and blades, and a range of geometric microliths made from them, was found in close proximity to the Middle Stone Age site; so close in fact that in each case the peripheral spread of debris from the two sites overlapped, although their central working floors remained distinct. Collections from the coastal sand dune or *teri* sites in the extreme south also suggest a continuous development from Middle to Late Stone Age traditions.

The site of Salvadgi in Mysore seems to have been used

during the Middle Stone Age and again in Neolithic times, but it is not clear whether it was also made use of by the Late Stone Age hunting people. The later phases of the Middle Stone Age are probably the least known part of the Stone Age sequence throughout the subcontinent. These are the industries which some archaeologists have referred to as Upper Palaeolithic, but as yet we do not even know whether they can be assigned to the Palaeolithic on temporal grounds – that is to say whether they belong to the Pleistocene period. At present also the persistence of the flake tradition appears to be so marked that any term which does not stress the continuity of this basic technological tradition appears to the present writers highly illogical (see page 28), and a more comprehensive term which does not by implication prejudge the position of the industries in a cultural or geological sense is therefore to be preferred.

CHAPTER 4

THE LATE STONE AGE

THE Late Stone Age throughout India and Ceylon is characterized by microlithic industries. There can be little doubt that
this cultural phase is entirely post-Pleistocene, indeed Late
Stone Age industries in many parts of India must be contemporary, in their later stages at least, with Neolithic and later
cultures. No industries of this period have been definitely
recorded in Pakistan as yet, but there are indications that they
are present in Sind and the former North West Frontier
Province, and adjacent tribal territories. If this is the case it is
most unlikely that they are absent in the Punjab and Baluchistan. We have seen that in southern India the change from
Middle to Late Stone Age – that is to say from the flake to the
microlithic tradition – appears to have been a process of continuous development rather than of sudden change. In Ceylon
Middle and Late Stone Age techniques are even more closely
integrated, although no example of a 'pure' Middle Stone Age
industry as such has as yet been recorded there. Farther north,
in regions such as Gujarat and western Central India, where a
considerable amount of work has been done on these problems,
the relationship between Middle and Late Stone Age traditions
has proved hard to pin down. At present there appears to be a
somewhat abrupt break between them in north-western India,
although even here there are vestiges of Middle Stone Age
techniques clearly discernible in many Late Stone Age assemblages. As with the tools of earlier periods, those of the Late
Stone Age have been found very widely in India. The only
major regions where they have not yet been recorded are the
Ganges plains and the northern mountains which overlook
them. But many of the finds are recorded only in the briefest
terms.

The plains of Gujarat are rich in sites of the Late Stone Age,
on river banks and on hillocks which are in many cases old
sand-dunes. Hollows scooped out by the wind in association

with the dunes hold water for part of the year following the monsoon season, and during this time each year the dunes must have provided ideal camping places from which to survey the surrounding plains and lie in wait for game animals when they came to drink. Excavations at one such site, Langhnaj, have shown a considerable period of occupation spanning changes in the soil which may represent minor climatic oscillations. Dune sand merges into a fixed soil cover, and this is later submerged by another layer of sand which is in turn fixed by the modern soil. A number of flexed burials were found at Langhnaj, and after examination the skeletons are considered to combine predominantly Mediterranean and Veddoid features. With the skeletons were beads of dentalium shell which must have been brought some distance from the sea. The total depth of deposits containing occupation debris is approximately 5 feet. A little below half-way up the section pottery makes its appearance in small quantity. Red, black and black-and-red sherds have all been found, the last recalling sherds from Rangpur III (see page 182). At a depth of 3 feet a copper knife was found, and somewhat higher up an iron arrowhead. Quartzite pebbles, a hammer stone, two small ground stone axes and a large quartzite ring stone, probably a macehead or a weight for a digging stick, were also among the finds. There are clear indications therefore that during the latter part of its occupation the inhabitants of Langhnaj were in contact with more settled Chalcolithic and Iron Age communities. The animal remains include those of several species of deer and antelope; the Indian rhinoceros (*Rhinoceros unicornis*); the Indian wild boar (*Sus scrofa cristatus*); the Indian wolf (*Canis* cf. *lupus*); cattle (probably *Bos indicus*) and/or Indian buffalo (*Bubalus bubalis*); rat, squirrel and mongoose. All the species recorded can be found in the savannah country of the subcontinent today, although several are nearly extinct or of restricted distribution.

The stone industry is based upon the production of small parallel-sided blades from carefully prepared cores. The blades are small, and both the bulbs of percussion upon them and the scars left upon the cores by their removal are very shallow. Therefore there can be little doubt that the blades were struck off by indirect percussion: that is, by means of a bone or hard wooden point placed on the core and struck with a hammer, rather as a cold chisel is used today. A classified list of stone tools found in the excavation has been published (Sankalia, 1966), and may be summarized as follows:

		per cent
Cores	70	5·31
Core-trimming flakes	20	1·53
Flakes	1117	85·90
Blades	59	4·67
Backed blades	5	0·38
Lunates	13	1·00
Triangles	3	0·0023
Trapezes	1	0·00107
Scrapers	2	0·00215
Points	1	0·00107
Plunging flakes	9	0·69

In general the tools are made of some kind of crypto-crystalline silica such as jasper, which is found in the form of small pebbles, brought down from the hills of Central India, in the gravels of the rivers which flow across the plains of Gujarat. A small proportion are made of quartz.

Central India is also rich in Late Stone Age sites. There are numerous small sites on hills or rising ground which command a view of the surrounding country, and they yield a fairly representative range of tools and a fair quantity of waste materials. The finds could well represent the debris of a spot where a family or small group of people camped for a period of time. Such sites are still favoured by tribal people as temporary or semi-permanent camping places to which they return from time to time. There are also a number of much larger factory sites, some of which cover an acre or more of ground, which in certain cases appear to have served other communities besides those which were responsible for the Late Stone Age industries. Nimkhera and Saliwara, Sakri and Kastara, two groups of sites near Jabalpur, appear to have been exploited by both Middle Stone Age and Late Stone Age tool-makers. But Barasimla in the same region seems to have been primarily a Late

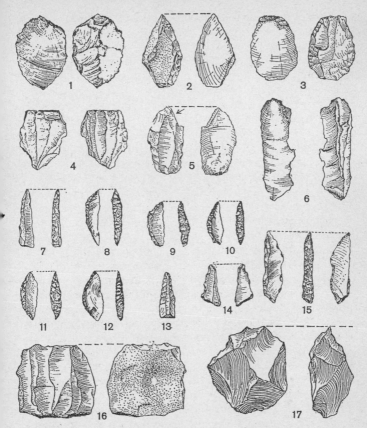

Figure 8. Langhnaj, Late Stone Age tools. 2:3 (approx.)
1–3, flakes; 4 and 16, blade cores; 5, burin; 6, blade; 7 and 15, backed blades; 8–12, lunates; 13, awl or borer; 14, triangle; 17, prepared core.

Stone Age factory site. Barkaccha and Siddhpur on the margin between the hills of Central India and the Gangetic plains give the impression that they may have served more advanced communities as well as the Late Stone Age hunters of the surrounding territory. Finally there are numerous rock shelters in Central India which contain occupation debris in the form of massive quantities of stone tools and waste material, varying amounts of bone and charcoal and other cultural remains. Many of these contain only shallow deposits consisting of little more than a few inches of dust and microliths disturbed by the feet of sheltering herd boys and their animals. Some however have been found to contain a greater depth of occupation (Plate 1).

Two shelters, Jambudip and Dorothy Deep near Pachmari, were excavated in 1930, and in 1961–3 two more were excavated at Lekhania in Mirzapur district by the Department of Archaeology of Allahabad University. All these yielded Late Stone Age industries throughout several feet of occupation deposit, with a certain amount of sterile cave filling below. The Lekhania rock shelters contained a number of burials, and they are associated with further sites, near by in the open, which are apparently contemporary. A bone sample from one of the skeletons gave a C14 date of 1710 B.C. The stone industry shows certain sequential changes and developments in each case, the tools becoming smaller, more delicately made and more varied in the upper layers. Pottery also makes its appearance at a certain point, and becomes more frequent towards the top. At Modi rock shelter on the Chambal valley the sequence is much the same, but the Late Stone Age occupation begins from bedrock. In no case has an occupation deposit containing a Middle Stone Age industry been recorded. Therefore the relationship between the Middle and Late Stone Age traditions is still uncertain.

Rock shelters excavated at Adamgarh hill in the Narbada valley present a clearer picture. A few tools of earlier industries were found in and upon the surface of a stony deposit which in places lay under that associated with the Late Stone Age. The Late Stone Age tools are found throughout a thick layer of black soil which varies from 50 to 150 centimetres in depth, and which sometimes lies on the earlier deposit, and sometimes on bed-rock. As there were no recognizable layers in the black soil the finds were recorded in measured levels. Trench one, of which a detailed account is given by the excavator, yielded almost 5,000 artifacts. It was cut into an undisturbed level surface in front of the rock shelter. In addition to the stone industry there was a quantity of animal bones, mainly concentrated between 25 and 40 centimetres from the surface, but also above and below this. Potsherds were found down to a maximum depth of 85 centimetres. Fragments of glass bangles were found at 20 centimetres, iron at 11 centimetres and haematite nodules at from 40 to 45 centimetres. There were also broken mace-heads and pebbles which appeared to have been used as hammer stones. Shells from between 15 and 21 centimetres have been dated by C14 to approximately 5500 B.C. – the first date so far for a primary Late Stone Age culture in the subcontinent. Of the stone industry R. V. Joshi writes:

Points and blades together form the bulk of the microlithic implements. Each of these may be divided into several sub-types. The primary distinction in the case of points is whether the tool is made on a nodule, a flake or a blade. The points on blades, which constitute the largest number, are further distinguished by taking into consideration the extent and position of the retouch. . . . In the case of the blades the basic types are simple blades and retouched blades.

In addition to these two basic groups he lists lunates; triangles which as a group grade into points; and occasional trapezoidal forms. A variety of scrapers are made on flakes, blades and cores, and notable among the last are those made upon blade cores. 'Borers, awls and burins do not constitute major tool types . . . but their presence is significant on account of their specific functions.' The great majority of the cores found in the excavation as a whole are blade cores. The finds are listed in the table on p. 84.

The animal bones found in the excavation include the domestic dog (*Canis familiaris*), Indian humped cattle (*Bos indicus*), water buffalo (*Bubalus bubalis*), goat (*Capra hircus aegagrus*), domestic sheep (*Ovis orientalis vignei* Blyth race *domesticus*), pig (*Sus scrofa cristatus*). There are also remains of a number of species of wild animals. These are Sambar, Barasingha and Spotted deer, hare, porcupine and monitor lizard. Wild and domestic animals are represented in approximately equal proportions, and a few of the bones of cattle, pig and spotted deer are charred. The association of the microlithic industry with the bones of domestic animals in this context in Central India raises a host of questions, and some of these

MICROLITHS AND OTHER ANTIQUITIES FROM ADAMGARH TRENCH 1.

Depths in cms.	POINTS — On Flakes	On retouched Blades	On unretouched Blades	Unclassified and broken	Borers and Awls	BLADES Retouched — Crescentic	Others	Simple	SCRAPERS — On Cores	On Flakes and Blades	Burins	TRIANGLES — Isoceles	Scalene	Trapezes	Tranchets	Cores	Animal Bones	Pottery	Charcoal	Glass Bangles	Iron Fragments	Haematite Nodules
10	29	11	7	13	3	6	18	17	1	1	—	—	—	—	4	3	—	—	—	—	—	—
20	—	38	5	107	3	20	64	85	20	9	1	6	25	1	4	67	—	—	—	—	—	—
30	21	51	24	163	3	13	114	263	54	9	3	10	45	6	4	118	—	—	—	—		—
40	42	319	33	259	5	67	324	315	52	6	2	10	27	2	5	64	—	—	—			—
50	11	135	22	233	6	28	210	281	63	11	—	14	25	2	2	47	—	—	—			—
60	10	184	27	125	3	26	121	113	57	7	—	6	13	1	—	44	—	—	—			?
70	2	45	3	1	—	8	16	73	9	—	3	—	1	—	—	—	—	—				
80	—	8	1	9	—	8	—	16	2	3	—	3	1	—	—	—	—	—				
TOTAL	115	791	122	910	23	176	867	1163	258	46	9	49	137	12	19	343						

will no doubt be answered by more precise dating and by further excavations in the same and adjacent regions.

Late Stone Age sites of all kinds are very numerous in western Central India, and many rock shelters and factory sites are extremely rich. Collectively the trenches at Adamgarh are said to have yielded approximately 25,000 microliths, and Morhana Pahar, excavated by A. C. Carlleyle in the late nineteenth century but never published in full, must have yielded a collection of comparable size if we can judge from the quantity of material which has found its way into museums in many countries of the world. Some of the factory sites, as we have already pointed out, cover an extensive area of ground. Throughout western Central India, both north and south of the Narbada rift, the general character of the industries appears to be consistent, allowing for a certain amount of variation in the quality and nature of the raw material. This includes a whole range of jaspers and agates, chalcedony, usually obtained in the form of pebbles from river gravels, and a certain amount of exceptionally fine-grained quartzite which appears to have been quarried, although no quarries have yet been located. R. V. Joshi's preliminary account of the vast collection from Adamgarh could well be taken to cover the whole region: 'A rapid scrutiny reveals the presence of a variety of blades – parallel-sided, plain or retouched, penknife-type etc.; points – crescentic, bi-marginally retouched, leaf-shaped, shouldered or tanged, and simple points on flakes; burins; scrapers; and miscellaneous cores.' He further points out that the so-called geometric microliths such as triangles and trapezoidal forms are very rare. This, in the opinion of the present writers, is often the case: in dealing with large collections these forms have tended to be picked out and given undue prominence. Burins noticed by us in many Late Stone Age collections in both Central and peninsular India also form a very small proportion of the finished tools, but they recur persistently. Frequently they are made upon fragments of quartz even when the rest of the assemblage is made of crypto-crystalline silica, and they are made in the same manner as the burins already described from Sanghao cave in West Pakistan, only in miniature. By far the greater part of the finished tools are made on fine parallel-sided blades, as in Gujarat, but the quality of both the material and workmanship here is considerably higher. Indeed, the technical perfection of these industries seems quite beyond that demanded for utilitarian purposes. Many of the semi-precious stones such as agates which were used for making microliths in Central India are still employed by jewellers and bead-makers who obtain many of their best stones from the gravels of the Narbada and other rivers – the same sources which supplied the Late Stone Age hunters.

Rock shelters are fairly numerous in Central India, particularly in the Vindhyan sandstone which lends itself to their formation. A fair proportion of them are decorated with drawings upon the walls and ceilings (Plate 3), the majority executed in varying shades of purple, red and light orange-brown. Some clearly belong to later times, but many of the drawings are equally clearly associated with the hunting cultures of Stone Age or immediately post-Stone Age times. They show animals of many kinds, including deer or antelope, wild pig, rhinoceros, elephant, buffalo, humped cattle (*Bos indicus?*) and monkeys, the majority of which are clearly wild species, but a minority – chiefly cattle – might be either wild or domestic. Then there are human figures, sometimes together with animals in hunting scenes and other large compositions, and sometimes alone or in groups, and finally there are objects and designs less easily identified.

A tentative chronology has been put forward for the rock art of Central and peninsular India (Wakankar, 1963) based upon style, context, superimposition and general indications of antiquity, which shows that it must cover a considerable period of time. Hunting scenes and game animals seem to be shown throughout in various styles, while as time goes on other subjects such as armed or mounted figures and horse-drawn chariots also occasionally appear. If the cattle which are sometimes shown are domesticated, the question remains, were the Late Stone Age occupants of the caves pastoralists themselves or did they prey upon the herds of neighbouring peoples? A number of scenes seem to depict cattle raids or the waylaying of travellers, and there can be little doubt that the Late Stone Age cave dwellers of Central India flourished alongside the

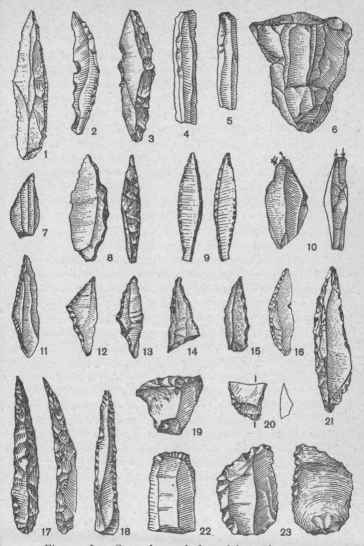

Figure 9. Late Stone Age tools from Adamgarh cave. 1:1

1, 3, and 21, backed blades; 4 and 5, blades; 2, 8, 11 and 16, lunates; 6, blade core; 9, double trimmed point; 12–14, triangles; 10, burin; 7 and 15, single trimmed points; 17 and 18, borers; 19, 22 and 23, scrapers; 20, transverse arrow-head.

Neolithic or Chalcolithic and possibly even later cultures of surrounding regions.

The eastern parts of Central India have been less thoroughly explored than the west, but it is already clear that Late Stone Age sites are to be found in considerable profusion there also, and the nature of the sites and the general character of the industries seem to be very similar to those farther west. At certain places somewhat different industries have been recognized. In the Singrauli basin for example a microlithic assemblage was found under a considerable depth of alluvium on the bank of a small affluent of the Rihand river, which in turn joins the river Son. The tools are made almost entirely of quartz, which is locally available from the quartz reefs and dykes of a granite area immediately to the south. The tools include rather crude attempts to produce small parallel-sided blades, a few lunates and a number of utilized flakes and fragments. The latter include two simple burins of the kind discussed above. The most remarkable feature of this collection is the group of bifacial points, the largest approximately 6 centimetres in length and the remaining five ranging from 3 centimetres down to less than 2 centimetres. These are made by the same techniques of flaking as the hand-axes of the late Early Stone Age and early Middle Stone Age, only on a very small scale, and they therefore differ from the bifacial points of other quartz industries in the extreme south, as we shall see. If this is indeed a single industry it provides a marked contrast to the microlithic blade industries in the western part of the Central Indian region.

At Birbhanpur on the Damodar river in West Bengal – the extreme eastern extension of the Central Indian hills – excavations were carried out at a group of microlithic sites which surface observations indicate covers approximately a square mile in all. The tools are made of quartz and other materials, and they occur in clusters upon an old land surface about 3 feet below the present surface, and also below this in what are considered to have been fissures caused by the drying out of the soil. A number of holes were noticed in the Late Stone Age land surface which the excavator tentatively interprets as postholes. This suggests that what we have here is a factory site or camping place – or both – upon which huts were erected by the microlith-makers. If the site was in use over a fairly long period of time the actual area of habitation no doubt moved about within the total area over which a surface spread of tools can be seen today. The climate during and immediately after the

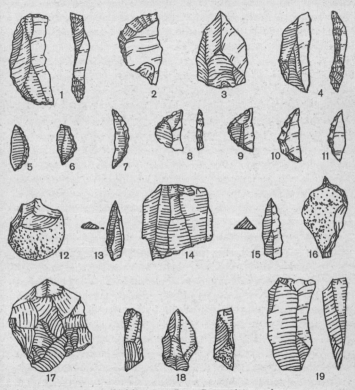

Figure 10. Birbhanpur, Late Stone Age tools. 2:3

1, 2 and 4–11, lunates; 3, pointed flake; 12, pebble core; 13 and 15, points; 14, blade core; 16, borer; 17, prepared core; 18 and 19, burins.

Late Stone Age occupation is thought to have been somewhat drier than at present, but follows an earlier phase of heavy precipitation and high humidity.

Birbhanpur did not yield such massive quantities of stone tools as the caves of western Central India, and the industry is of a somewhat different character. This is partly due no doubt to the high proportion of quartz used – 68·7 per cent of the stone tools and factory debris excavated. The blades and blade cores, whether in quartz or other materials, are not quite so fine; the points and lunates are broader, and a significant proportion of them are made on flakes rather than blades. The excavator classifies the industry from the excavations, excluding surface finds, as follows:

Blades	Lunates	Points	Borers	Burins	Scrapers	Total
106	42	60	19	12	43	282
37·5%	14·8%	21·2%	6·6%	4·2%	15·3%	

The total number of finished tools (282) are only 5·1 per cent of the whole assemblage excavated, of which 6·8 per cent are cores, and 87·9 per cent are flakes. These figures definitely suggest a factory site. Both triangles and trapezoidal forms are absent from the excavation, although one doubtful specimen of each was noticed on the surface. This, together with the absence of pottery and of crested guide flakes – an inevitable by-product of the manufacture of fine parallel-sided blades – is taken by the excavator as an indication of greater antiquity than that of the industries of the upper layers of the caves farther west. The present writers are inclined to agree with this conclusion, although the absence of crested guide flakes and so called geometric forms could be ascribed to the use of such a high proportion of quartz, which would make the production of parallel-sided blades by orthodox means difficult. Another argument in favour of the greater antiquity of the Birbhanpur industry is the weight of evidence for the late survival of the western industries which we have already discussed. The excavator rightly makes the point that there is no specific evidence in the form of carbon dating for the date of this industry, and it may in fact have survived as long as the others but remained out of touch with more advanced peoples. He also notes that quartz and crystal seem to have been preferred for the manufacture of borers and burins. The latter are of the same kind as those described earlier from western Central India. They are classified by him into four groups, but are all fairly simple and unspecialized, and utilize the natural angularity of the quartz. One only regrets that this excavation did not yield human or animal skeletal remains.

Throughout eastern Central India the occurrence of Late Stone Age tools has been briefly recorded, both in the open and in rock shelters, but little further systematic work has been done. But there is no doubt that their distribution extends throughout West Bengal, Bihar and Orissa, and southwards into Andhra Pradesh. Before considering southern India we must look at one more group of sites on the west coast.

A group of coastal sites around Bombay were described by K. R. U. Todd (1950). These are situated chiefly on headlands and small rocky islands overlooking the sea, or on rising ground near the banks of streams. The industry has the basic characteristics of all those we have discussed so far, but with a certain admixture of larger tools such as scrapers and points – many of the former made on flakes. Blades and blade cores, lunates and points made on both blades and flakes are the predominant forms, as they are in all north Indian Late Stone Age industries. Burins are found, as before, in a limited variety of simple forms, and made on flakes and pieces of raw material, which in this case is largely jasper. There are also occasional perforated stones, made by the technique of pecking used in making stone axes in Neolithic times. These were probably used as weights for digging sticks and perhaps for other purposes as well. Fragments of pottery found with the stone tools may well be contemporary. The situations chosen by these people show that they must have had boats of some kind, and that they must have relied on fishing as a staple part of their economy. It is possible that these sites were the temporary or permanent homes of coastal fishing communities who latterly were contemporary with Neolithic, Chalcolithic and perhaps even later peoples. The stone industry has a distinct character of its own which quickly becomes modified as one moves inland.

Inland sites in Maharashtra yield somewhat impoverished assemblages without the fine finish of the Central Indian industries or the distinctive blend of Middle and Late Stone Age traditions seen at the coastal sites. The same can be said of the assemblages from the western edge of the Deccan plateau, where the familiar pattern of sites upon small hillocks and ridges continues. This pattern is seen again in Andhra Pradesh, where a large number of microlithic sites were found more than forty years ago in the lower Godavari valley, by L. A. Cammiade, and many more have been found throughout the region since. The tools in the Cammiade collections are made in a range of different kinds of crypto-crystalline silica and occasionally quartz. They give the impression that their closest affinities are with eastern Central India, but both regions deserve further study before anything definite can be said about this.

Moving southwards from any of the regions we have just mentioned, Bombay, upland Maharashtra or northern Andhra, we approach a new region in terms of Late Stone Age techno- logy. The Late Stone Age industries so far recorded in the southern part of the Indian peninsula are predominantly based upon milky quartz. This is in part due to the granite rocks underlying so much of the country, in which quartz veins and dykes are readily found. The jaspers and chalcedonies so common in the volcanic rocks farther north are in short supply, but they do occur in places and they are represented in many river gravels. Both earlier and later peoples found these sources, but many of the southern Late Stone Age assemblages are almost a hundred per cent quartz. This was first noticed in Mysore where the change takes place between the districts of Raichur and Bellary. In Raichur, Stone Age factory sites on the banks of the Krishna, one of which we have already men- tioned, produce an industry comparable to those we have dis- cussed from regions farther north, and based largely upon pebbles of jasper taken from the river gravels. As in the majority of the north Indian sites, excepting Birbhanpur, only a very small percentage of the tools were made of quartz. A late Middle Stone Age site lay in close proximity, and the source of supply was common to both. Again, at many Neo- lithic sites in the same region, river pebbles of jasper and similar materials are the basis of a stone blade industry. Whether the blades were made at the same factory sites – and perhaps even by the same people – as the tools used by the Late Stone Age hunters is an interesting subject for research. There seems little doubt that the same sources of supply were exploited continuously from Middle Stone Age to Neolithic times. By contrast both to the south of Raichur, in the former Mysore State, and to the west, Late Stone Age hunters seem to have preferred to make their tools of quartz.

A group of sites at Jalahalli in the vicinity of Bangalore produced a distinctive quartz industry in which both the technique of striking flakes from small carefully prepared discoidal cores and that of making microlithic blades are represented. The latter is rather poorly developed, probably on account of the intractable nature of quartz. The same range of tools is found as in the industries farther north, including scrapers of several kinds, burins, awls, lunates and points. This group of industries might in fact be described as the translation into quartz of all the elements seen in the microlithic industries we have described from Raichur, the lower Godavari region, inland Maharashtra, or even Gujarat. One new feature makes its appearance, a transverse arrow-head. A closely similar assemblage was found at Kibbanahalli to the north-west of Bangalore, and isolated assemblages of quartz microliths have been recorded from Giddalur in the Eastern Ghats, and Calicut in Malabar on the west coast. A large number of sites yielding quartz tools of this and earlier periods have recently been found in Goa. Quartz tools have also been reported lying on top of ruined buildings in the Buddhist city of Nagarjunakonda in southern Andhra Pradesh. The implications of this are remarkable, and although the city itself is now submerged by a dam the surrounding regions deserve investigation. In Belgaum district, at the top of the Western Ghats a quartz industry is reported from Barapedi cave, and at Sanganakallu, a granite hill in Bellary district, quartz flakes were found below the lowest levels of Neolithic occupation.

On the east coast, south of Madras, another distinctive group of coastal sites has been discussed by several writers. The tools are associated with a group of old sand-dunes, on what are taken to be two former shore lines at 50 and 20 feet respectively above the present sea level. These dunes are locally known as *teri*, and hence the industry associated with them has come to be known as the teri industry. The dunes were in process of formation when the first hunters, or more probably fishermen, camped among them. Later they became fixed, due to the growth of vegetation and the formation of soil, almost certainly as the result of a slight increase in rainfall. Then drier conditions returned and the sand began to move once more. The wind moved the sand, but left the stone tools and factory debris, sometimes on the surface of the old subsoil. The industry from the dunes on the 20-foot shore line is made approximately of fifty per cent quartz and fifty per cent light brown chert. The flake tradition is more strongly represented here than in the Mysore quartz industries, and small discoidal cores and the flakes struck from them are characteristic tools of the industry; so also are lunates and transverse arrow-heads and retouched points of various kinds. Blades and blade cores are represented, but they are rather a minor element in the industry as a whole. The majority of the finished tools are made either on flakes or on chips of raw material – it is often impossible to know which, as reworking has removed any indications there might have been. This might be described as a micro-lithic industry based upon flakes. There are also scrapers of various kinds, a few rather problematic burins, and a large number of utilized flakes, cores and fragments of raw material. In addition there is a small proportion of very fine bifacial points. These are unlike anything found in Late Stone Age industries elsewhere in the subcontinent, with the exception of Ceylon, and they can only have been made by the very special-ized technique of pressure flaking. The industry found in dunes associated with the fifty-foot beach appears to be a somewhat less developed flake industry without microliths. Recently this has been called in question, and the suggestion made that the whole range of tools is found throughout. There is of course no reason to suppose that the dunes were only inhabited when the sea was at a higher level than at present: they provide a sheltered camping place within reach of the sea and of lagoons and estuaries suitable for fishing and fowling. Fishing com-munities on the coasts of India still live in situations of this kind, building their huts among sand-dunes which are far from stable in order to be near their fishing grounds. As in the case of the Bombay sites, there seems little doubt that this is the industry of a Late Stone Age fishing community.

As yet there are only a few radiocarbon dates, and no other absolute datings for sites of this period as there are for later cultural periods. Evidence for climatic change during or immediately after the main period of occupation has been recorded at Langhnaj, Birbhanpur and Adamgarh, and at the teri sites. But without some means of relating these to one another in terms of absolute time there is no means of knowing whether these changes were merely local, due perhaps to the effects of human activities in the vicinity, or were part of more widespread climatic changes perhaps affecting the whole continent.

The Late Stone Age or 'Mesolithic' industries of India must be associated with people much like the modern 'tribal' groups in more remote regions who live (or lived until less than a century ago) primarily by hunting and gathering, only sometimes augmenting this by trading with more advanced communities or by going out to work for them. This too could well have been the practice of later 'Mesolithic' communities who established contact with Neolithic or Chalcolithic neighbours. The bow and arrow are used by hunting peoples throughout India and Ceylon today, and they are represented in the cave art of the Late Stone Age in Central India, therefore it seems highly probable that they are associated with this phase throughout. The small tools of this period were clearly intended for hafting as composite tools and weapons – there are analogies for this from many parts of the world. This method makes for economy in the quantity of stone needed, and for lightness, as much of the tool is made of wood, mastics, etc., which are lighter than stone, while stone forms only the points, barbs and cutting edges. It also allows for a great variety of tools to be made from a limited range of forms, and it is particularly suitable for making arrow-heads of all kinds. If the advent of the bow and arrow did not actually coincide with the advent of microliths, it must certainly have had its heyday in Late Stone Age times.

The Late Stone Age of Ceylon exemplifies all that we have said about this period in India. Our knowledge of earlier phases is limited to a single hand-axe, but this particular cultural phase has been exceptionally well recorded, first by the Sarasin brothers who visited Ceylon in 1907 and by the Seligmans (1911), then by the excavations of Hartley in 1913 and 1914 and more recently by the researches of Dr P. E. P. Deraniyagala. The Sarasins and the Seligmans each carried out small excavations in caves, the latter in one which was actually occupied by a Vedda family. They both found quartz microliths together with larger tools, such as pounders and hammers of various kinds of stone, animal bones and bone tools throughout, and pottery in increasing quantities in the upper layers. Objects of iron were also found in the topmost levels, where the quality of the stone industry tended to decline. The industry has been found in caves and at surface sites in southern Ceylon, in the mountainous part of the island, and at one site in the north, near Jafna, under four feet of earth. This last is not far removed from the teri sites of southern India. Both the Sarasins and the Seligmans considered the Vedda tribes, who then inhabited the remoter parts of the southern mountains, where many of the caves and related surface sites were found, to be the direct descendants of the Late Stone Age inhabitants of the caves. Some doubt has since been cast on this on account of the intermixture of later peoples, but there can be no doubt that they represent a continuous tradition of hunting, gathering, and living for part of each year in the caves which only finally gave way to the pressures of agriculture and industry at the beginning of this century. Ever since the beginning of the Iron Age, which in Ceylon may very well antedate the arrival of settlers from north India, from the fifth century B.C. onwards, the hunting tribes must have been steadily drawn into relations with more advanced communities, but like many of the 'tribal' people of India they managed to retain their own cultural identity.

The large factory site of Bandarawela which covers four small hillocks in the plateau country of southern Ceylon was excavated by Hartley. The excavations showed only a few inches of soil above a gritty layer two to three inches deep containing tools, debris and charcoal. This lay upon the surface of the decomposing gneiss of which the hills are formed. In the course of two short seasons of one month each 4,768 finished tools were recovered, together with a large but unspecified quantity of factory waste. All except three tools were of quartz. Unfortunately the collection has been divided, and it is therefore impossible to give percentages for the various tool-types found. Hartley's classified list of tools found in his second season's work is of some interest, although the categories into which he divides his collection are rather different from those of more recent workers in this field. It reads as follows:

1	Lunates	264
2	Semi-lunates	188
3	Irregular	11
4	Rhomboidal	1
5	Angular	52
6	D-shaped	78
7	Beaked	17
8	Curved points	322
9	Straight points	33
10	Drill points	0
11	Borers	3
12	Arrowheads	8
13	Blades	4
14	Chisels	2
15	Hollow scrapers	2
16	Round scrapers	32
17	Quartz pebbles	2
18	Gneiss pebbles	5
	Blanks	6
	Uncertain	45
	Total:	1,075

From our own observations of collections in museums in Britain we can confirm that, as in the teri industry, blades and blade cores are comparatively rare, but their presence shows that the technique was known. Larger tools such as scrapers and utilized flakes, cores of all kinds and fragments of quartz are abundant, and both awls and burins are similar to those in Indian Late Stone Age industries. What is remarkable about this industry is the variety and perfection of the microliths. Lunates and transverse arrow-heads predominate, varying from thick segments of up to 4 cm. in length down to less than one centimetre. These groups grade into one another and also

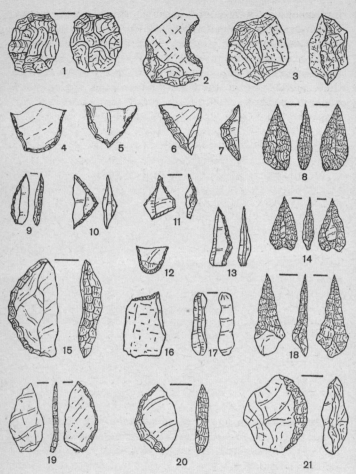

Figure 11. Bandarawela, Ceylon, Late Stone Age tools of quartz. 2:3

1 and 3, prepared cores; 2, hollow scraper; 4–6 and 12, tranverse arrow-heads; 7, 9, 15, 19 and 20, lunates; 8, 14 and 18, bifacial points; 10, triangle; 11, borer; 13, trimmed point; 16, burin; 17, blade; 21, convex scraper made on a flake struck from a prepared core.

into smaller groups of trimmed points, triangles and trapezoidal forms. Bifacial points (Hartley's arrow-heads) like those in the teri industries are also found in relatively small numbers, but show considerable variety of form. Discoidal cores prepared for the removal of flakes, similar cores already struck, and the flakes produced from them are all present in fair numbers. Some of the finest tools can be seen to be made either from flakes of this kind or from blades – more often the former – but the majority have no bulb of percussion or other definite indication of how they were made. This can sometimes be accounted for by its removal in process of making the tool, but it occurs so frequently as to suggest that there must be some other explanation. The charcoal found at Bandarawela is suggestive, especially in the light of the method of shattering quartz recorded in the Andaman Islands. The Andamanese heated pieces of quartz in their fires and then struck them with a stone while still very hot. The result was a quantity of sharp slivers and fragments which they used for shaving and general cutting purposes without further preparation. The adoption of such a method would explain the marked preference for quartz seen here and in much of south India. Once this method was established it must have been less tedious than the preparation of cores, and the removal of flakes or blades one by one. But it does not entirely explain the use of fifty or sixty per cent of quartz at the teri sites or at Birbhanpur. The small fragments of quartz were particularly suitable for incorporating in the composite tools of the Late Stone Age. This also explains why its use was favoured then, but not so much in earlier times when quartz was flaked by the same method as other kinds of rock; nor was it favoured by the Neolithic and Chalcolithic inhabitants of the granite regions who went to considerable trouble to obtain good-quality jasper and chert from which they could make large quantities of parallel-sided blades for their day-to-day needs.

CHAPTER 5

EARLIEST SETTLEMENTS OF BALUCHISTAN AND THE INDUS PLAINS

ON present showing the slow but cumulative stages of the Old World Neolithic revolution took place in the Middle East. Archaeological research during the past half century has gradually pushed its horizon back in time, until with the recent discoveries at Jarmo, Jericho and Catal Huyuk it rests somewhere between the ninth and seventh millennia B.C. How long it took for the new ways of life to spread into the Iranian plateau and thence northwards to Central Asia is not yet precisely known; but at such sites as Sialk and Djeytun it may well have been before the close of the sixth millennium B.C. How and when it reached the valleys and foothills of Baluchistan and Sind on the eastern borders of the Iranian plateau is even more obscure. The environment offered by this region has much in common with the Fertile Crescent and it might be expected that in ancient times this similarity was if anything even stronger. Thus it comes as something of a surprise to discover that in 1966 the earliest settlement in West Pakistan for which a radiocarbon date is available is not much older than 3500 B.C. However, it must not be forgotten that compared to the Middle East planned exploration in this area is still in its infancy, and further work may well give evidence of earlier settlements to bridge the apparent gap. That this may happen has already been suggested by the recent discoveries of one writer. Be this as it may, the picture presented today suggests that there was a considerable time lag between the appearance of a food-producing way of life in the Middle East, and even Iran, and in any part of the Indian subcontinent.

Our purpose in the following chapters is to trace the main outline of the culture sequence in the several regions of India and Pakistan and to learn something of the relations of the different regions and different periods. We shall deal with the following main culture phases: the pre-Harappan cultures in the Indus valley and Baluchistan, the Harappan civilization, the problem of the Aryan invasions, the Neolithic–Chalcolithic spread to the east of the Indus valley, the introduction and spread of iron working, the emergence of city states in north India and the beginnings of history. The rapid growth of our knowledge of certain regions particularly in India, during the past two decades, and the growing body of radiocarbon dating determinations make possible a far clearer picture of the earlier phases than could have been drawn even a decade ago. We are now required to place less reliance than hitherto upon cross-datings with what are often tenuously dated materials from earlier excavations in Iran. Therefore we shall attempt to emphasize the evidence of excavated cultural sequences and radiocarbon dates rather than such cross-dating, particularly as relatively little new evidence of the latter kind has come to light since the publication of Piggott's *Prehistoric India* in 1950.

EARLIEST SETTLEMENTS IN BALUCHISTAN

The earliest settlements attested by archaeology lie in north, central and possibly southern Baluchistan. In this arid mountainous region, in the isolated valleys often at heights of four to five thousand feet above sea level, there are many traces of early settlement. In the north these are particularly common in the Quetta valley, and to the east in the valleys of the Loralai and Zhob rivers. Today, the modern population eke out a hard existence. The climate is moderate, but the rainfall is less than 10 inches a year. Wheat is the main crop, and fruit and vegetables flourish with the aid of irrigation.

Kili Ghul Mohammad is a small mound approximately 100 yards long and 60 yards wide, lying about two miles from the modern city of Quetta. Here in 1950 Fairservis carried out a small exploratory excavation only 3·5 metres square, reaching virgin soil at a depth of 11·14 metres. Hence in the lower levels the area excavated was very small indeed. Period I, the lowest of the four cultural phases revealed at the site, produced radiocarbon samples from a hearth in its uppermost levels. These have given dates of 3688 and 3712 B.C. Below there is a further deposit of nearly 4 metres in thickness, doubtless representing

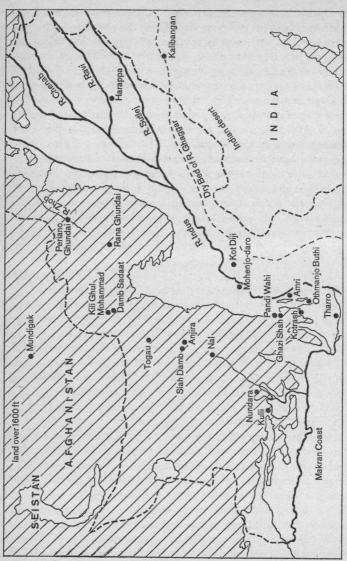

Figure 12. Map of pre-Harappan settlements of the Indus system and Baluchistan

a considerable time duration. The cultural data of this period indicate that the inhabitants had domestic sheep, goats and oxen, and certainly by the end of the period constructed houses of mud brick or hard packed clay. Their material equipment included blades of chert, jasper or chalcedony, and a broken rubbing or grinding stone, but no metal objects. Awls or points of bone were also found, but no pottery was discovered, and hence the excavator treats the period as pre-ceramic, although on so small a sample this is perhaps to overstate the case. There followed two further periods, II and III, the earlier yielding crude handmade and basket-marked pottery. These levels contained further house walls of mud brick, and a material culture otherwise little different from that of the preceding period. The predominant pottery had a red or yellow-red surface with a yellowish body, and a coarser ware with sandy body also occurred. In period III the first copper was found along with distinctive pottery, both wheel- and handmade, decorated with black or red painted designs including simple geometric motifs.

There are several sites in north and central Baluchistan which may on comparative grounds be associated with Kili Ghul Mohammad II and III. In the Loralai valley the mound of Rana Ghundai was excavated by Brigadier Ross in the late 1930s and an extensive sequence revealed. The lowest occupation (period I) was some 14 feet in thickness, and consisted of a series of living surfaces and hearths in which no trace of any structures was discovered, although these may have been of mud-brick and hence undetected. Ross suggested that this level represented a sort of nomadic occupation. Throughout this period plain handmade pottery occurred along with bone points and a stone-blade industry. Animal bones included those of sheep, goat, ass and Indian cattle (*Bos indicus*). The four equine teeth recorded by Ross in this period have been shown by Zeuner to be most likely those of a hemione or semi-ass, and by themselves they certainly do not provide evidence of the domestication or even presence of the horse. Fairservis revisited the site in 1950 and confirmed Ross's observations of the sequence. He discovered in period I sherds of painted pottery distinctly reminiscent of those of Kili Ghul Mohammad II. He also studied the trial excavations of the neighbouring

site of Sur Jangal made in 1927 by Sir Aurel Stein, and concluded that the earliest period of occupation there was contemporary with at least the later part of Rana Ghundai I.

In central Baluchistan, in the Surab valley, the recent excavations of Miss de Cardi have revealed a related picture of the
earliest settlements at Anjira and Siah-damb. In the first phase
(Anjira I), immediately upon the natural gravel, there was no
sign of structures, but ash and stone suggested the domestic
rubbish of a semi-nomadic community. A chert-blade industry,
including a small number of backed blades and lunates, occurred along with bone awls, spatulas, and a small bead. The
pottery was of a fine buff ware, wheel-thrown and often with
burnished red slip; it included both plain and decorated sherds,
the latter painted with motifs comparable with those of Kili
Ghul Mohammad II. Anjira I was followed by a further shallow deposit of about 3 feet associated with house walls of river
boulders. The pottery may again be compared with that of Kili
Ghul Mohammad II–III, and included a substantial number
of cream-surfaced, handmade, and basket-marked sherds. Although there are as yet no radiocarbon datings to relate the
evidence of Rana Ghundai or Anjira to that of Quetta, there is
a sufficient cultural uniformity, and even relationship of specific
details of ornamentation, to make cross-dating over the relatively short distances possible.

Further evidence of the character of the earliest settlements
in this region comes from south-east Afghanistan, where at
Mundigak, on a now dry tributary of the Arghandab river,
J.-M. Casal has excavated a most important sequence. The
initial occupation (periods I, 1, and I, 2) did not reveal any
structures. Then followed a level containing walls of pressed
earth, and in the upper layers of the period mud-brick made
its appearance. Thus here too the first settlers seem to have been
semi-nomadic. A terracotta figurine of a humped bull occurred
in period I, 3 (Plate 7 A No. 1). From the prestructural phase
onwards pottery is present, including painted ware (Figure
13), apparently for the most part wheel-thrown. Some characteristic painted designs are similar to those of Kili Ghul
Mohammad II and Anjira I. Bone awls, alabaster vases, stone
blades and beads in (?) steatite, lapis lazuli and frit, all make

their first appearance during this period. So do objects of copper, including a needle and a small bent blade. The whole impression of the Mundigak period I assemblage is of closer proximity to sites of Iran, and reveals a greater diversity of crafts, etc., than the sites of Baluchistan. Thus there is reason to infer that the first waves of influence felt in north and central Baluchistan followed the ancient trade route across southern Afghanistan and the plain of Kandahar.

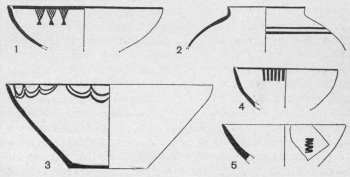

Figure 13. Mundigak I painted pottery. 1:6

There is as yet no clear evidence of any settlements of this period in southern Baluchistan or the Makran coastal region. That they exist is to be expected, but as yet there has been less scientific excavation there, and we must await further work.

BALUCHISTAN AROUND THE CLOSE OF THE
FOURTH MILLENNIUM

Somewhere, around the end of the fourth millennium B.C. – the date is hypothetical and as yet attested by no radiocarbon samples – important cultural changes seem to have occurred in the sites of north and central Baluchistan. What these changes signify is not quite clear, but they may well have involved the arrival of new influences or people from the west. Their interest is emphasized by the fact that they coincided with, and clearly contributed to, the extension of settled life on to the vast plains of the Indus system. With this period in all parts of Baluchistan a great proliferation of settlements and development of material culture seems to have occurred. As a result of the excavations of the past fifteen years the cultural picture is now becoming clearer, but it was still a perplexing mass of vaguely related data when Piggott wrote in 1950.

Because Mundigak appears to represent the line along which these new influences arrived in Baluchistan we shall first consider what developments took place there. In period II at Mundigak the houses are well constructed and the settlement is notably more compact than in the earlier period. In one house a well with a brick head was discovered. Many of the rooms had hearths constructed in the centre. The pottery of this period, by contrast to that of the first, was mainly handmade, and undecorated, suggesting cultural stagnation. On the other hand the second period produced the first crude stone disc seal (Plate 7 B, No. 1), and the first of a series of bifacially worked stone leaf-shaped arrow-heads. Mundigak III, in which there are six phases of construction, represents a time of great activity, the structures forming a logical development of those of the preceding period. A cemetery was discovered at the foot of the mound with contracted burials in its earlier phase, and in its later phase, more commonly, communal ossuaries. The pottery shows an increasing proportion of wheel-made vessels and an exciting range of painted decoration (Figure 14). In particular black geometric designs on a red surface and polychrome designs appear – both having many parallels at other sites of Baluchistan. The stone-blade industry continues and there is a considerable increase in the use of both copper and bronze. In III.6 a bronze shaft-hole axe and a shaft-hole adze were found (Figure 31, No. 4). Terracotta figurines are numerous and include the humped bull and crudely formed human females (Plates 6 and 7 A). There are numbers of flat stone seals, both square and circular (Plate 7 B). The whole assemblage from period III shows many features reminiscent of Sialk and Hissar, and this too suggests actual contacts with Iran. A radiocarbon date for III.6 of 2360 B.C. appears to be plausible.

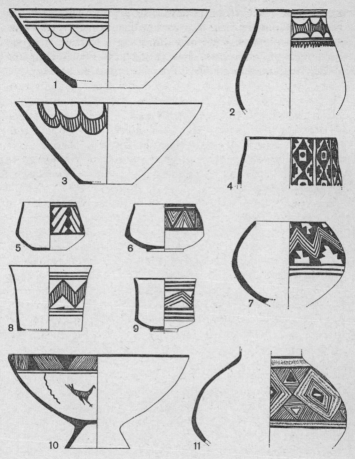

Figure 14. Mundigak III, painted pottery. 1:6

Mundigak IV saw the transformation of the settlement into a town with massive defensive walls and square bastions of sun-dried bricks. The main mound was capped with an extensive building identified as a palace, and another smaller mound with a large 'temple' complex. The brick walls of the palace had a colonnade of pilasters (Plate 4 B). The city was destroyed, and twice rebuilt during the period. An increasing quantity of pottery was decorated with a red slip and black paint, with a growing use of naturalistic decoration showing birds, ibex, bulls and *pīpal* trees (Figure 15). Female figurines of the 'Zhob mother goddess' type are found, and these have

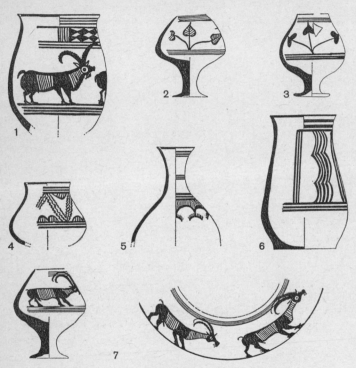

Figure 15. Mundigak IV, painted pottery. 1:6

their closest parallels in Damb Sadaat III and Rana Ghundai IIIc (Plate 6, Nos 4 and 5). This suggests that Mundigak IV corresponds with these periods in its earlier phase, while in its later phase it is contemporary with the Harappan period. Further support for this may be found in the male head with hair bound in a fillet, in white limestone, assigned to Mundigak IV.3 (Plate 4 A). This piece has a certain relationship to the celebrated priest-king of Mohenjo-daro even if the relationship is not a direct one.

The developments we have just witnessed at Mundigak appear to be closely paralleled in the Quetta valley. At the open-

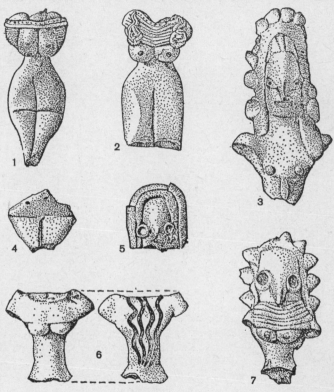

Figure 16. Damb Sadaat, terracotta figurines. 2:3
1 and 5, surface; 2 and 4, period II; 3, 6 and 7, period III.

ing of this period, i.e. around the beginning of the third millennium, the settlement at Kili Ghul Mohammad came to an end, but the sequence is taken up by a new site some ten miles south at Damb Sadaat, also excavated by Fairservis. Here too there is a noticeable advance in the scale of the houses, but mud-brick is still favoured, and hearths and bread ovens were found. There were three phases of occupation, of which the earliest (I) produced two radiocarbon dates of 2625 and 2528 B.C. and the second (II) three dates of 2554, 2425 and 2220 B.C. In the third phase a more ambitious structure with brick walls of monumental proportions was constructed. The material culture of the three phases is homogeneous; distinctive figurines of terracotta, both human female and animal forms, were found in periods II and III (Figure 16). Among the animals the humped bull with painted decoration was noteworthy. Two button seals of clay occurred in periods II and III (Figure 17),

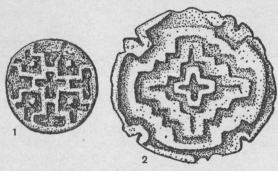

Figure 17. Damb Sadaat clay seals. 2:3
1, period II; 2, period III.

and copper objects in the earlier period included a dagger blade. Bone tools and a stone-blade industry, mainly of chert, continued, as did the alabaster bowls. The presence of numbers of grinding slabs and stone balls, perhaps used as corn-crushers, attests the preparation of cereals. Once again varieties of painted pottery proliferate, and the Quetta ware with its black-on-buff bichrome decoration shows numerous parallels with Mundigak III. The beginnings of this style are found in Damb Sadaat I and its elaboration continues through periods II and III. Polychrome decoration (named 'Kechi Beg polychrome' after the type-site) occurs in Damb Sadaat I and II; and a painted grey ware (named Faiz Mohammad grey) is another feature. A characteristic of the plain pottery is a surface roughening, as in the Quetta 'Wet' ware, while another variety of this ware has circular stamping on the shoulder of the vessel. The similarities of form, fabric and design point to a general relationship between Damb Sadaat I–III and Mundigak II–III.

In the north-east lobe of Baluchistan, in the Loralai and Zhob valleys, further convincing concordances may be found. Here as yet there are no radiocarbon dates. At Rana Ghundai in the Loralai valley the second major period (II) coincides with an important change and the introduction of a new, finely made painted pottery with friezes of humped bulls in black, upon a buff-to-red surface. These vessels are frequently in the form of bowls or cups, often with a ring base or a hollow pedestal. Period III follows, and is divided by its excavator into three sub-periods. The division was traced by him in a stylistic evolution of the painted pottery. In IIIA appears a bichrome painted style with red-on-red tones, occurring also nearby at Sur Jangal in period III. In the upper levels of this period there appear a number of wares with parallels in Quetta, including the 'Wet' ware, polychrome akin to that of Kechi Beg, and a painted style akin to Faiz Mohammad ware. The third period ended with a conflagration and was replaced by a very different potting tradition. A larger excavation is required to provide a more certain chronology for the Loralai valley.

From the Zhob valley in the extreme north of Baluchistan further evidence comes from the site of Periano Ghundai, excavated by Sir Aurel Stein in 1924 and revisited in 1950 by Fairservis. The earliest phase here seems to coincide with Rana Ghundai IIIC. The finds include leaf-shaped bifacial arrowheads, stone blades and female figurines of the sort commonly known as 'Zhob Goddesses'. A distinctive type of surface roughened ('Wet') ware again suggests its date. Another special feature of Periano Ghundai was the large terracotta figurines of humped bulls. The assemblage from this site is discussed in greater detail by Piggott and Fairservis.

In central Baluchistan, de Cardi's recent work at Kalat provides a valuable extension of our knowledge of this period, or at least of its earlier half. Anjira III seems to coincide with Damb Sadaat I–II, and Anjira IV with the flowering of Damb Sadaat II–III. Here the principal painted pottery was that named after the type site of Togau, fine red ware with painted designs including friezes of animals, usually caprids. De Cardi has traced the stylistic evolution of this motif in the succeeding levels of the excavation. Other characteristic painted wares are bichrome and polychrome, the former with cream or red slip, and decoration in red or black. These same varieties are found again in Anjira IV. Also common in this last period are the black-coated Anjira ware, and a surface-roughened ware having obvious affinities with the Quetta 'Wet' wares.

The situation in south Baluchistan for this period still lacks clarity. There may well be significance in the resemblances of the polychrome wares from the Nal cemetery to those of Mundigak III and Anjira IV; while as Dales has recently suggested the non-cemetery materials from Nal may be somewhat later and compare with those of Damb Sadaat III, Mundigak IV and Rana Ghundai IIIC. It is probable too that during this later period the Kulli culture began to develop in south Baluchistan. The distinctive decoration on the Kulli pottery clearly emphasizes its position as a link between southern Iraq and Iran and the lower Indus. It seems probable that the Kulli culture survived well into Harappan times. The full excavation of a Kulli site is one of the many desiderata of the later prehistory of West Pakistan.

PRE-HARAPPAN SETTLEMENTS IN SIND, PUNJAB AND
NORTH RAJPUTANA

During the period of the earliest settlements of Baluchistan we must visualize, on the basis of the limited evidence available, that the remainder of the Indian subcontinent was inhabited by tribal communities whose technology was based primarily upon stone, and whose principal tools were the bow and arrow, the trap, the snare and the digging stick. It is probable that in the varied environments offered by the peninsula there were many different local cultures based upon fishing, hunting and food collecting. It appears at present that around the end of the fourth millennium B.C. the first major expansion of the Neolithic–Chalcolithic way of life took place, with the colonization of the great tracts of alluvial land in the valley of the Indus and its tributaries. But we must be cautious in accepting this without reservation, for there is at least one assemblage of retouched stone blades, reputedly found with sherds of pottery near Karachi, that may indicate a much earlier stage of Neolithic settlement than any so far recognized there. The expansion to which we refer is one of tremendous importance, since it can now be seen to provide a uniform environment and cultural basis upon which at Amri, Kot Diji, Harappa and Kalibangan the foundations of the first Indian civilization were laid.

The Indus plains offer a very different environment from the upland villages of Baluchistan. Today the whole landscape is largely man-made; embankments and irrigation canals effectively mask its ancient shape, but it is still possible to envisage how it must have appeared to the first settlers. The main channel of the Indus flows through a wide expanse of alluvial floodplains which, with the recession of the annual inundation of June to September, are of extreme fertility. Wheat and barley sown at that time ripen by the following spring, without either ploughing or manuring of the ground. The banks of the river and of its subsidiary channels are not cultivated and must then, as now, have supported a dense cover of tamarisk and scrub. Once the agricultural potentials of the new alluvium were realized, and means were discovered of overcoming the problems of protecting settlements on the flood-plain from inundation, an entirely new type of life became possible. On present showing this development took place somewhere around the opening of the third millennium B.C.

The southern group of sites is that associated with the type-site of Amri. The settlements are still for the most part well above the flood-plain of the Indus and are found rather in tributary valleys, such as Othmanjo Buthi, or on piedmont ground, situated between the western hills and the plain. Amri is outstanding, both because it was here that Majumdar by his excavations of 1929 first demonstrated the existence of a pre-Harappan phase lying beneath the Harappan culture, and because some thirty years later the excavations of the French team directed by J.-M. Casal have provided a clear and certain picture of the stages of this change. The ancient settlement here lies within a mile of the river Indus, on the right bank. It is situated on the alluvial plain, but above the flood line.

The pre-Harappan occupation of Amri is divided into two periods, the first being further subdivided into four phases. In the earliest of these (IA) no structures were discovered, but it yielded a number of ditches, buried storage jars and other pottery. Most of the pottery was handmade, a few sherds having bichrome and many others monochrome decoration, including motifs recalling the Togau C ware and thus probably contemporary with Anjira III–IV (Figure 18). Fragments of copper and bronze, a chert-blade industry and numbers of stone balls (perhaps slings or bolus stones) completed the assemblage. The second sub-period followed without any break, and contained two phases of mud-brick buildings, with bricks of irregular sizes and in some instances footings of stone. The pottery constitutes a definite development from that of the earlier phase and includes a wide range of painted motifs, and the chert blades and bone tools continue. The third phase (IC) represents the high point of the Amri culture and contains no less than four structural phases. Houses are built of both mud-brick and stone, and a curious feature is presented by multiple small compartments about a yard square which seem to have served as platforms, probably to raise buildings above ground level. The pottery now includes a majority of wheel-thrown vessels, and shows a wide variety of painted motifs, mainly geometric, in both plain and polychrome styles, with brown or black, and ochre or orange-upon-pink (Figure 19). The range of forms is a direct development from the earlier phases; the other categories of the material culture, bone points, stone blades, etc., continue. The final phase of the first period is represented by only one building level and a continuation of the essential features of the culture. From this period comes a beautiful painted sherd with a humped Indian bull, and another painted vessel has a row of quadrupeds, two of which appear to be caprids and one a carnivore, perhaps a cheetah or a dog.

In discussing the external affinities of the Amri culture we must regret the absence of any radiocarbon datings and base our estimates upon cross-dating to other excavated sites. The earliest phases (IA–B) provide links with Anjira III, Kili Ghul

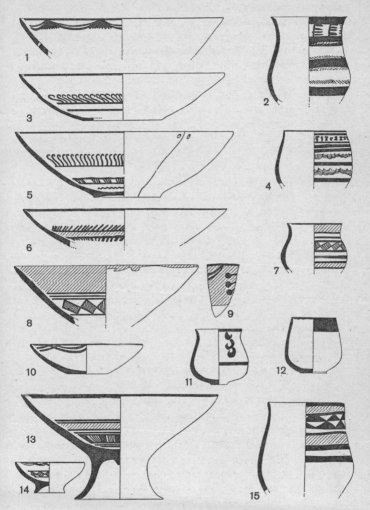

Figure 18. Amri IA, painted pottery. 1:6

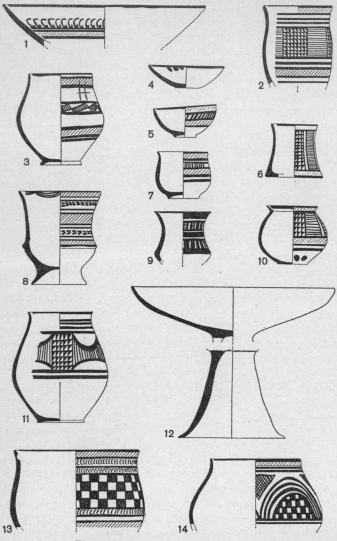

Figure 19. Amri, painted pottery. 1:6
1–10 and 12, period IB; 11, 13 and 14, period IC.

Mohammad III–IV, and Mundigak III; while the last phase ID gives comparisons with the upper levels of Mundigak III and Anjira III–IV. The presence of a few sherds of Harappan pottery in this level and the further correspondences with Kot Diji, to be discussed below, are significant. Period II at Amri follows without any cultural break, but after a general levelling and reconstruction of the site. It is divided into two phases, A and B, and is characterized by an increasing presence of sherds of Harappan type alongside the Amrian. It may thus be regarded as transitional between the purely Amrian culture of I and the Harappan of III. From period II the cross-datings of pottery are with Mundigak IV.1 and Damb Sadaat II, and more especially with Kot Diji and sites of the Indus valley proper. There is a suggestion that the site was burnt at the end of the period.

A number of sites have been identified as belonging to an equivalent pre-Harappan, Amrian phase. In the south, on a promontory which in those days was probably on the coast, although now far inland, behind deltaic formations, is the fortified settlement of Tharro (Tharri Gujo). Another fortified site is at Kohtras Buthi, south-west of Amri. To the north lie other small sites such as Pandi Wahi and Ghazi Shah.

About a hundred miles north-east of Amri, on the left bank of the Indus, today some twenty miles from the river, but still near one of its ancient flood channels, lies Kot Diji. The ancient site is somewhat similarly placed to Amri, located on the solid ground below a small rocky outcrop on which a medieval fort was constructed (Plate 8 B). There are indications at various points that the early settlement was subject to floods and that stones were piled up as a protection against their action. The site was excavated in and after 1955 by the Pakistan Archaeological Department, and the published results are of great interest although they leave many questions unanswered. The first settlement was constructed upon bed-rock, and immediately above it were discovered house floors, contained within a massive defensive wall of which the lower courses were of limestone rubble and the upper mud-brick. The wall was strengthened by bastions and preserved in places to a height of 12–14 feet. Within this great wall there were some 17 feet of occupation deposit, the lower portion being excavated only in a restricted area. Throughout the upper 10 feet, house walls of stone and mud-brick occur, and it is probable that further excavation below this level would reveal similar structures. The material culture included a chert-blade industry with some serrated blades, and other blades reportedly bearing 'sickle gloss'. A small number of leaf-shaped arrow-heads, unfortunately not illustrated, suggest parallels with Periano Ghundai I and Mundigak II–V. Stone querns, pestles, balls (corn-crushers, sling or bolus stones?) and at least one fine terracotta bull were found. It is not clear whether there were any objects of copper, but a fragment of a bronze bangle is reported. The pottery was of a distinctive character with restrained use of painted decoration (Figure 20). It was mainly wheel-thrown and much of it was decorated with plain bands of brownish paint. An interesting motif appears to have developed from bands of loops and wavy lines into the well known fish-scale pattern which later appears on Harappan pottery. As in Amri II, in the later levels of Kot Diji I many characteristic Harappan forms occur. The excavators report a clear typological evolution of the principal forms throughout the period. Of the painted pottery one may note the common bichrome with a cream slip and red-, sepia- or black-painted decoration; parallels for this ware are found in Mundigak III.5 and IV. A small number of vessels had distinctive painted motifs. The roughening of the outward surface of some vessels is reminiscent of Anjira III–IV and Damb Sadaat II–III.

The early occupation of Kot Diji closes with evidence of two massive conflagrations and is replaced with a mixed but predominantly Harappan culture. The date of this event, carrying with it as it does the suggestion of violent overthrow and conquest, is suggested by the radiocarbon evidence. The pre-Harappan occupation yielded three samples: one from near the beginning of the settlement gave a date of 2605 B.C.; and two others from nearer the top, 2335 and 2255 B.C. respectively. A fourth date of 2090 B.C. corresponded with the second great conflagration. The comparison of the pottery of Amri and Kot Diji should provide an all-important check on their relative ages. There is little doubt that Amri IA–C is earlier than the beginning of Kot Diji. Parallels between Amri ID and IIA and B, unfortunately not well represented in the excavations, and Kot Diji, are more numerous. But even here there is considerable individuality in the two assemblages. The suggestion is clearly that in pre-Harappan times there were fairly marked divergences in potting tradition.

About thirty miles west of Kot Diji on the right bank of the Indus lies Mohenjo-daro, now some three miles from the river,

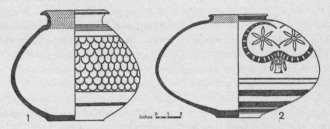

Figure 20. Kot Diji, pre-Harappan pottery

but squarely on the flood-plain. The continuing deposition of alluvial silt with each year's floods has raised the whole land surface in this area more than 30 feet since Harappan times, and as the water table has risen correspondingly archaeologists have so far been unable to plumb the lower levels of this vast site. It is tempting to speculate that here, too, beneath the Harappan occupation there may lie a pre-Harappan culture corresponding to that of Kot Diji. Support for this may be found in such pre-Harappan features as surface roughened ware reported in the lowest levels reached by Mackay. Further support is probably to be found in the exciting results of the borings conducted in the HR area by Dales and Raikes. Here occupation deposits were encountered to a depth of 39 feet below the modern level of the plain. In the same way at Chanhu-daro Mackay reported further occupation levels below the water table and speculated that these too might well contain a pre-Harappan, or Amrian culture. Pottery of probably related facies has been reported from sites in Bahawalpur, notably at Bhoot, south of Khairpur, and at Jalilpur in Multan district, and it is to be expected that a comparable pre-Harappan phase may be found in that area.

Related pre-Harappan cultures seem to have extended very widely. Pottery was discovered by Wheeler during his excavations at Harappa in 1946, in stratified positions both under the defences, in the earliest structural level of the defences, and among the mud-bricks of the rampart. Wheeler with brilliant foresight drew the inference that this pottery represented a pre-Harappan culture phase, but in the light of Kot Diji and Kalibangan it can be seen that, in all probability, he had stumbled on part of the brick rampart of a pre-Harappan settlement at Harappa itself. It therefore seems legitimate to add Harappa to the list of pre-Harappan sites, and to expect further excavation at the great citadel mound to reveal a brick-walled settlement analogous to those of Kalibangan and Kot Diji.

There remains one further site at which excavation has revealed a related sequence. This is Kalibangan, on the bank of the now dry course of the Ghaggar river, about 120 miles south-east of Harappa, and 300 miles east-north-east of Kot Diji. Here excavations have been undertaken by the Archaeological Survey of India since 1959 with impressive results, although as yet only short summaries have been published in *Indian Archaeology*. The pre-Harappan settlement was found beneath the Harappan citadel mound as at Kot Diji and Harappa. There were five building phases, all the structures being of mud-brick of a standard size different from that of the Harappan period (Plate 9). The settlement was surrounded by a massive rampart of mud-bricks, though whether as defence against floods or human agencies cannot be said. Pot-like hearths were found in the rooms. One house contained a series of ovens both above and below ground. A feature of the material culture was a stone blade industry, with some serrated blades. Shell bangles, steatite disc beads and beads of various other materials were found. Copper and bronze were rare, but copper objects included a bangle and more than one flat axe.

The pottery of this early period is varied and of great interest (Figure 21). The range of forms and painted motifs differs quantitatively from those of either Amri or Kot Diji, although it shares one important element, particularly with the latter. As at these sites, some features anticipate the Harappan ware, including the presence of such forms as the offering stand. The predominant pottery (Fabric A) is red or pink with black, or bichrome black and white painting. Among painted motifs may be noticed a distinctive arcading, a 'moustache-like' bifold

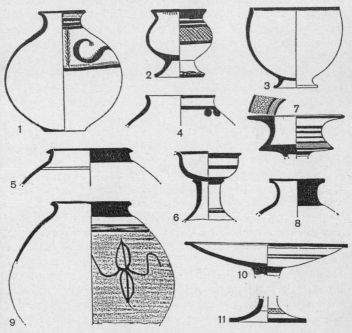

Figure 21. Kalibangan, pre-Harappan pottery. 1:8
1–4, fabric A; 9, fabric B; 5, 7, 8, 10 and 11, fabric C; 6, fabric E.

scroll also found at Kot Diji, as well as occasional plants, fish and cattle (Plate 8 A). One group of pots of Fabric B shows a surface roughening technique somewhat similar to the Quetta 'Wet' ware but sometimes overpainted with animal or other motifs. Another group (Fabric D) has elaborate incised or combed decoration on the inside of open bowls or basins, a technique seen occasionally in Amri II (Figure 22). On the whole the pottery of Fabric A is distinct, while that of Fabrics B, C, D and E is closer to that of Kot Diji and Amri, both in point of manufacture and of painted decoration, with plain bands of red and black. An extensive series of radiocarbon samples has been obtained at Kalibangan, those for the pre-Harappan period ranging between 2370 and 2100 B.C. A cluster of six between 2100 and 2000 B.C. gives dates for the beginning of the Harappan period provocatively close to that obtained at Kot Diji.

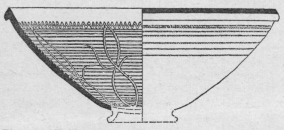

Figure 22. Kalibangan, pre-Harappan bowl, fabric D. 1:8

In his explorations in 1950–53 Shri A. Ghosh, the former Director General of Archaeology in India, discovered many sites in the valley of the Ghaggar river and its tributary the Chautang, producing a pottery which was apparently identical to the pre-Harappan pottery of Kalibangan. This complex he named the Sothi culture, but so far little has been published regarding it, and it remains a somewhat shadowy entity.

To summarize the evidence presented in the previous pages. The earliest settlements so far reported in the whole Indian subcontinent are in the upland valleys of Baluchistan and southern Afghanistan. At a somewhat later date, probably around the opening of the third millennium B.C., a cultural complex named after the type-site of Amri appears in the piedmont zone to the south-east of Baluchistan, abutting on the Indus flood-plain. A distinctive settlement pattern, still if we may judge from the material culture having its primary links with Baluchistan, developed there and after a series of evolving stages gave way to a culture of purely Harappan type. Further north at Kot Diji and Harappa a somewhat similar culture is indicated as developing, perhaps slightly later, in settlements beneath the Harappan levels. The pottery of these two sites is distinguishable from that of Amri both in the relative austerity of its painted decorative patterns and in its range of forms; but it is still largely wheel-thrown and still suggests Baluchi ancestry. Finally at Kalibangan a comparable sequence is observed, probably having a life span slightly later than or nearly contemporary with that of Kot Diji, but possessing a pottery which introduces many new painted motifs and a rather wider, and incidentally less closely Baluchi, range of forms.

In all these cases the material culture provides hints of an intermediate period when forms and motifs emerge which are later identified as Harappan. At Amri and Kot Diji there is important evidence of a general destruction by fire coinciding with the emergence of the new 'Harappan' culture. What is particularly exciting in these recent excavations is the repeated evidence of continuity from pre-Harappan to Harappan times, suggesting that a large if not a major element in the Harappan civilization must derive from the pre-Harappan culture of the Indus valley itself. Another interesting feature is the evidence of massive fortification walls in the pre-Harappan period. The destruction at Kot Diji may nevertheless indicate that the actual transition from the pre-Harappan culture to the Harappan coincided with attack from outside. It remains to comment upon the already considerable uniformity of culture over so wide an area during this pre-Harappan phase. When the indications of further settlements around and between the excavated pre-Harappan sites are taken into account, it may be concluded that there were at least three subregions of this culture: the central, including Kot Diji and Harappa, and hypothetically also Mohenjo-daro; the southern or Amrian with closer ties with southern Baluchistan; and the eastern or Kalibangan with suggested (and still largely hypothetical) affinities with a pre-Harappan Indian culture phase. This leads us to frame certain very interesting questions. For instance, how large did the settlements at the central sites become, and did they already contain the essential elements to warrant their being regarded as cities? What were the Indian cultures which influenced the Kalibangan province, and what in turn were

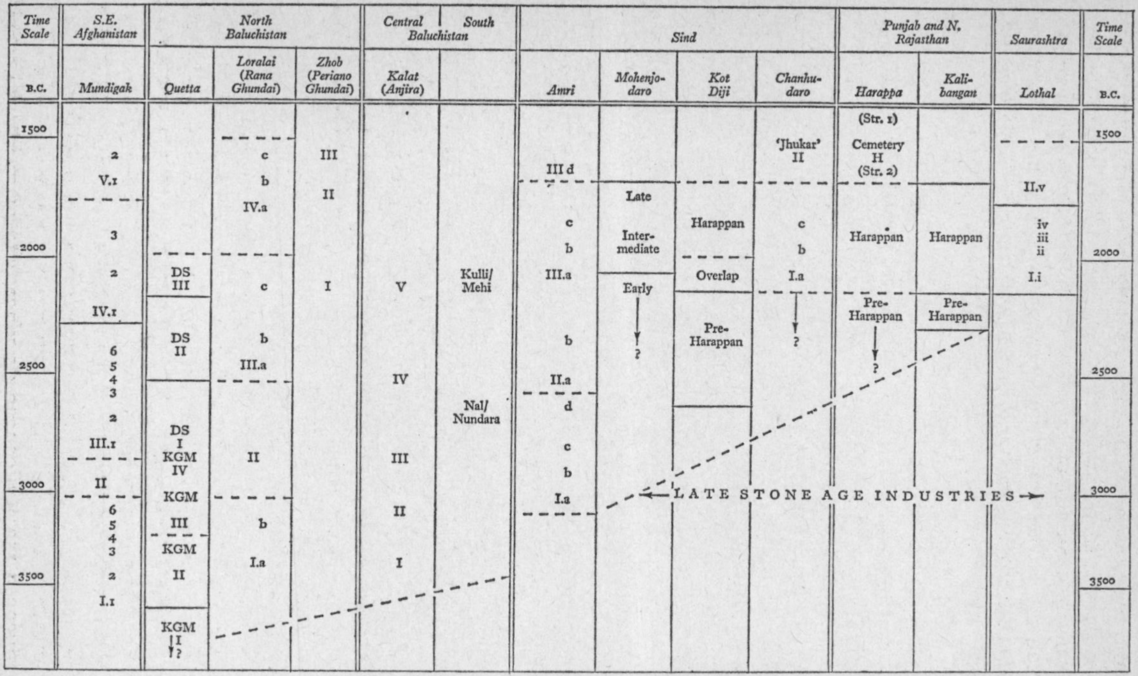

Time Scale B.C.	Saurashtra	Punjab and N. Rajasthan		Sind				South Baluchistan	Central Baluchistan	Zhob	North Baluchistan	Quetta	S.E. Afghanistan	Time Scale B.C.
	Lothal	Kali-bangan	Harappa	Chanhu-daro	Kot Diji	Mohenjo-daro	Amri		Kalat (Anjira)	Zhob (Periano Ghundai)	Loralai (Rana Ghundai)	Quetta	Mundigak	
1500	II.v		(Str. 1) Cemetery H (Str. 2)	'Jhukar' II		Late	III.d		V	III	c / b / IV.a	DS III	2 / V.1	1500
2000	iv iii ii / I.i	Harappan	Harappan	c / b / I.a	Harappan	Inter-mediate	c / b / III.a	Kulli/ Mehi	IV	II	c / b / III.a	DS II	3 / 2 / IV.1	2000
2500		Pre-Harappan	Pre-Harappan	?	Overlap	Early	b / II.a	Nal/ Nundara	III	I	II	DS I / KGM IV	6 5 4 3 / 2 / III.1	2500
3000				?	Pre-Harappan	?	d / c / b / I.a		II		b / I.a	KGM III / KGM II	II / 6 5 4 3 / 2	3000
3500									I			KGM I ?	I.1	3500

LATE STONE AGE INDUSTRIES

Figure 23. Pre-Harappan and Harappan sequence of Baluchistan, Sind and Punjab (chart 1)

their cultural antecedents? And finally, do the five or more centuries of pre-Harappan culture in the Indus valley provide the matrix within which the extraordinary and in so many ways peculiarly Indian civilization developed, to burst out suddenly and brilliantly during the closing centuries of the third millennium B.C.?

CHAPTER 6

THE INDUS CIVILIZATION AND THE ARYAN INVASIONS

IT has been remarked that books on the prehistory of India and Pakistan are often Indus valley centred. If this be true, it is understandable, for until recently the Indus civilization occupied the centre of our knowledge. The past two decades have changed this, and we venture – at the risk of erring in the other direction – to try to put the civilization in a better perspective. Its importance is however still unique, both because it represents a great and astonishing cultural achievement and because it may be seen as the formative mould for many aspects of classical and even modern Indian civilization. In this chapter we shall direct our discussion mainly to questions of sequence, and of the extent of the civilization, and in later chapters we shall touch upon various salient features. The preceding pages have shown how the stage is set in the Indus valley and Punjab and how there is a direct cultural continuity between the pre-Harappan and the Harappan periods. It is in the light of this that we may now proceed.

The present evidence, either of archaeological sequence or of absolute dating, does not permit any certain conclusion of the rate at which the Harappan culture expanded nor of where the new culture traits first evolved, apart from the pre-Harappan cultures of the Indus valley. There is some evidence both at Mohenjo-daro and Harappa of a general cultural evolution, but the earlier excavations of Marshall and Vats are not helpful on this point. We feel that the expansion was something of an 'explosion' and that it represented among other things an outcome of the successful control of the tremendous agriculturally productive potentialities of the Indus plains. The refinement of the archaeological evidence concerning the development of the civilization and of its regional variants, and the consequent possibilities of discovering the first centres of

the culture and of tracing its diffusion, are thus desiderata of
the research programme of the coming decades.

We have already mentioned the environment of the Indus
valley and the opportunities it offered once the annual inundation had been understood. There is no good evidence of any
drastic change in climate during the past four or five millennia
in this region. Thus while it is reasonable to expect a slightly
higher rainfall throughout the area before the natural vegetation cover was reduced by man's steady intensification of agriculture and grazing, no major shift in climate need be postulated. A vital necessity of settlement on the Indus plain itself
would have been flood defence, and here it seems that burnt-
brick must have played an important role. For in those areas
where stone was not readily available (and this includes the
majority of Harappan sites) mud-brick would have been
rapidly destroyed by rain or flood water. Thus the discovery
and utilization of burnt-brick was one factor. It has sometimes
been suggested that the Indus valley could not have produced
sufficient timber for this operation, unless the climate were
damper than today. But Lambrick, writing with many years
of administrative experience of the Sind, has shown that timber growing along the riverine tracts today is sufficient for all
the burnt-bricks made in the province, and anciently cannot
have been less abundant.

The area enclosed by a line joining the outermost sites at
which the material culture of this civilization has been discovered is little less than half a million square miles, considerably larger than modern West Pakistan. Within this area over
seventy sites are known, of which the great majority lie on the
plains of the Indus and its tributaries, or on the now dry course
of the Hakra or Ghaggar river which once flowed to the south
of the Sutlej and then southwards to the east of the Indus, with
the Sind desert on its left bank. Outside the Indus system to
the west a few sites occur on the Makran coast, the farthest
being Sutkagen Dor near the modern frontier of Pakistan and
Iran; these were probably ports or trading posts in a separate
culture region. The uplands of Baluchistan appear to have
been outside the Harappan zone. To the east of the Indus
further sites occur on or near the coast beyond the marshes of

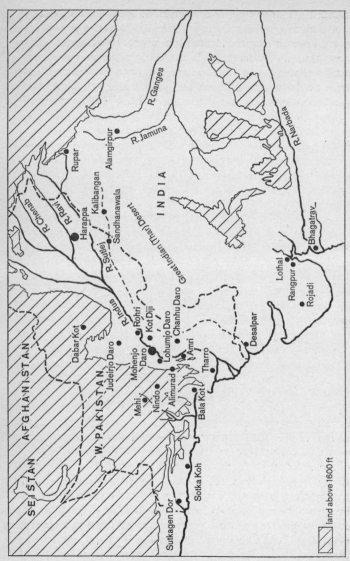

Figure 24. Map of principal sites of the Harappan civilization

Cutch (Kacch), the most impressive being the trading post at Lothal, on the gulf of Cambay; while at the mouth of the Narbada river the small settlement at Bhagatrav marks the southernmost extent of the culture so far recognized. One other significant extension is beyond the Indus system towards the north-east, where the site of Alamgirpur lies beyond Delhi, between the Ganges and Jamuna rivers.

Of all the Harappan sites two stand out, both on account of their size and of the diversity of the finds excavations have revealed. These have generally been hailed as cities, the twin capitals of this extensive state.* The southern is Mohenjodaro on the right bank of the Indus. Here the Indian Archaeological Survey under Sir John Marshall, and later Mackay, excavated between 1922 and 1931; after the partition of India and Pakistan in 1947 further work was done by Sir Mortimer Wheeler, and more recently by Dr George Dales of Pennsylvania University. In all these excavations the bottom of the Harappan occupation has never been reached, let alone the level of the first settlement, because, as we have already seen, the alluvial deposition of the centuries has raised the level of the plain by more than thirty feet, and the water table has risen correspondingly, so that reaching the lower levels presents special difficulties. The second and northern city is Harappa on the left bank of the now dry course of the Ravi

* It is perhaps hardly necessary to mention that this glib sentence conceals the cold archaeological truth, that up to today there is no positive evidence that the cities were capitals, either of separate states or of a unified 'empire'. For any society lacking written records, or whose script is still undeciphered, evidence of such matters as political conditions is clearly hard to come by, and is at best inferential. Generations of archaeologists have felt that some such interpretation better fits the Harappan evidence than any other, but necessarily it remains hypothetical. The reader must therefore draw his own conclusions from the available data: the apparent uniformity of weights and measures, the common script, the uniformity – almost common currency – of the seals, the evidence of extensive trade in almost every class of commodity throughout the whole Harappan culture zone, the common elements in architecture and town-planning, the common elements of art and religion. Even if the political and economic unity is admitted, there remain the profound and tantalizing problems of how it came about and how it was maintained. These have yet to be tackled satisfactorily.

in the Punjab. The vast mounds at Harappa were first reported by Charles Masson in 1826, and visited by General Cunningham in 1853 and 1873. Their rediscovery some sixty years later led to the Archaeological Survey's excavations between 1920 and 1934, directed by Pandit M. S. Vats. A short but important further excavation was made in 1946 by Sir Mortimer Wheeler: the natural soil was reached and evidence of a pre-Harappan culture phase revealed. In the earlier excavations of both these sites a mass of information was obtained relating to their planning and architecture, and much material relating to arts and crafts and to the way of life of the people was recovered. However, the excavations prior to 1947 did not achieve a satisfactory picture of the development of the cities, and in the absence of radiocarbon dating no absolute chronology was obtained.

A second series of sites have in some cases features which recall the basic layout of the cities, and although smaller, they may reasonably be regarded as provincial centres of government. Among them several have been excavated. Most recent in point of time is Kalibangan, where extensive excavations of the Harappan township are still in progress. From the viewpoint of technical excellence this work is among the finest so far done in the subcontinent and does credit to the Indian Archaeological Survey. Kalibangan shares with Harappa and Mohenjo-daro the layout of citadel and lower town, and it has produced a series of radiocarbon datings (Figure 70). At Kot Diji the excavators also treat the site as comprising a citadel and outer town of Harappan style. It was excavated in 1958, but the publication is somewhat unsatisfactory. Other large sites which may also be included in this category are Sandhanawala in Bahawalpur and Judeirjo-daro in Sind north of Jacobabad, but these have not as yet been excavated, nor has the great mound at Dabar Kot in the Loralai valley of north Baluchistan, apart from trial trenches made by Sir Aurel Stein. Farther south in Sind are Amri and Chanhu-daro, the former on the right and the latter on the left plains of the Indus. The French excavations have revealed much interesting information at Amri and have shown not only the pre-Harappan development, but also three distinct phases of Harappan occupation, as well as an immediately post-Harappan period. Chanhu-daro was excavated in 1935–6 by Mackay and produced a great deal of interesting material relating to the two latter periods.

Among other excavated sites we may mention Sutkagen Dor on the Makran coast where Sir Aurel Stein dug some trial trenches. More recently Dales has shown the existence of a great fortification around the Harappan outpost there. Perhaps the most important excavation of the post-war period has been that at Lothal. Here the Indian Archaeological Survey's team, under the direction of S. R. Rao revealed a great artificial platform with streets and houses of regular plan, and a series of building phases which have been dated by a number of C14 samples. Beside the township was discovered a remarkable brick dockyard connected by a channel to the gulf of Cambay (Figure 67). Two other smaller sites excavated in recent years are Rojdi in Saurashtra, and Desalpar in Cutch (Kacch) district. Both provide evidence of an initial occupation in the Harappan period, and of continuing occupation during post-Harappan times. Finally mention may be made of two outlying sites at Rupar in the Punjab and at Alamgirpur in Uttar Pradesh, at both of which recent excavations have established the presence of Harappan or late-Harappan settlements. The extension of the civilization eastwards towards the Ganges–Jamuna Doab raises various interesting possibilities which must await the research of coming years.

As a result of more than thirty years of excavations at these sites, there is a great body of evidence relating to the life of the civilization which produced them. Much of the detailed description will be given in later chapters, but here we shall summarize the main outlines which present themselves to the observer. Our overwhelming impression is of cultural uniformity, both throughout the several centuries during which the Harappan civilization flourished, and over the vast area it occupied. This uniformity is nowhere clearer than in the town-planning (Plates 10 A and 10 B). The basic layout of the larger settlements, whether cities or towns, shows a regular orientation, with a high citadel on the west dominating the lower town (Figure 66). Probably the latter was originally more or less square. Equally careful was the oriented grid of streets which intersected the blocks of dwellings. The widths of the streets seem to have been determined by a modulus. The imposition of this new layout on the older pre-Harappan settlement at Kalibangan, with its haphazard disposition, dramatically emphasizes the suddenness and completeness of the change (Plate 9). A similar uniformity is found throughout the Harappan structures. There is a remarkable standardization of brick sizes, both of burnt- and mud-bricks, and this too is in basic contrast to that of the pre-Harappan period. The skill of the bricklayers is particularly clear in the great public buildings of the citadel complexes, for example in the great bath at Mohenjo-daro (Plate 11), and in the granaries at both cities. On the other hand one cannot but be struck by the monotonous regularity of the plain undecorated brickwork of the acres of uniform houses of the lower town at Mohenjo-daro. Another feature of the towns that calls for attention is the care expended on domestic bathrooms and latrines, and on the chutes which linked them to brick drains running down the streets. At intervals the drains were connected with soakage pits or sumps, and their maintenance implies some sort of highly effective municipal authority.

The mainstays of life must have been extraordinarily like those of recent centuries in the Indus valley. Wheat and barley were the main crops; leguminous plants, field peas and dates were other items of diet. Sessamum and mustard were used, presumably for oil. We shall have more to say regarding the system of agriculture in a later chapter. Among domestic animals were sheep, goats and cattle, and the domestic fowl was also kept. It is not clear whether bones of pig and buffalo indicate the presence of domesticated stock, or only that these animals were hunted for food. Several varieties of deer were certainly hunted. The discovery of fragments of woven cotton is of great interest, attesting the antiquity of an industry for which in later times India has been particularly famous.

A similar uniformity of culture can be observed in the technology of the Harappans: indeed it is as strong as in the town-planning, and so marked that it is possible to typify each craft with a single set of examples drawn from one site alone. It is not yet established whether this uniformity was achieved by the centralization of production, linked with efficiency of distribution, or whether by other factors, but in either case it calls for special study. A standard range of tools of copper and bronze is recorded at site after site (Figure 25). Many among

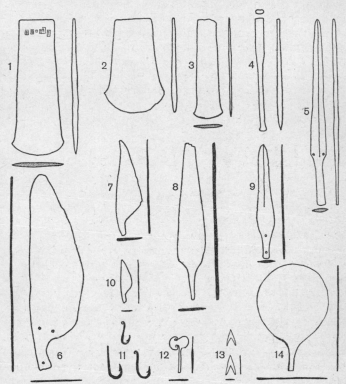

Figure 25. Mohenjo-daro, Harappan copper and bronze tools and weapons. 1:10

them set the pattern for later Indian types for centuries to come. The majority exhibit what Piggott called 'competent dullness', a simplicity of design and manufacture linked with adequate, but not great functional efficiency. The range of bronze and copper vessels is technically more worthy of remark (Figure 73). There is little doubt that such special objects as the cast bronze figures of people or animals, or the little model carts (of which nearly identical examples come from sites as far apart as Harappa and Chanhu-daro) were the products of special-ists' workshops in one or other of the cities (Plate 16 B). In spite of the commonness of metals, stone was not abandoned, and chert blades were prepared from cores which in turn had probably been exported from such great factories as that at Sukkur (Sakhar) (Figure 26). This craft, which demands com-

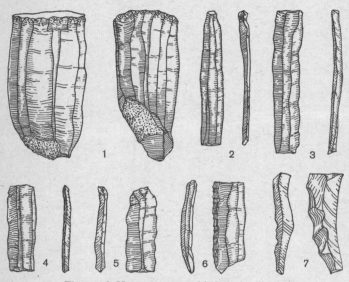

Figure 26. Harappan stone-blade industry. 1:2

parison with the stone-blade industry of the Neolithic–Chalcolithic cultures of peninsular India, shows a sort of effortless competence, without apparently any desire to pro-duce novel or special results. On the other hand the products of the potters must have been mainly local, and the uniformity of forms and painted decorations which they display (Figures 27 and 28) cannot be accounted for by trade. How it was achieved is not easy to determine; mere uniformity of wheels or equipment cannot alone supply the answer, even though it must have played a substantial role. The ubiquitous terracotta figurines of people and animals, both male and female, deserve no special mention (Plates 17 A and 20 A). They may have been toys, or in some cases cult figures of mother goddesses.

There were numerous highly developed arts and crafts. Among them that of seal-cutting calls for comment (Plates

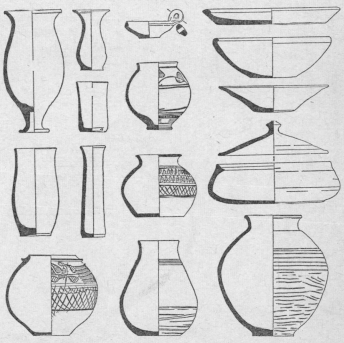

Figure 27. Harappa, Harappan pottery. 1:8

13 and 14). The seals were sawn from blocks of steatite and cut as intaglios, then toasted in a small furnace to harden and glaze the surface. Their importance was doubtless linked in some way with their role in trading activities, but for the modern observer of even greater interest are the short inscriptions in the unknown Harappan script and the subjects of the intaglio, many representing scenes of a cultural or religious character. The bead-maker's craft was also remarkable,

and the long barrel beads of carnelian rank among the technical achievements of the Harappans. So too must have done the art of shell inlay, unfortunately known only from fragments of shell; and the manufacture of objects of faience. Of stone and metal sculpture very few examples are known, but these range in quality between excellence and comparative crudity (Plates

Figure 28. Harappa, Harappan pottery. 1:10

16 A and C). Summing up we may say that technical uniformity over so great an area is probably unique in the ancient world and that Harappan technology deserves Childe's acclaim as 'technically the peer of the rest' (that is, of Egypt and Babylonia). But its limitations should not be overlooked. The majority of the products are unimaginative and unadventurous, in some ways reminiscent of the products of the Roman provinces, but also suggesting that the people of Harappa had their eyes on things not of this world. There are signs of an

innate conservatism, which in many respects demands comparison with Indian conservatism of later times.

Other categories of information are less easily obtained by excavation, but include aspects of life and culture which are essential if a full and balanced picture is to be obtained: thus from variations of house sizes, and from localization of groups of 'barracks', some scholars have inferred class differences even amounting to slavery. The same evidence has been used to suggest the presence of a 'caste' structure like that of later times. Again the presence of great granaries on the citadel mounds and of the 'citadels' themselves, have suggested, partly by analogy with Middle Eastern cities, the presence of priest-kings or at least of a priestly oligarchy who controlled the economy, civil government and religious life of the state. The intellectual mechanism of this government and the striking degree of control implicit in it are also very worthy subjects of research.

The language of the Harappans is at present still unknown, and must remain so until the Harappan script is read. Broadly there would appear to be two main contestants: that it belonged – however improbably – to the Indo-European or even Indo-Iranian family; or that it belonged to the Dravidian family. In spite of the careful analysis of the corpus of Harappan inscriptions – now in the region of 2,500 – by Hunter, Langdon and others, the task of decipherment remains problematic. Numerous attempts have been – and are still being – made, but none so far can inspire much confidence. In recent years the most significant advance has been the certain proof, offered by B. B. Lal, that the script was written from right to left. The shortness of the inscriptions, nearly all on seals or amulet tablets, further renders decipherment difficult. The uniformity of weights and measures is another indication of the efficiency of state control throughout a large area.

There are many traits which appear to anticipate features of the religion of Vedic times or later Hinduism. We shall notice below the probable existence of temples and stone cult icons in the cities. The seals have been generally agreed to contain a body of information on religious beliefs. It is evident that such motifs as the *pīpal* leaf, or the *svastika*, were already of religious significance for the Harappans. There is a suggestion of a religion dominated by one great God, who convincingly shares many of the traits of the later Śiva, being a *Yogi*, a Lord of Beasts, whose cult was associated with fertility and the *lingam*, and who in later times had the epithet *Mahādeva* (great God) (Plate 14, No 2), and by a great Mother who equally shares traits of Parvati, the spouse of Śiva known also as Mother, and Devi, the Goddess. There is an indication of the cult of trees or tree-spirits, and of the special significance of various animals (Plate 14, No 5). Taking all in all, we are left with a very clear sense at least of elements of the Harappan religion, and we cannot fail to see in them much that continues in subsequent Hinduism.

The information that has been gathered on such topics as the economy, social system, government or religion, was largely the product of chance finds in the earlier excavations. It is to be hoped that as archaeological research in India and Pakistan advances further excavations may be conducted with the aim of answering specific questions and elucidating specific problems.

The earlier excavations at Mohenjo-daro and Harappa revealed surprisingly little clear evidence of the Harappan burial customs. However, in the final seasons at the latter site Vats discovered the post-Harappan Cemetery H (to be discussed below), and between 1937 and 1941 a second, Harappan burial ground known as Cemetery R 37. Both these were further investigated by Wheeler in 1946. Since 1940 three other Harappan cemeteries are reported, although none is yet published; at Derawar in Bahawalpur, discovered by Stein, at Lothal, and at Kalibangan. The two latter have been excavated. It appears that the predominant burial rite was extended inhumation, the body lying on its back with the head generally to the north. Quantities of pottery were placed in the graves, and in some cases the skeleton was buried with ornaments. A number of graves took the form of brick chambers or cists, one at Kalibangan being of unusual size (4 × 2 metres), and from Harappa is reported a coffin burial with traces of a reed shroud. At Kalibangan two other types of burial were encountered: smaller circular pits containing large urns, accompanied by other pottery, but, perplexingly, no skeletal remains, at any rate in the examples so far excavated; and more orthodox burial pits with what are evidently collected bones. From the Lothal cemetery comes evidence of another burial type with several examples of pairs of skeletons, one male and one female in each case, interred in a single grave (Plate 18 B). It has been suggested that these may indicate a practice akin to *sati*. Until more is published, or further research is done, it does not seem possible to add to Marshall's speculations regarding the burials inside Mohenjo-daro itself, but it is evident from all these other finds that the regular cemeteries wherever they have been discovered were disposed around the perimeter of the settlement.

We shall now turn to a more detailed discussion of Harappan chronology and internal development, and the circumstances of the downfall of the civilization. The first estimate of the duration of the occupation at Mohenjo-daro was made by Sir John Marshall in 1931. His estimate, based upon general concordances with Mesopotamia, was from 3250 to 2750 B.C. In the following year C. J. Gadd published a paper listing a number of Indus, or Indus-like, seals discovered in Mesopotamian sites, particularly Ur, and discussing their ages. Here, apart from two examples which were listed as pre-Sargonid, the majority of finds of seals belonged to the Sargonid and Isin–Larsa periods, and might therefore be expected to indicate active trade contacts between 2350 and 1770 B.C. A few seals were also found in Kassite contexts indicating a yet later date. Since then Piggott (1950) and Wheeler (1946, 1960, etc.) have reviewed the evidence, including cross-dates to the as yet imprecisely dated sites of Iran (Hissar, Giyan, etc.), and other categories of objects apparently imported into Mesopotamia, etched carnelian beads, stone house-urns, etc. There has been general agreement upon an overall span of 2500–1500 B.C. with principal trade contacts with Mesopotamia between 2300 and 2000 B.C. In the past twenty years little additional evidence has come to light to change this view, so far as archaeological cross-datings are concerned. However, in 1955 Albright concluded that the end of the civilization must have been around 1750 B.C. in order to coincide with Mesopotamian evidence. The advent of radiocarbon has provided a welcome new source of information on what must otherwise have remained a very vague position, and may well necessitate a revision of the earlier views. Already by 1956 Fairservis had seen in the radiocarbon dates of his excavations in the Quetta valley a need to bring down the dating of the Harappan culture to between 2000 and 1500 B.C. In 1964 Shri D. P. Agrawal, of the flourishing radiocarbon laboratory attached to the Tata Institute of Fundamental Research in Bombay, was able to plot some two dozen dates, including those from Kot Diji, Kalibangan and Lothal, and to draw the conclusion that the total time span of the culture should be between 2300 and 1750 B.C. This evidence appears to us to be on the whole most plausible.

In view of the proximity of Kot Diji to Mohenjo-daro, it seems improbable that any great time lag would be experienced in the culture sequence of the two. Thus the radiocarbon dates relating to the general destruction by fire which heralds the intermediate period following the end of the pre-Harappan at Kot Diji, and any dates relating to the subsequent developments, would be of tremendous interest. Unfortunately the published report on Kot Diji leaves some vital gaps. The detailed description of the layer numbers of two of the four samples is not clearly stated, but we gather that only one date, 2090 ± 140 B.C., relates to the final destruction at the end of the Kot Dijian occupation. With this we may compare the series from Kalibangan, where a cluster of dates between 2100 and 2070 B.C. indicates the beginning of the Harappan period, and two dates around 1770–1670 B.C. indicate its conclusion. At Lothal another series gives dates between 2080 and 1800 B.C. (±115 and 140 years respectively), and a single date from a late level at Mohenjo-daro gives 1760±115 years.* There is a surprising conformity in these dates. They suggest a period of not more than four centuries for the Harappan civilization, between 2150 and 1750 B.C. We are inclined to accept them with the proviso that unknown variables may be found which demand some general modification. Yet even allowing a margin of 100 years, an initial date of 2250 B.C.

* A recently published series of dates from Mohenjo-daro, obtained by G. F. Dales, gives the Mature Harappan a span of 2154–1864 B.C.

would seem acceptable and in no way goes against the ad-
mittedly imprecise evidence afforded by the Mesopotamian
finds. Acceptance of this chronology carries with it the implication that trade contacts with the Middle East prior to 2150
B.C. would have been with the towns of the pre-Harappan
Amrian culture in the lower Indus.

There is another category of dating evidence which may be
invoked, in the textual references from Mesopotamia to objects
imported from Meluhha (probably the Indus Valley or
Western India), or the entrepots of Tilmun (probably in the
Persian Gulf, perhaps Bahrain) and Magan (perhaps in
Southern Arabia or on the Makran coast). There is good
reason to suppose that many of these objects originated in
India, and therefore the dates of this literature are likely to be
significant, at least of the period of maximum trade activity
on the part of the Harappans, if not of the duration of the
civilization. The first reference is in the time of Sargon of
Agade (c. 2300 B.C.), but the volume of literature only grows
during the third dynasty of Ur (2130–2030 B.C.) and the subsequent Larsa dynasty (2030–1770 B.C.). Thereafter they
markedly decline. They therefore suggest that the maximum
trade contacts coincide almost exactly with the duration of the
civilization indicated by the radiocarbon samples. It seems
likely that a critical reassessment of dates ascribed to seals and
other Indus objects from Mesopotamia would also tend to confirm these results. The discovery of a 'Persian Gulf' seal at
Lothal highlights the interest attached to finds at Failaka,
Bahrain and other sites on the southern shores of the Persian
Gulf. In recent years the Danish expedition working in this
area has discovered a large number of these distinctive seals,
some almost identical to imported specimens found at Ur and
other sites in Mesopotamia. Most recently Buchanan has reported the impression of one such seal on a dated cuneiform
tablet of the tenth year of king Gungunum of Larsa, that is
about 1923 B.C. according to the middle chronology. Thus almost for the first time, a find from a Harappan site, although
unhappily not from a well-stratified context, can be cross-
dated to the historical chronology of Iraq; and is not found to
conflict with the radiocarbon chronology we are following. Of

all the findspots of these seals and of objects supposedly imported into Mesopotamia from the Indus region, Frankfort's
excavations at Tell Asmar in the Diyala valley supply perhaps
the most convincing evidence of the age. But there seems even
so to be some latitude in the interpretation of the evidence.
According to Buchanan the earliest seals and imports are not
earlier than the late Agade period, and he concludes that 'the
Mesopotamian evidence therefore does not require a date for
the mature Indus civilization much, if at all, before the twenty-
third century B.C.'. If this conclusion is correct, it means that
there is no substantial conflict between the Indian and Mesopotamian evidence.

At almost every site of the Harappan period there is at least
some evidence of internal development. Unfortunately much
of the earlier work at Mohenjo-daro and Harappa was of such
a kind that its analysis is now scarcely possible, while the more
recent work at Kalibangan or Lothal is still incompletely
published. It is thus not easy to make a close comparison of
the development at each site, although one is led to feel that
parallels might be found, if only more evidence were available.
At those sites where excavation has revealed a pre-Harappan
phase below the Harappan (Amri, Kot Diji, Kalibangan) there
is in each case an indication of cultural continuity. Even when
at Kot Diji a massive burnt layer intervenes, the evolution of
decorative motifs on pottery continues. At the same three sites
there is further a transitional level in which both styles of pottery are found together. Of this level there is no evidence at
Chanhu-daro or Mohenjo-daro, as the height of the subsoil
water prevented excavation below a certain point, but at
Mohenjo-daro Mackay's deep digging in Block 7 of the DK
area revealed an early period, related by him to the 'Early'
eighth stratum of Marshall on the Citadel mound, which produced some pottery of non-Harappan type, for example some
incised comb decoration, recalling the pre-Harappan Fabric
D at Kalibangan. This may indicate that the early period
reached in the excavation at Mohenjo-daro goes back to the
transitional phase of the other sites.

At Harappa, Mohenjo-daro and Chanhu-daro the early
period ends with the massive brick platforms of the citadel

areas, and above are found the remains of the high period of the civilization. At Mohenjo-daro this included three principal structural levels of Marshall's intermediate period and was succeeded by a great and disastrous flood, and by three levels of the late period; at Harappa there were six structural levels of which the uppermost produced some pottery of Cemetery H type. At Kot Diji there are also apparently six or seven building phases within the Harappan period, while at Kalibangan nine are reported. At almost every site there succeeds a 'late' period during which planning and construction decline, brickbats from former houses are reused, new motifs appear on pottery, etc. This is generally seen as a decline, though whether associated with natural calamities or with political factors is still far from clear.

Around 1750 B.C. the uniform culture of this great area broke up: apparently with different results in Sind and the south, and in the Punjab and the north. What was the cause of this breakdown? Several causes have been suggested. Lambrick has recently proposed that calamitous alterations of the course of the Indus above Mohenjo-daro may either have driven population from desiccated areas to Mohenjo-daro, or have caused the desiccation of the lands around the city, and thereby weakened it, making it an easy prey to barbarians from the west. Marshall and Mackay stressed the repeated flooding of the city, and saw too in the vagaries of the Indus a possible cause of decay. This view has recently been modified by Raikes who, as a result of his study of the exposed flood-deposits and borings made at Mohenjo-daro, and of related observations elsewhere, has invoked tectonic movements downstream as responsible for mighty lake formation and silting. All three of these theories need not entirely exclude one another. But Raikes's theory raises serious difficulties which require elucidation before we are ready to accept it. Marshall, who dated the civilization almost a thousand years earlier than we have done, saw no connexion between its downfall and the Aryans. But Childe (1934) and Wheeler (1946) have shown that with revised chronology there is every possibility of invoking Aryan, if not Rigvedic Aryan, agency for the destruction. The unburied skeletons lying in the streets of

Mohenjo-daro are very suggestive. We may now, from the position suggested by radiocarbon dates, envisage yet another possibility – even if a remote one. If, as we have seen, the Harappan civilization with its remarkable cultural unity, came into existence only around 2150 B.C., it is necessary to admit that not only the end of the cities, but even their initial impetus may have been due to Indo-European speaking peoples. It is interesting to notice that recent work in Greece and Asia Minor suggests that the earliest movements traceable to Indo-European peoples there – those associated with the Minyan ware – may also be assigned to a nearly similar date.

THE ARYAN INVASIONS

As we have already seen, not only are languages of the Indo-European family the most widely spoken in modern India and Pakistan, but also the Rigveda is revered as the fountainhead from which all later Indian religion and philosophy developed. It is therefore of great interest to know when the Indo-European speakers entered the subcontinent and whence they came; and we now propose to consider briefly the archaeological evidence relating to their arrival. It is generally agreed that the expansion of the Indo-European languages in some way coincided with the domestication of the horse and its subsequent use with light war chariots. The wild species of horse appears in late Pleistocene times on the south Russian and Ukrainian steppes, and thence eastwards towards Kazakhstan and Central Asia. It is therefore to be expected that domestication would have taken place somewhere in this region. According to Zeuner the evidence formerly adduced from such sites as Anau and Sialk for a date in the fifth or fourth millennia B.C. relates to bones of half-asses (hemiones) and not to true horses. At present all that can be said is that domestication probably took place some time before 2000 B.C. and that the adoption of the war chariot dates from the opening of the second millennium. One of the earliest references to this spread is in the Chagar Bazar tablets of Samsi-Adad (*c.* 1800 B.C.), in the Khabur of north Syria. There is also inscriptional evidence from about that time for Indo-European languages spreading into the Iranian region. The Kassite rulers of Babylon at the opening of the sixteenth century bore Indo-European names, as did the Mitannian rulers of the succeeding centuries. A treaty of the Hittite King Subiluliuma and the Mitannian Mattiwaza of *c.* 1380 mentions the names of Mitra, Varuna and Indra, gods of the Rigvedic Aryans themselves, and among the Boghaz Keui tablets is a treatise on horse-training by Kikkuli of Mitanni using chariot-racing terms in virtually pure Sanskrit.

The archaeological evidence relating to all these movements, both in Iran and in India and Pakistan, is much less precise, and indeed it almost always lacks any clear hallmarks to establish its originators as Indo-Europeans. In north Baluchistan, Piggott has drawn attention to the thick layers of burning which indicate violent destruction of whole settlements at about this time at Rana Ghundai, Dabar Kot, etc. In South Baluchistan the cemetery at Shahi-tump, dug into an abandoned Kulli settlement, shows copper stamp seals, a copper shaft-hole axe (Figure 31, No. 2) and footed and legged bowls. The seals may be compared with Iranian examples from Anau III and Hissar III; the shaft-hole axes, unknown until this time in the Indian subcontinent, are of west Asiatic type and compare with those from Maikop and Tsarskaya in south Russia. A date of *c.* 1800 B.C. is quite acceptable. At Mundigak in period V the picture is rather different. On the main mound a considerable reconstruction of a massive brick structure is found over the ruins of the palace of period IV. The massive structure is perhaps in some way connected with the brick granaries of the Harappans and may well indicate a need for fortified storage of grain. Copper stamp-seals, of patterns sometimes reminiscent of those of Shahi-tump, make their first appearance during period IV, and continue into V. Copper pins with spiral loops, also reminiscent of Shahi-tump and Chanhu-daro, appear in IV (although related types are reported already in II, while shaft-hole axes and adzes are already present in III.6). None of these finds however is datable in itself.

Evidence of a rather different kind is available in Sind, where at Amri, Chanhu-daro, Jhukar, Lohumjo-daro and other sites, the occupation continues, apparently without a major break, with a distinct culture named after the type-site of Jhukar. The most extensive evidence of invasions was discovered at Chanhu-daro. Here a shaft-hole axe (Figure 31, No. 1) and copper pins with looped or decorated heads recall Shahi-tump and more significantly Hissar III*b*. Circular, or occasionally square, stamp-seals of stone or faience again recall Hittite parallels from Asia Minor, and also Shahi-tump. Another foreign trait is a small cast bronze cosmetic jar (or mace head) comparable to examples from Luristan and Hissar III. In contrast to such objects the distinctive Jhukar pottery, a buff ware with red or cream slip often in bands, and bold painting in black, suggests a real degree of continuity with local Harappan and even west Indian traditions, and leads us to infer that a substantial element of the population survived the invasion. The picture in this way is generally comparable to that of Saurashtra although the two regions show important differences. By contrast with the Harappan pottery, a fair proportion of the Jhukar ware gives evidence that it was finished by beating, after removal from the wheel. This later becomes a typical Indian potting technique.

At Mohenjo-daro direct evidence of a Jhukar occupation is wanting, perhaps because of natural causes, but on the other hand the numerous groups of hastily buried or unburied corpses left in the streets of its final occupation, and the buried hoards of jewellery and copper objects seem testimony enough to the proximity of foreign barbarians. More precise evidence of their presence at Mohenjo-daro in the upper levels is found in the copper shaft-hole axe-adze, whose Iranian parallels date from *c*. 1800 to 1600 B.C. (Figure 31, No. 7); while two dirks and two daggers with thickened mid-rib and rivet holes, are also of this time (Figure 25, Nos. 5 and 9). We shall see below that thickened mid ribs of bronze and copper appear to have spread into the peninsula of India between 1500 and 1300 B.C. The bronze pin with spiral loop, found by Mackay at a depth of 18·4 feet in the DK area, must indicate an earlier importation, and so too may the animal-headed pin discovered in the same part of the site. Their Iranian or Caucasian origin nevertheless seems established.

At Chanhu-daro and at the mound of Jhangar on the other

side of the Indus, the Jhukar phase is succeeded by one producing a poor grey-black burnished pottery with incised decoration. This ware is quite different from the earlier painted
traditions, and no other evidence of the material culture of its
makers is known. An inferior painted ware is also found. Some
of the Jhangar forms, and more particularly the incised patterns, are reminiscent of those occurring in paint in Saurashtra
at Rangpur and Somnath, during our phase 4 (see page 182),
and may thus be expected to date to *c.* 1000 B.C. In Saurashtra
too, incised grey ware, often of crude make and of related forms
is found. The most distinctive 'Jhangar' form from Chanhu-
daro was a triple jar whose analogues are at Shahi-tump and
Sialk, Necropolis B, thus reinforcing our view of the date.

The period coinciding with the end of the Harappan civilization in the north of the region, in the Punjab, is of a rather
different character from that of the Sind, and may well prove
of fundamental importance to our understanding of later
Indian civilization. A bronze animal-headed pin found at
Harappa near the surface in area J suggests connexions with
western Iran and the Caucasus between 1500 and 2000 B.C.
All over the citadel mound at Harappa, and in the topmost
stratum of the area F immediately to the north, Vats discovered
a decadent period of structures of reused brick, and pottery
including a significant quantity similar to that discovered in
Cemetery H (see pages 313–14). Even in the second stratum of
the citadel mound instances of pottery of this sort were noted.
As this pottery is clearly identified only in the cemetery, we
propose to refer to the culture to which it belongs as the Cemetery H culture. Wheeler showed conclusively by his excavation in 1946 that the cemetery bore a stratigraphic relationship
to the cemetery (R37) of the Harappan period. Between the
two there intervened a great mass of debris, mainly Harappan
pottery, including some late-Harappan forms such as footed
goblets. Above and into this debris burials of Cemetery H were
dug at two levels. In the lower (stratum II) were extended
inhumations accompanied by quantities of pottery, while in the
upper (stratum I) were fractional burials in large urns, without
accompanying grave goods. It has not so far been definitely
established whether these two are contemporary, or whether

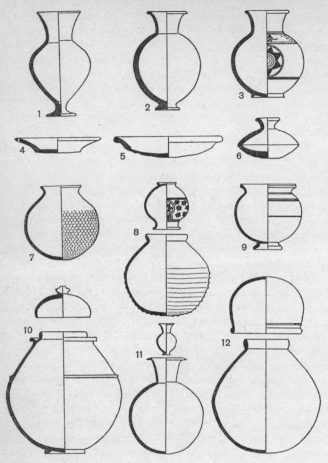

Figure 29. Harappa, Cemetery H pottery. 1–6, 1:8; 7–12, 1:16

the lower is earlier, as Vats believed. The latter would clearly represent an important change in burial customs during the period.

We are given almost no information by the excavators about the other aspects of the related material culture: thus at present all we have to go by is the pottery (Figure 29). Our view is that

the differences between it and the earlier Harappan pottery
have been overemphasized, while the many technical similarities and even the forms have not been given sufficient attention. A substantial range of forms – the urns themselves, the
carinated vessels, the graceful footed vases – are no doubt
foreign to the Harappans; the painted decoration with its distinctive stars and ring-and-dot patterns, is also foreign. On
the other hand the whole feeling of the pottery, with its
monotonous red slip and black painting, suggests a continuity
of potting tradition, and must indicate an integration of existing potter communities with the newcomers, whoever they
were. This conclusion was reached by Vats, who supported it
by a careful consideration of relative stratigraphy. He stated that
the Cemetery H culture was the final stage of the Harappan,
and continuous with it; but that it must indicate the presence
of foreign conquerors or immigrants. In our view this is a fact
of great interest, suggesting the sort of cultural fusion which
may be represented by the Cemetery H culture itself. The date
of this event is not easy to estimate with precision. It may be
expected to open at about the time when the Harappan period
ends (i.e. *c.* 1750 B.C.). The pottery shows affinities with wares
from far to the west in Iran, near the borders of Mesopotamia,
particularly Tepe Giyan (Strata II–III), and Djamshidi II,
dated between 1400 and 1550 B.C. or somewhat earlier, and
with Susa D. At these sites stars and birds occur in registers in
a manner strikingly recalling those of Cemetery H. This unfortunately does not help us to a very precise date. Certain of the
evolved Harappan forms, particularly the offering stands,
may be compared with those from Rangpur IIB and C (see below page 180–81). Altogether, we feel that this period may extend over some two centuries or more in the Punjab, probably
between 1750 and *c.* 1400 B.C. Its geographical extent is suggested by sites reported in Bahawalpur, and by pottery from
Rupar and Bara to the north-east. The pottery from the latter
site shows some resemblances of painted decoration to that
of Giyan IV. It is also probable that among the sites with
Harappan or late-Harappan affinities recently reported from
Saharanpur district to the east, some may belong to this phase.
From the Punjab we turn to the north-west to consider the

growing body of evidence of folk movements into this area during the second millennium. From Fort Munro in the foot-

Figure 30. Copper dirk from Fort Munro

hills west of Dera Ghazi Khan comes a beautiful bronze dirk with a fan-shaped decoration on the pommel of its hilt (Figure 30). This piece is very close to dirks from Luristan and Sialk VI and should date to *c.* 1150 B.C. At Moghul Ghundai, in the Zhob Valley, Sir Aurel Stein excavated cairn graves which Piggott assigns to the period of Cemetery B at Sialk (*c.* 1000–800 B.C.). These graves produced an array of bronze objects typical of the latter site, including a tripod jar, horse bells and a bangle. In some of the graves iron arrow-heads were found, but these are in no way out of keeping with the probable date. At Shalozan, high up in the Kurram valley, a characteristic trunnion axe of copper was discovered, belonging to type III of Maxwell-Hyslop's classification, and comparing with examples from Hasanlu and other Iranian sites, where they belong to the second millennium and indicate contacts between Anatolian and Iranian smiths (Figure 31, No 5). A somewhat perplexing surface find is a golden stag from the Hazara district of the Punjab, now in Peshawar museum. This piece has a distinctly Caucasian appearance and may be compared with many examples of various metals from the south-west Caspian at such sites as Talyche, Samthavro and Lenkoran, where they date from *c.* 1450 to 1200 B.C.*

---

* The age of this piece is open to debate. M. Bussagli has assigned it to the Animal style of the Scytho-Sarmatian period, and dates it accordingly to the last centuries B.C. (*La Civiltà dell'Oriente*, 4, pp. 137–8, and Pl. 191). We can only comment that it is far removed from other Indian objects which exhibit the influence of the Animal style at that period (for example, some of the pierced ring-stones of Mau-

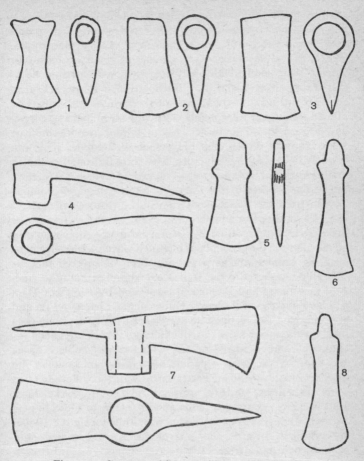

Figure 31. Copper and bronze objects of the Western group. 1:4 (approx.)

Shaft-hole axes: 1, Chanhu-daro (Jhukar culture); 2, Shahi-tump cemetery; 3, Mundigak III.6. Shaft-hole adze: 4, Mundigak III.6. Trunnion axes: 5, Shalozan; 6 and 8, Gilgit, Karakoram. Shaft-hole axe-adze: 7, Mohenjo-daro

ryan date), and appears to us to be considerably earlier. It is difficult to believe that at so late a date it would exhibit no trace whatsoever of contemporary Indian influence.

In 1958 Professor Jettmar photographed the residue of a large hoard of bronze objects discovered shortly before at a spot far up the Indus valley, high in the Gilgit Karakoram. This included several good specimens of trunnion axes of a similar type, along with shaft-hole axes with narrow necks (Figure 31, Nos. 6 and 8). This hoard also suggests Iranian contacts during the second half of the millennium. It may be argued – however improbably – that the stray items of copper and bronze found in these western border regions indicate trade contacts rather than movements of peoples. This can scarcely be said of the grave sites with their thoroughly Iranian equipment. Taking the two categories of evidence together, the outline is beginning to emerge of a series of waves of immigration from the direction of Iran during the second half of the millennium, some penetrating deep into the valleys of the northern mountains. The graves of a group of people who may be taken as the descendants of one such wave of Indo-Iranian-speaking immigrants have recently been discovered in considerable numbers by the Italian expedition working at such sites as Butkara and Barama in Swat, and by Professor Dani and his associates of Peshawar University at Thana in Swat and at Timurgara in Bajaur. The graves are usually drystone cists built on the lower slopes of the valleys. The grave goods include plain grey and red pottery with pedestal goblets, flasks and bowls whose nearest parallels are in Giyan I and in the two Necropoles at Sialk. Partly burnt bones are deposited in some of the urns, while other graves have complete skeletons. Iron is a rare occurrence. This may be taken to indicate new waves of Indo-European speaking peoples entering the Indian subcontinent towards the end of the second millennium. Radiocarbon dates from Butkara and Barama range between 713 and 440 B.C.

We shall be returning to the archaeological evidence for Aryan movements east of the Indus later, but a few more stray metal finds may be mentioned here. A copper hoard from Khurdi in the Nagaur district of Rajputana included a fine bowl with long protruding channel spout, of a form with numerous analogues in both pottery and metal at Giyan I, Sialk (Necropolis B), etc.; another simple bowl of copper reminiscent of examples from Sialk, and a flat double axe of copper (Plate 21A). From copper hoards at Fatehgarh and Bithur in Uttar Pradesh, and from a site in the neighbourhood of Kallur in Raichur district, well to the south in the peninsula, have come swords or dirks of copper or bronze with midribs and 'antennae' hilts (Plate 21B), compared by von Heine-Geldern to examples from the Koban culture of the Caucasus and there datable to *c.* 1200–1000 B.C. A copper spearhead with somewhat similar hilt from Chandoli in Maharashtra (Figure 50, No 12) comes from strata dated by radiocarbon to *c.* 1330 B.C., and a fragment of a similar piece comes from Navdatoli. Identical spearheads were found in a grave at Gezer in Palestine, datable to the close of the XVIII Egyptian dynasty, and therefore contemporary with the Chandoli piece. All of these stray finds may do no more than indicate indirect contact, but they appear to be consistent with the movement of peoples from Iran and perhaps even from the Caucasus region into India.

It is in the light of this archaeological evidence that the Rigveda must be read. It has hitherto been tantalizingly difficult to point to any archaeological culture which may be that of the Vedic Aryan tribes; but now at last there appears to be a probability that the two categories of evidence may shortly be superimposed upon each other. It is believed that the Veda – on account of its great sanctity – was not reduced to writing until the time of Sayana (in the fourteenth century A.D.), and thus that it was passed down in oral traditions for about thirty centuries. None the less, from the time when its hymns were collected and arranged, probably before 1000 B.C. they have been preserved syllable by syllable with incredible accuracy, and while the language changed with time so that their original meaning became more and more obscure, the hymns were passed down immutably from Brahman teacher to pupil. The picture the hymns present is of barbarian tribes, glorying in their swift horses and light chariots, with sheep, goats and cattle, cultivating at first barley and wheat and later rice. They made tools and weapons of *ayas*, a metal which, being occasionally described as red in colour, must have been either copper or bronze. Iron (at first known as black metal to distinguish it) is not mentioned in the Rigveda, but in later Vedic literature, from the time of the Atharvaveda and the *Samhitas* of the Yajurveda, it becomes increasingly common.

The Vedic hymns are addressed to Indo-European gods such as Indra, the warrior charioteer whose thunderbolt destroyed their enemies and who brags of his inebriation on the sacred *soma* drink; Agni, the fire god, who also shares something of this warlike character as the consumer of the enemy, as well as being the intermediary between gods and men; Varuna, the Asura or righteous king; Mitra, with solar characteristics, and so on. Their cult revolved around the fire sacrifice. The Aryan funeral rites are of interest: cremation and burial were evidently both in vogue.

The geographical horizons of the Rigveda are relevant to our inquiry. On the west they are bounded by the western tributaries of the Indus, the Gomatī (modern Gomal), the Krumu (modern Kurram) and the Kubhā (modern Kabul) rivers. Other rivers are mentioned even to the north of the Kabul, notably Suvāstu, the modern Swat. This latter signifies 'fair dwellings' and may therefore indicate Aryan settlements in this beautiful valley. The centre of Rigvedic geography is the Punjab. The rivers most often referred to are the Indus itself, the Sarasvatī and the Drishadvatī and the five streams which collectively gave their name to the Punjāb (five waters), the Śutudrī (Sutlej), Vipās (Beas), Parushnī (Ravi), Asiknī (Chenab), and Vitastā (Jhelum). The eastern horizons are the Jamunā river and at the end of the period the Ganges.

From the Veda it is evident that the Aryans were not the only inhabitants of the region, for which they themselves used the name *Sapta-Sindhava* or land of seven Indus rivers, and that their original stay was not entirely peaceful. We learn of a people called *Dāsas* or *Dasyu* (the word later means 'slave') who were dark-complexioned, snub-nosed, worshippers of the phallus (*śiśna deva*), etc. They were rich in cattle and lived in fortified strongholds, *pura*. We learn of another people, the *Panis*, who were also wealthy in cattle and treasures. Although many of the hymns refer to battles between one Aryan tribe and another there is an underlying sense of solidarity in the fight against the Dāsas, and Indra is named *Purandara*, the 'breaker of cities'. Already in the Veda the first encounters of Indra (the Aryan people personified) and the fortified settlements of the Dāsas were being forgotten and the Dāsa rulers were regarded as demons. We hear of a city named Nārminī destroyed by fire, and of a battle on the banks of the Ravi at a place named Hariyūpīyā (which Indologists are ever more confidently identifying with Harappa). Professor Burrow has recently shown the unambiguous character of such references as, 'Through fear of thee the dark-coloured inhabitants fled, not waiting for battle, abandoning their possessions, when, O Agni [fire], burning brightly for Puru [an Aryan tribe], and destroying the cities, thou didst shine' (VII. 5.3). He has further recognized the importance in both the Rigveda and later Vedic texts of the word *arma*, *armaka*, meaning ruin. For instance, in the Rigveda we read, 'Strike down, O Maghavan [Indra], the host of sorceresses in the ruined city of Vailasthānaka, in the ruined city of Mahāvailastha [Great Vailastha]' (I.133.3). There were then, in the time of the Rigveda, great ruin-mounds which the Aryans associated with the earlier inhabitants of the area. The same idea recurs in a later Vedic text, the *Taittirīya Brāhmana* (II. 4, 6, 8), in the statement that, 'The people to whom these ruined sites belonged, lacking posts, these many settlements, widely distributed, they, O Agni, having been expelled by thee, have migrated to another land.' Also in one of the later Vedic texts we read, 'On the Sarasvatī there are ruined sites called Naitandhava; Vyarna is one of these'; and, for the archaeologist perhaps even more suggestively, 'He should proceed along the right bank of the Drishadvatī, having reached the ruined site near its source he should proceed towards the right,' etc.

Such, briefly, is the picture presented by the Rigveda. It provides us with a geographical provenance and with two fairly sure termini, the overthrow of the Harappan cities, in *c.* 1750 B.C., and the introduction of iron around 1050 B.C. Against this evidence we must consider that of archaeology, both the earlier and less positive part discussed in this chapter and the later part discussed in the following chapter. Archaeology is as yet only on the threshold of revealing the information which will be needed to pin down the authors of the Rigveda, but we feel fairly confident that the researches of the last decade or so have made a large contribution towards this end.

CHAPTER 7

NEOLITHIC–CHALCOLITHIC SETTLEMENTS OF INDIA BEYOND THE INDUS SYSTEM

IN Chapters 5 and 6 we traced the earliest settlements so far reported in the subcontinent, in Baluchistan, and the dramatic spread of settled life on to the plains of the Indus river system during the first half of the third millennium. Then we saw the growth of the vast Indus valley civilization towards the close of the millennium and we associated its disappearance at about 1750 B.C. with the eastern movements of barbarous tribes of Indo-European-speaking horse and chariot riders, with new and more efficient bronze weapons. Almost all the events we discussed took place within the confines of West Pakistan, except for extensions along the coast as far as the Gulf of Cambay, and in the eastern Punjab towards Delhi. We now move on to discuss the appearance of settlements in the rest of India.

It was, until recently, thought doubtful that any culture with a food-producing economy existed in these areas until relatively very late times. Thus in 1948 Sir Mortimer Wheeler would only allow the 'Stone Axe' culture at Brahmagiri to extend back to the first half of the first millennium B.C. Even before the advent of radiocarbon dating, however, the flood of new excavations which he unleashed had shown in one region after another an extensive range of cultural horizons, so that it became necessary to envisage far earlier dates. We can now see that in at least two regions Neolithic cultures existed which are, chronologically speaking, pre-Harappan. Yet the picture is still remarkable for its general lateness, and for the prolonged conservatism which seems to have prevailed in many parts. We must recall too in this context our observations upon the use of the term Neolithic and Chalcolithic in South Asia (page 28).

The attention of archaeologists has for over a century been directed towards the often very large numbers of stone axes, both flaked, edge-ground, fully ground, and pecked (or hammer-dressed), discovered widely as surface finds. In the most general terms five main groups of axes can be distinguished: (*a*) a Northern group, from the Vale of Kashmir; (*b*) a Southern group, spreading over the Peninsula, south of the Godavari river; (*c*) an Eastern group, including many finds from the Assam hills; (*d*) a Central group from the hills of Central India, south of the Ganges valley; and (*e*) an Eastern-Central group from the hilly regions of Bihar, Orissa and Chota Nagpur. It may be assumed that these distributional groups have some cultural-historical significance, and therefore we shall consider them as entities. It is at once apparent that the state of our knowledge of the different areas is very uneven, and that in some the task of establishing a chronological or sequential framework has barely begun.

THE NORTHERN GROUP

This comprises a small number of sites in the Vale of Kashmir. Only one has so far been excavated, but it provides valuable evidence of the culture sequence. Burzahom is situated on a terrace of Karewa clay above the marshy flood-plain of the river Jhelum, about six miles north-east of Srinagar. A trial excavation was made some thirty years ago by the Yale-Cambridge expedition, but serious work was only taken up after 1959 by the Archaeological Survey of India. The earliest occupation (I), which radiocarbon dates indicate to be before *c*. 2375 B.C., took the form of a series of pits dug into the soft clay. The largest were presumably pit-dwellings, and post-holes around the perimeter indicated roofs. Hearths are found near the entrances. The material culture included coarse grey or black burnished pottery often with mat-marked bases (Figure 32); a wide range of bone points, awls, needles and harpoons (Plate 22 A); stone axes, frequently pecked and ground, of both oval and oblong section; ring stones, and a distinctive pierced rectangular chopper or knife of a kind hitherto unknown in India (Plate 22 B). The absence of a stone-blade industry is significant. There is as yet no clear evidence of the subsistence of these people, though it appears that hunting played an important part. Grindstones or querns are notably absent.

In period II, whose date is not yet clearly established, but

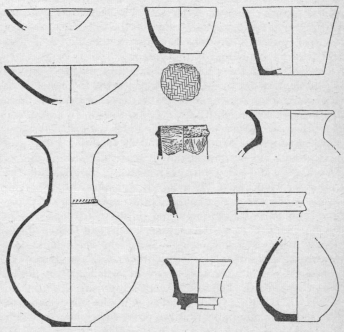

Figure 32. Burzahom I and II, pottery. 1:8

which a long run of radiocarbon dates suggests to have continued at least until *c.* 1400 B.C., the stone and bone industries of I continue, but there are traces of houses of mud or mud-brick, sometimes with mud plaster. A single copper arrowhead is reported from the end of this period. Also to this period belonged a number of burials, chiefly of crouched skeletons in oval pits, without grave goods. In some cases red ochre had been put over the body, and one skull had been trepanned during life. Dogs were also sometimes buried with their owners. Another peculiar feature without parallel in the subcontinent was the evidently purposeful burial of animals, such as dogs, wolves or ibex. A third period, associated with the construction of a massive megalithic circle or part-circle, saw a new pottery of coarse red ware replacing that with grey or black burnish, although apparently there is still no evidence of the presence of iron. Exploration has revealed about nine other sites of the Burzahom culture in the adjacent terraces of the Jhelum river. Further finds of ground stone axes in Kangra district probably belong to this group.

In discussing the origins and affinities of the Northern Neolithic, certain things at once strike the eye as foreign to the Indian tradition. Among them are the forms of the bone tools, the rectangular perforated stone knife, the pit-dwellings, and the placing of domestic dogs in the grave with their masters. Each one of these features is found in Neolithic cultures of north China, the perforated knife in particular being a characteristic trait, and a dog burial is reported in the Ang-Ang-Hsi culture of Manchuria. The dog was apparently almost a cult animal in the Shilka cave culture of the upper Amur; and dogs were until recently sacrificed and buried with their owners among such peoples as the Gilyaks, Ulchis and Goldis of this region. A bone industry, including harpoons, is also a frequent occurrence of north Chinese Neolithic sites. The Burzahom axe industry is of an unspecialized sort which may as lief be compared with the collections of the Swedish Expedition to Mongolia, as with anything Indian. On the other hand, the Burzahom ceramic industry is not obviously comparable with any Chinese Neolithic pottery. In short, the Burzahom 'Neolithic' appears as a sort of hunting-based culture whose affinities are with the 'Neolithic' and surviving hunting people of the peripheral regions north and north-west of China and of Central Asia. Another feature which demands consideration is that although this culture must have coexisted with the pre-Harappan and Harappan developments in the Indus valley and Punjab, there is no indication that the two enjoyed any contact whatsoever. The question of relations with the other Indian Neolithic groups is more problematic, and we leave it on one side for the present.

1 Baghai Khor, Mirzapur district: a typical Central Indian rock shelter

2 (*below*) Vedda family
encamped in a rock shelter,
Ceylon

OPPOSITE
3 A (*above*) Chariot group,
Morhana Pahar, Mirzapur
district
B (*below*) Rock painting
of a herd of animals, perhaps
goats, from same site

4 A (*left*) Sculptured head
in limestone, Mundigak,
period IV (height 9.3 cm.
B (*below*) Palace building
from Mundigak, period
IV, Afghanistan

OPPOSITE

5 A (*above*) Painted pots
from Mundigak, period
III.6
B (*below*) Painted pots
from Mundigak, period
IV

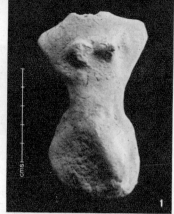

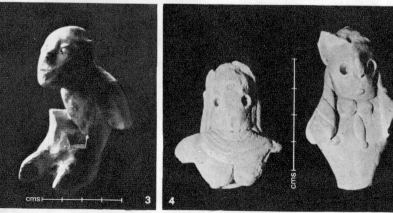

6 Female figurines of terracotta, Mundigak: 1, period III.1; 2–4, period IV.1; 5, period IV.2

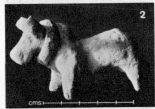

7 A (*left*) Cattle figurines of terracotta, Mundigak: 1, humped bull, period II.2; 2, humped bull with collar, period IV.2; 3, head of bull, period IV.1; 4, painted humped bull, period IV.3
B (*below*) Stone button seals, Mundigak: 1, period II.2; 2–4, period III; 5–7, period IV

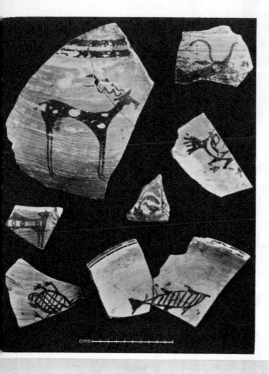

8 A (*left*) Pre-Harappan painted pottery from Kalibangan

B (*below*) Kot Diji, general view of excavations. The stone foundations of the pre-Harappan defensive wall are visible in the foreground

OPPOSITE

9 (*above*) Pre-Harappan settlement beneath Harappan citadel, Kalibangan

12 A (*above*) Mohenjo-daro: representation of ship on a stone seal (length 4·3 cm.) B (*centre*) Mohenjo-daro: representation of ship on terracotta amulet (length 4·5 cm.) C (*below*) Lothal: general view of Harappan dockyard. The main settlement lies on the left, and the spillway can be seen in the left foregroun

13 Mohenjo-daro: seals with animal
motifs. 1, Indian humped bull;
2, Indian elephant; 3, water buffalo with
feeding trough; 4, pair of antelope;
5, bull of primogenius type with manger;
6 Indian rhinoceros; 7, mountain goat

14 Mohenjo-daro: seals with mythological or religious content.
1, composite animal, starfish with head of bull; 2, seated figure
identified as a god, possibly prototype of Siva; 3, composite animal
bull-elephant-tiger; 4, composite animal, bull-antelope;
5, mythological scene.

15 Mohenjo-daro: stone sculpture of bearded head (height 19 cm.)

16 A (*left*) Harappa: two views of small stone figure (height 9·3 cm.)
B (*top right*) Mohenjo-daro: bronze figure of dancing girl
(height 10·2 cm.)
C (*bottom right*) Harappa: stone dancing figure (height
10 cm.)

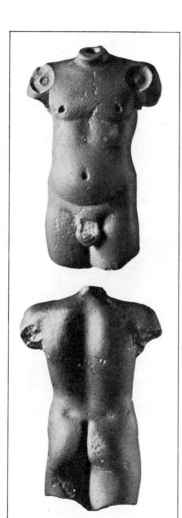

18 A (*right*) Seal of 'Persian Gulf' type from Lothal (diameter 2·5 cm.)
B (*centre*) Lothal: burial and double burial of Harappan period
C (*below*) Mohenjo-daro: terracotta cart

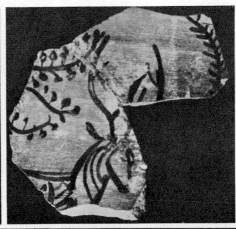

19 Lothal: painted pottery of Harappan period

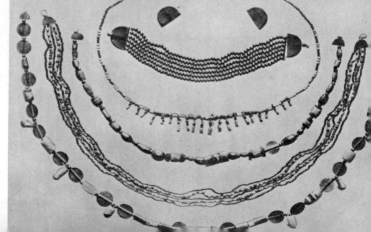

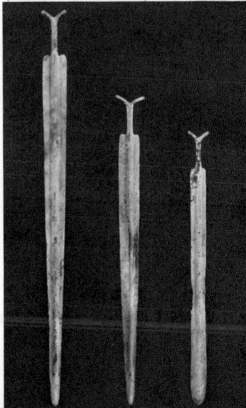

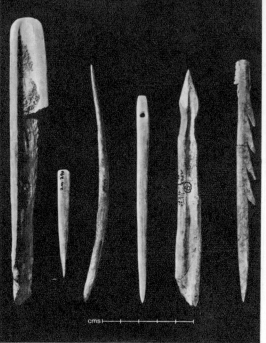

22 A (*above*) Bone and
antler tools from
Burzahom, Kashmir
B (*below*) Ground and
pecked stone tools from
Burzahom. 1, 4, 6 and 7,
ground and pecked stone
axes; 2, rectangular
harvesting knife with
pierced holes; 3, hammer
stone; 5 ring stone

OPPOSITE
23 A (*above*) Neolithic burial
from phase II,
Tekkalakota
B (*below*) A typical
Neolithic hill settlement
in northern Mysore,
Piklihal, Raichur district

24 A (*above*) Modern Boya hut in Tekkalakota village
B (*below*) Excavation of Neolithic hut floor in hill settlement above
Tekkalakota village

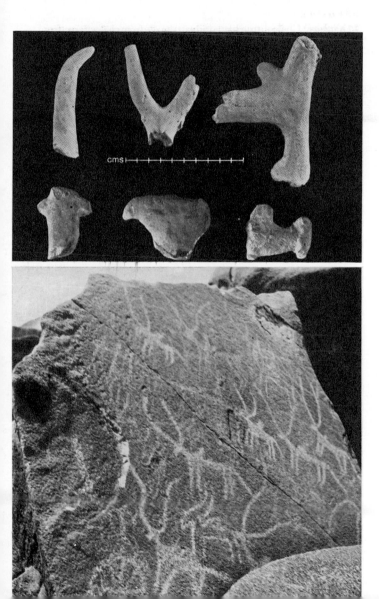

26 A (*above*) Hoof impressions from floor of cattle-pen in ash-mound
B (*below*) Excavation of ash-mound at Utnur, Mahbubnagar district

OPPOSITE

27 A (*above*) Chalcolithic blade industry made from chalcedony, from
Chandoli, Poona district
B (*below*) Channel-spouted bowl from period IIID, Navdatoli

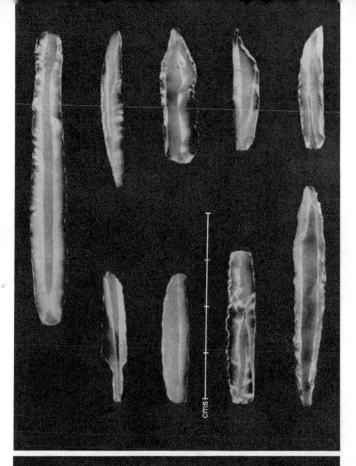

28 A (*above*) Painted pot of Malwa ware,
Daimabad, Ahmadnagar district
B (*below left*) Navdatoli: high-necked
vessel from Chalcolithic level
C (*below right*) Water pot of
Jorwe ware, Navdatoli

29 A (*above*) Painted pottery of Malwa and white slipped wares from Navdatoli, period III
B (*below*) Painted Malwa ware from same site, period III

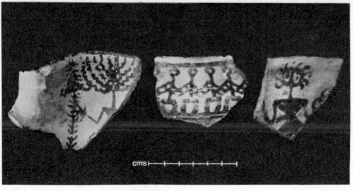

30 A (*left*) Black-and-red ware from Iron Age graves at Yelleshwaram, Andhra Pradesh
B (*below*) Bronze lid and dog from urn burial[s] at Adichanallur, Tinnevelly district, Madras

OPPOSITE

31 A (*above*) Points and arrowheads of bone, horn and ivory from Chirand, Saran district, Bihar. Period IA: 1–6, 8 and 9; Period IB: 7 and 10–12
B (*below*) Bronze lid and cock from urn burials at Adichanallur

32 A (*above*) Iron Age cist graves from Brahmagiri, Mysore, showing port-hole and grave goods
B (*below*) Iron Age pit burial from Maski, Raichur district, with grave goods and extended skeleton

THE SOUTHERN GROUP

The presence of very large numbers of ground stone axes in the Karnatak region, in the valley of the river Krishna and its tributaries, was first established by Bruce Foote. Largely on account of the foundation provided by his researches, it has now become the best documented of the Neolithic groups we are considering. Since 1947, when Sir Mortimer Wheeler excavated at Brahmagiri, there have been excavations at several settlements, such as Sanganakallu (1948, 1964–5), Piklihal (1951), Maski (1954), Tekkalakota (1963–4), and Hallur (1965). In addition 'ash-mounds' at Utnur (1957) and Kupgal (1965) have been excavated and shown to be Neolithic cattle-pens. At present radiocarbon dates are available for no less than five sites in this area. The southern extension of the culture is represented by the site excavated at T. Narsipur at the confluence of Kaveri and Kapila rivers, and the neighbouring Hemmige near Mysore; the eastern, towards the coast, by the excavations at Nagarjunakonda and at Paiyampalli in North Arcot district. It is possible, on the basis of comparisons, to provide some sort of tentative sequence for the periods which precede the introduction of iron at these sites:

1. The earliest settlements were made by a people who possessed a ground stone-axe industry and a somewhat rudimentary flake or blade tradition. It is evident that they had domesticated cattle, sheep and goats. Their pottery was predominantly handmade grey or buff-brown, but a less common ware had a black or red burnished slip, often with purple-painted decoration. A feature of the grey ware was the use of bands of red ochre applied after firing. Other noteworthy features of this early pottery are the applied ring feet and hollow pedestals, recalling those of pre-Harappan Amri or Kalibangan. The settlements were usually made on the tops of granite hills, or on levelled terraces on the hillsides, or on saddles or plateaux between two or more such hills (Plate 23 B). They also made forest cattle stations, probably for seasonal grazing (Plate 26 B). Terracotta figurines are predominantly those of humped cattle (Plate 25 A), and rock paintings and rock bruisings around the settlements are also

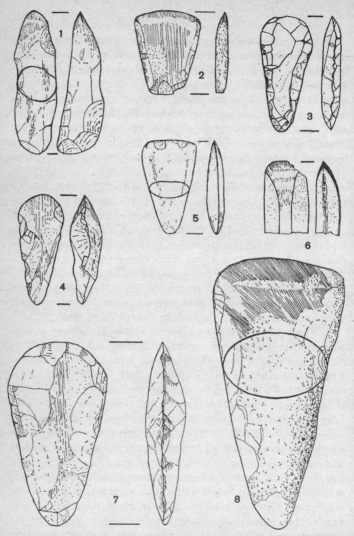

Figure 33. Stone axes from Bellary district, south India. 1:3

predominantly of cattle (Plate 25 B) (see page 298). From the earliest levels numbers of rubbing stones and querns are found, suggesting some sort of grain production. This phase is represented by the occupation at Utnur, the lower Neolithic of Piklihal, Maski I, and parts of the Brahmagiri IA. It is dated by the radiocarbon results from Utnur from *c.* 2300 to 1800 B.C., and in the complete absence of metal it may be regarded as a primary Neolithic phase.

2. During the second phase some important developments took place. Mud floors are in evidence, and circular hutments of wattle and daub on a wooden frame (Plate 24 A). The stone-axe industry proliferated, but without any clear evidence of typological development. There is a great increase in the number and regularity of stone blades prepared from small blade cores of various siliceous stones. Red and black slipped wares more or less completely disappear from the range of pottery: on the other hand new elements appear, suggesting contact with regions to the north. Among these are perforated vessels, and the practice of roughening the outer surface of vessels in a manner reminiscent of that employed in Baluchistan in pre-Harappan levels, and spouts make their first appearance. There is nevertheless a basic continuity discernible between these two periods. Phase 2 is in evidence at Piklihal (upper Neolithic), Brahmagiri (parts of IA and IB), Sanganakallu I.1, Tekkalakota I and Hallur IIA (layers 10–11). The occupation of Hallur I (layers 12–14) and T. Narsipur appears to date from the beginning of this phase and represents a southern, slightly later extension of phase I. The first metal objects, of both bronze and copper, appear with increasing frequency towards the end of this period. Radiocarbon dates from Tekkalakota I, Hallur and Sanganakallu I.1 suggest that it extends from between *c.* 1800 and 1500 B.C.

3. A third phase is in evidence particularly at Tekkalakota II and Hallur (layers 8–9) and perhaps Paiyampalli. It is also present at Piklihal (intrusion), Sanganakallu I.2 and Brahmagiri, although not discernible in the excavated sections. It coincides with an increase in the number of tools of copper and bronze, although the axe and blade industries in stone continue (Figure 50). A copper fish-hook was discovered at

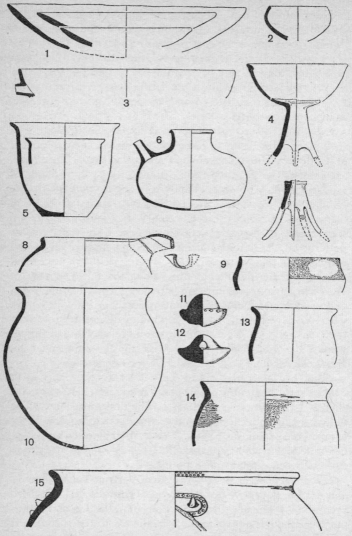

Figure 34. Piklihal and Brahmagiri, Neolithic pottery.
1:8, last piece 1:12
1–9, 11–15, Piklihal; 10, Brahmagiri.

Hallur. In pottery a new and harder surfaced grey and buff ware becomes common, together with an entirely new wheel-thrown unburnished ware with purple paint, akin to the Jorwe ware of Maharashtra (see below, page 197). The presence of a bone of *Equus cabalus* in the beginning of this phase at Hallur is suggestive, particularly if it is considered in conjunction

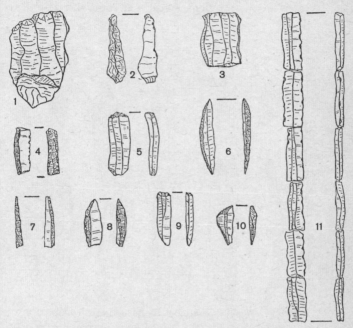

Figure 35. Piklihal, Neolithic stone-blade industry. 2:3

1 and 3, blade cores; 2, primary guide flake; 4, section of backed blade; 5 and 9, truncated blades; 6, lunate; 7, 8 and 10, broken lunates or points; 11, sections of utilized blades.

with an extensive group of rock paintings showing horses and riders, and with such exotic metal objects as the Kallur bronze swords (Plate 21 B). Few radiocarbon dates have as yet been published for this period, but comparing it with the Jorwe phase in Maharashtra, whence it must have derived its new traits, it may be expected to have extended from *c.* 1400 to 1050 B.C.

The three phases show every indication of remarkable continuity, and settlements once established do not appear to have shifted. Stone axes occur throughout in large numbers, and fine stone blades in the two later phases. The blade industry commands our attention because it shows many features in common with those of the Late Stone Age of Central India and the Deccan. The excavations reveal that somewhat less than

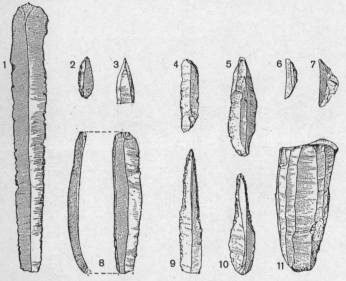

Figure 36. Maski, Neolithic stone-blade industry. 2:3
1, 5 and 8, blades; 2, 6 and 7, lunates; 3, point; 4, truncated blade; 9 and 10, awls;
11, blade core.

three quarters of the assemblages are blades, without retouch, and frequently with both bulb of percussion and distal ends snapped off (Figure 35, No 11). Reworked, backed or truncated blades occur in small numbers (around four to five per cent of the total), and lunates, points or borers, together occupy only about two per cent of the total. There can be little doubt that the predominant blades were hafted in gum to make composite knives or sickles, but evidence is lacking in this region so far. All told, the industry compares closely with that of Chal-

colithic sites in Maharashtra and Malwa. As far as can be seen
the economy depended throughout largely on cattle-raising, but
varieties of gram and millet (*Dolichos biflorus* and *Eleusine cora-
cona*) are reported at Tekkalakota I and at Hallur in phase 2.
There is also apparent uniformity of burial customs: extended
inhumations, usually with some grave goods (Plate 23 A). In
one case, a male, these consisted of two stone axes and five
large blades, and in another, a female, a spouted pot and a deep

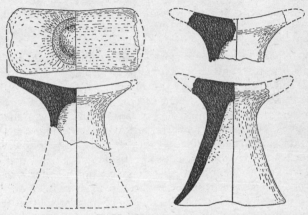

Figure 37. T. Narsipur, pottery headrests. 1:4

(?) milking vessel. Infants were buried in pottery urns. Burials
of all types appear to have been among the houses of the settlement rather than in separate burial grounds. In the third phase
multiple pot burials at Tekkalakota are reminiscent of those of
Maharashtra during the Jorwe phase. From a burial at Narsipur, and from other phase 2 contexts, come pottery headrests
of a distinctive form (Figure 37).

Neolithic axes have been found in surface collections, often
in quantities, far beyond the nuclear region we have just considered, particularly towards the south-east, where they have
been found in large numbers in the Shevaroy and Javadi hills,
and thence eastwards towards the Tamil coastal plains, southwards to Madura and even the extreme south of the peninsula.
There is as yet no evidence that this distribution extends into

Ceylon. The relative age and cultural contexts of these finds have still to be established. It seems important, now that so much excavation has been done, that archaeology should advance beyond the stage of mere typological classifications. Therefore we shall not discuss in detail the several classificatory systems that have been proposed. The most common tool is the stone axe with medial ground edge, with a generally triangular form and curved blade, and an oval or lenticular median section. Full grinding is usually reserved for small, flattish axes, and pecking for larger tools made from suitable raw material. The commonest axe form is that often spoken of as a pointed-butt axe.

In inquiring into the origins of this culture a number of points present themselves. The pottery of phase I shows two main influences. The grey burnished ware, including the variety with unburnt red ochre paint, occurs again in Maharashtra from the beginning of the Daimabad settlement and is suggestively closer to the early pottery of Burzahom than to anything else in the subcontinent at that date. There is however a broad similarity of craft between this grey ware and that of Hissar, Turang Tepe and Shah Tepe in north-eastern Iran. The red or black painted pottery is more likely to be of north-western origin, and must ultimately be related to the pre-Harappan pottery of Baluchistan and the Indus system. The stone-axe industry is also reminiscent of the Kashmir Neolithic, rather than of the stray axes from the Iranian region. The stone-blade industry is peculiarly difficult to pin down. In phase 1, at Sanganakallu, Hallur, T. Narsipur, etc., the blade element is at best poorly represented, or even quite absent, being sometimes replaced by a quartz industry. This could well indicate a continuation from the Late Stone Age industries of the region. The presence from the beginning of *Bos indicus* as a dominant culture trait certainly suggests initial influence from the north-west. Finally the human physical types, now becoming known from Neolithic graves at several sites, in all cases fall within a 'Caucasoid' or 'Mediterranean' range.

During the second phase the blade industry develops, perhaps as a result of contact or trade with Late Stone Age groups; other traits suggest influences from the 'Malwa' phase

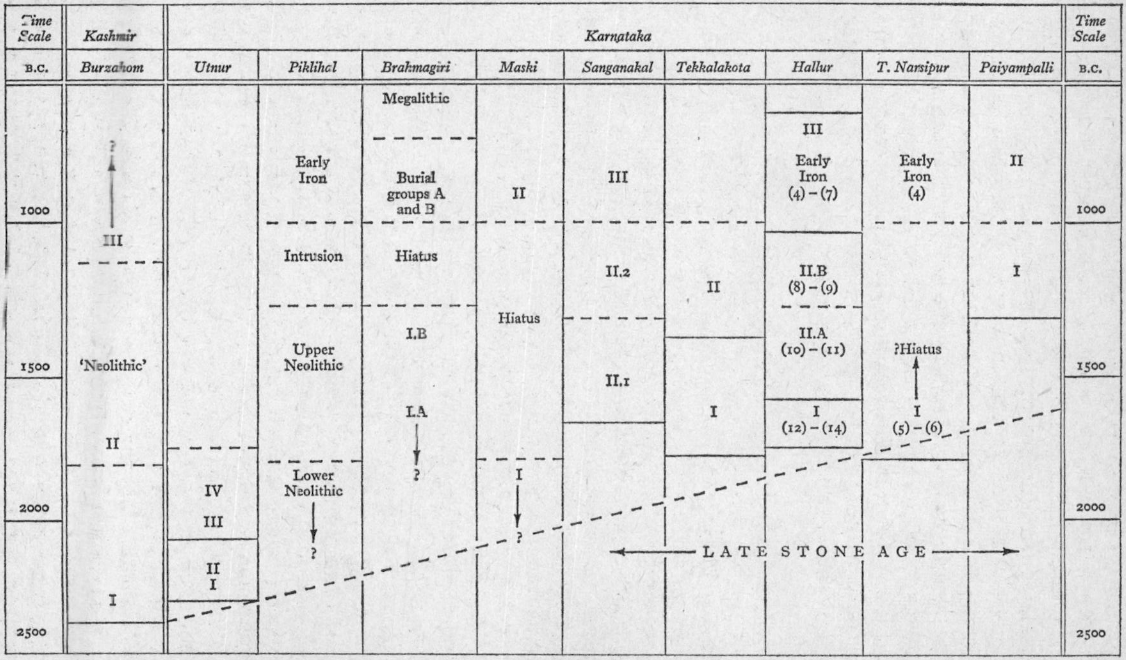

Figure 38. Neolithic–Chalcolithic sequence of Kashmir, Karnataka, etc. (chart 2)

to the north. The third phase shows even stronger external influences; in particular we note the intrusive 'Jorwe' type pottery, and the copper and bronze objects with Jorwe or even post-Harappan affinities (fish-hooks, double axes, etc.). The hypothesis has been advanced that this Southern Neolithic originates as a result of movements of people and cultures into the subcontinent from the east. The evidence is not sufficient to warrant either complete confirmation or rejection of this, but if it is to be maintained it must be in the face of the several more positive indications of north-western connexions we have outlined above.

THE EASTERN AND OTHER GROUPS

From the hill areas of Assam come many further surface collections of stone axes. These have been treated typologically, for so far only one very small excavation has been made, and this does not reveal any clear sequence, or any dates. So far as surface collections go, there appear to be certain broad divisions. Thus from the Garo Hills some sites produce almost nothing but flaked, or flaked and edge-ground axes of unspecialized triangulate form. Examples of such collections are from Ronchigiri and Rongram. The one excavation to which we referred was at an open site, Daojali Hading in the North Cachar Hills. It was carried out by Dr T. C. Sharma and members of the University of Gauhati. It is not clear whether the finds were *in situ* or redeposited, but the rich deposit included large numbers of stone axes, bones, and quantities of sherds of cord-impressed and striated beater-impressed pottery. Among the stone tools were large numbers of small ground axes of rounded form, and numbers of small shouldered adzes with angular outline (see Figure 39). Both these are types not encountered in the Northern or Southern groups. They are types which have an extensive distribution in China and Southeast Asia and a long and respectable ancestry there. So too has the pottery, in so far as it can be identified. Its affinities seem to be with south China, recalling the pottery of the Neolithic sites around Hongkong. No metal was encountered in the excavation.

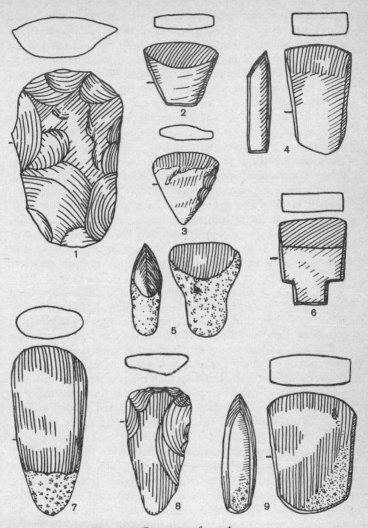

Figure 39. Stone axes from Assam. 1:3

1, North-East Frontier Agency; 2, 3 and 6, Cachar hills; 4 and 8, Garo hills; 5, 7 and 9, Naga hills.

Surface materials from other parts of Assam largely agree with those of the North Cachar hills and the excavated site of Daojali Hading. It is notable that in both the Garo and Naga hills, a peculiar rounded-shouldered, quasi-tanged tool is common. This too appears to have eastern affinities, and the entire collection (excluding that from the Garo hills) may be taken as indicating culture contacts with south China, Burma and Yunnan. It is as yet impossible to determine whether the Neolithic settlements of the Garo hills shared a cultural as well as typological relationship with either the Southern or Northern Neolithic groups, or whether the axes merely represent an earlier stage of development of those of the Eastern. In assigning any sort of tentative date to the Neolithic of Daojali Hading and Assam two things need to be borne in mind: (a) the lower limit must be considered in relation to that of the Chinese Neolithic, and may be of unexpected antiquity; (b) the Assam hills are tribal areas down to the present, and stone tools may well have persisted in use until very late times.

A number of surface collections of stone axes have been made in the hills south of the Ganges valley, in Mirzapur and Banda districts and adjacent areas. These constitute our fourth or Central group. Unhappily little is known of these collections, and so far no site associated with them has been discovered, let alone excavated. A study of collections made by Cunningham and Rivett-Carnac many years ago and now housed in the British Museum shows that the great majority of the tools are triangulate axes, with curved medial ground edges. They thus conform to the main type from the Southern group. One or two however were small axes of rounded form, whose prototypes are found in the Assamese collections. Some of the axes have depressions on the face, apparently to assist hafting. One part of the collection stands out, comprising mainly heavily patinated basalt flakes, apparently debris from a factory site. This group also included broken, unfinished axes again typologically close to those of the south. In the absence of any better evidence we may note the following points regarding age. Stone axes have been found in a number of excavations of Chalcolithic sites to the south of the area

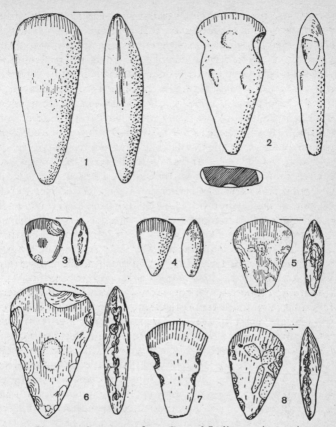

Figure 40. Stone axes from Central India. 1:4 (approx)

(Daimabad, Nevasa, Sonegaon, etc., see below, pp. 193), and Early Historic sites in the immediate vicinity on the Ganges plains (Bhita). Further, a late Stone Age factory assemblage from Mirzapur included one broken stone axe. The hills have been occupied until today largely by tribal people, who although preserving a very primitive way of life have long since used iron for all essential cutting tools. Therefore it is not yet established whether anything approaching a primary Neolithic culture ever flourished in this area.

The fifth group comprises surface collections from eastern Bihar, the western extensions of Bengal and parts of Orissa, again largely, though not exclusively, coming from hilly country which until recently was occupied by tribal people. Here too very little excavation has been done. At Kuchai, in the Mayurbhanj district of Orissa, a small excavation by B. K. Thapar of the Archaeological Survey revealed a deposit of stone axes, some of rectangular form, along with coarse gritty red pottery, stratified above a Late Stone Age assemblage. Another collection was made in the Sanjai valley by Anderson in 1917, but it is not clear whether the tools were *in situ*. A number of surface collections have been published, in particular a large collection from the Santal Parganas made by a Norwegian missionary named Bodding. Of this more than a third were of axes of generally triangulate form with medial edge; about another third were of small axes, the majority having either a somewhat rounded form or a tendency to rectangularity, but still with medial edge-grinding; and a much smaller proportion were of rectangular celts and small adzes with square shoulders (Figure 41). The tools of the second and third categories are reminiscent of those found in Assam, and beyond. Those of the first are closer to the Southern and Central groups. It is interesting to notice that some of the surface collections contain tools exclusively or nearly exclusively of the first category. This may indicate here, as in Assam, the presence of an earlier, less evolved industry, or of a Neolithic phase having more in common with the Southern group, being antecedent to one with Eastern affinities. An alternative hypothesis would see this region as a frontier zone in which the traits of two separate cultural traditions meet. Certainly it may be regarded thus in terms of anthropology. Until more work is done here it is impossible to discuss the question further. With regard to dating we may note, firstly, that stone axes have been found stratified below Early Historic levels in an excavation at Tamluk, in West Bengal, along with ill-fired pottery (hitherto unpublished), and in late Chalcolithic or early Iron Age levels in Pandu Rajar Dhibi III and IV in the Ajay valley, Burdwan District, West Bengal. Secondly, they have been found in Early Historic contexts at Sonepur, Prahladpur and Bangarh

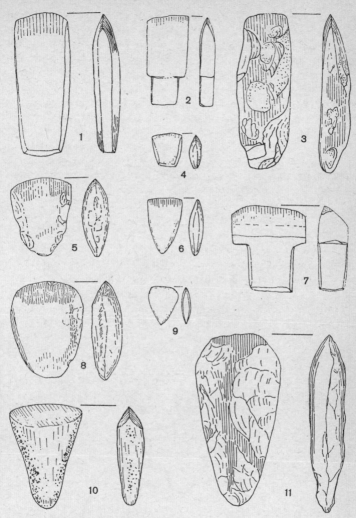

Figure 41. Stone axes from Santal Parganas, eastern Central India. 1:3 (approx.)

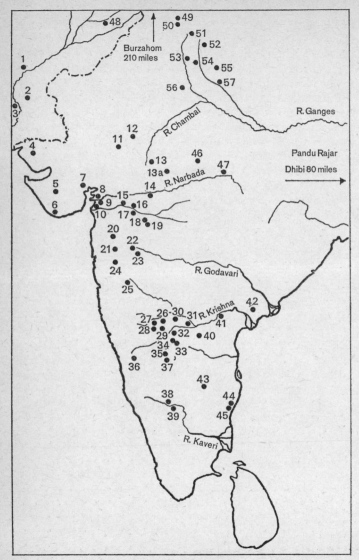

Figure 42. Map of Neolithic and Chalcolithic sites east of the Indus system

to the north of the area, all sites on or bordering upon the Ganges plains. It is thus premature for us to attempt to decide whether anything amounting to a primary Neolithic culture ever existed here, and also what affinities such a culture may have had with those of adjacent regions.

To summarize, there is a clear suggestion of a pre-metal Neolithic stage of settlements in Baluchistan, almost certainly a diffusion from western Asia. In this region the cultures were soon enriched by copper, so that we may refer to them as 'Chalcolithic', and later by bronze. In Kashmir and beyond the Indus system in India there is as yet no clear evidence of a

KEY TO FIG. 42.

Sind	1. Jhukar		30. Kallur
	2. Chanhu-daro		31. Utnur
	3. Amri		32. Tekkalakota
			33. Sanganakal
Saurashtra	4. Desalpar		34. Kupgal
	5. Rojadi		35. Kudatini
	6. Somnath		36. Hallur
	(Prabhas Patan)		37. Brahmagiri
	7. Rangpur		38. T. Narsipur
	8. Mehgam		39. Hemmige
	9. Telod		40. Patpad
	10. Bhagatrav		41. Nagarjunakonda
			42. Kesarapalli
South-east Rajputana	11. Ahar		
	12. Gilund	*Tamil Nad*	43. Paiyampalli
			44. Gaurimedu
Malwa	13. Nagda		45. Mangalam
	13a. Kayatha		
	14. Navdatoli	*Central India*	46. Eran
			47. Tripuri
Maharashtra	15. Bahurupa		
	16. Prakash	*Punjab*	48. Harappa
	17. Savalda		49. Rupar
	18. Bahal		50. Bara
	19. Tekwada		
	20. Nasik	*Ganges-Jamuna*	51. Bargaon
	21. Jorwe	*Doab*	52. Ambakheri
	22. Daimabad		53. Alamgirpur
	23. Nevasa		54. Hastinapura
	24. Chandoli		55. Ahicchatra
	25. Sonegaon		56. Noh
			57. Atranjikhera
Karnataka-Andhra	26. Watgal		
	27. Billamrayan Gudda		
	28. Piklihal		
	29. Maski		

continuation of this broad diffusive process until late- or post-Harappan times. On the other hand we find evidence in at least three regions of pre-metal Neolithic cultures, albeit in absolute time they may be somewhat later than Neolithic stages farther west. At least the first two of these are now dated by runs of radiocarbon to what in absolute time is a pre-Harappan period. In Kashmir the culture is probably associated with a hunting economy, and there is as yet no proof of agriculture or domestication. Equipment and burial customs lead us to associate the Neolithic of Kashmir with Neolithic or near-Neolithic cultures right across central Asia into southern Siberia and the north-western frontiers of China. Apparently it had little or no contact with the western Chalcolithic cultures. On the other hand several elements, such as the stone axes and the grey burnished pottery, appear, however distantly, to have some relationship to the axes and pottery which appear, almost simultaneously, in south India.

The southern Neolithic culture is associated from the beginning with people possessing herds of cattle (*Bos indicus*), sheep and goats, and developing in course of time a stone-blade industry. It also shares traits with the north-western Chalcolithic cultures, but its origin is still obscure. It passes through three distinct phases, of which the second and third see a steady increase in the still small number of copper or bronze tools. These two phases we may regard as secondary Neolithic or Chalcolithic. In Assam there is a suggestion of an 'Early' Neolithic with possible relations with the two previous groups, and also perhaps with those of south China, and there is more certain evidence of a mature Neolithic with very definite south Chinese and Southeast Asian affinities. These phases are as yet not dated. Eastern Central India sees the farthest extent of this culture group along with indications of an earlier, undifferentiated stone-axe industry which is found throughout Central India. In these parts of eastern and Central India tribal peoples have survived into recent times, and we may suspect that a good deal of our surface evidence relates to very secondary Neolithic cultures.

THE EXPANSION OF POST-HARAPPAN SETTLEMENTS

The rediscovery of the post-Harappan culture sequence in region after region of India has been one of her archaeologists' most remarkable achievements in the past two decades. As more material becomes available in published form, the picture of this period of later prehistory, or protohistory as it begins to deserve to be called, is becoming clearer. But the information we have is still far from being sufficient to make a complete cultural reconstruction. There can be little doubt that this phase is one of cultural expansion eastwards and southwards from the Indus valley, and we shall try to trace this stage by stage.

We begin in the Kathiawar peninsula which, it will be re-called, was an area colonized by Harappan civilization. It would seem that during the Harappan period – if not even before it – settlements came into being which had a local culture of their own. At Lothal, throughout the occupation, a sprinkling of local pottery is found, including a distinctive black-and-red ware and a cream-slipped ware. The purely Harappan occupation of this site seems to have ended around 1860 B.C., and the succeeding period II is characterized by new pottery forms and styles of painting, including animals of striking naturalism*. This 'sub-Harappan' phase produced two radiocarbon dates of 1856 and 1809 B.C., and it must, we feel, indicate the partial withdrawal of colonial rule and the emergence of an independent provincial culture. Apart from Lothal there are three principal excavations where the subsequent development can be followed; these are Rangpur, Somnath (Prabhas Patan) and Rojdi. Between them these sites give a complete sequence from the Harappan down to the arrival of iron. We shall summarize here the main phases of this development, as recognized at present:

1. Harappan. During this period settlements showing a combination of Harappan and local pottery came into exist-ence. Rangpur IIA is our main source of information for this period; Rojdi IA is also probably contemporary, as too may be

*In some publications periods I and II at Lothal are referred to as A and B respectively.

Desalpar IA, in Cutch. It will be interesting as research advances to see whether it is possible to differentiate Harappan settlements such as Lothal from other sites, and whether the local cultural elements predominate at some sites more than others. One would like to know, for example, whether Harappan seals or sealings are found at the smaller sites. From what is already published it appears that, if not seals, at least inscribed potsherds are noticed at Rangpur and Rojdi.

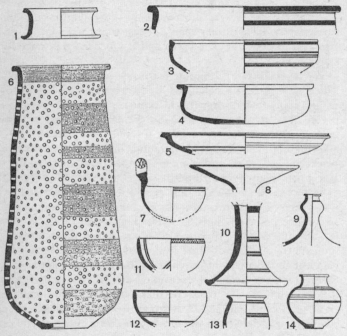

Figure 43. Rangpur IIA, red ware pottery. 1:6

2. Post-Harappan. This phase is represented by Lothal II, Rojdi IB, Rangpur IIB, and by the earliest settlement at Somnath (Prabhas Patan) IA. At both Lothal and Rangpur it is marked by a decline, following no doubt the withdrawal of Harappan trade and influence. The pottery and other items of material culture continue without any marked break, but

elaborate town-planning and drainage, so characteristic of Harappan culture, disappear. This period should commence around 1800 B.C., and at Rangpur the occupation is of about 12 feet in depth. A radiocarbon date for this period from Rojdi gives 1745 B.C.

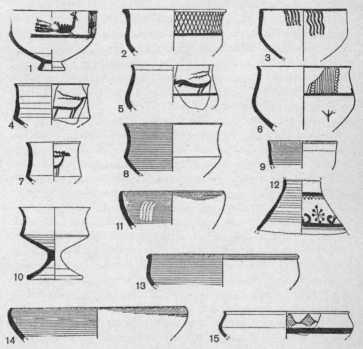

Figure 44. Rangpur pottery. 1:6

Period IIB: red ware, 1. Period IIC: red and lustrous red wares, 2, 3 and 5–7. Period III: red and lustrous red wares, 4, 10, 12 and 15; black-and-red ware, 8, 13 and 14; white-painted black-and-red ware, 9 and 11.

3. The third period coincided at Rangpur IIC with something of a revival. This may be equated with Rojdi IC and Somnath IB. Again there is no real break with the preceding period. Some further distinctive Harappan forms of pottery, such as the footed goblets and the terracotta cakes disappear, and new painted motifs are found on the pottery, including

examples of antelopes and bulls. A bright red burnished
pottery known as the Lustrous Red ware makes its appearance.

4. The final development of the series corresponds with
Rangpur III, Somnath IIA (and perhaps B), and Rojdi II.
The Lustrous Red ware becomes a dominant trait, as do the
painted antelope and bull motifs, and a wide range of geometric designs painted on small carinated bowls. Another new
and highly significant trait is the black-and-red pottery, often
with white-painted designs (Figure 44, Nos. 8, 9, etc.).

The stone-blade industry of the Harappan period, made of
imported materials, gives way in all the subsequent phases to a
blade industry of locally available jasper and agate, but copper
tools are found throughout. A study of the large quantity of
plant remains obtained from Rangpur showed the cultivation
of rice already in Period IIA, and some millet, possibly
bājrā (*Pennisetum typhoideum*) in Period III. Interestingly the
trees identified are mainly acacias, tamarisk and albizzia, indicating a dry forest and therefore a climate little different
from that of today. The sequence we have just witnessed is not
as yet fixed by any later radiocarbon dates, but as iron appears
at Somnath in the subsequent period, IIIA, we may with
some confidence conclude that the fourth phase ends about
1000 B.C. Considering this evidence, and noting the remarkable
continuity from the Harappan period forward, we may well
ask at what stage Indo-Iranian languages were first introduced.
Already before the Christian era Somnath was associated with
Shri Krishna, the hero of the Mahābhārata story, who became
identified with an incarnation of Vishnu. Another feature of
the sequence is the way in which it apparently parallels that of
Sind, where also a post-Harappan (Jhukar) culture phase succeeded fairly directly after the Harappan. Coastal Gujarat is
an eastern extension of this region, where sites around the
estuary of the Narbada river give evidence of a similar sequence:
phases 1 and 2 are represented at Bhagatrav, phase 2 alone at
Mehgam and Telod, and phases 3 and 4 at Hasanpur, all in
that area. The explorations and excavations carried out by the
late P. P. Pandya and by Shri S. R. Rao and others have
revealed only five Harappan settlements; of the first post-
Harappan phase (our 2 above) over fifty new settlements have

so far been identified; of the second (our 3) over ten more; and of the third about four additional new settlements. Clearly this indicates a continuing increase in population.

About two hundred miles north-east of the Kathiawar peninsula, in the hilly country east of the Aravalli range, a somewhat different culture has been brought to light in recent years, called the Banas culture after the river of that name. Certain features suggest that it may have played a significant role in the formation of later Indian civilization, but neither of the principal excavated sites, Ahar or Gilund, has so far been fully published. In this area no Harappan sites are yet known,

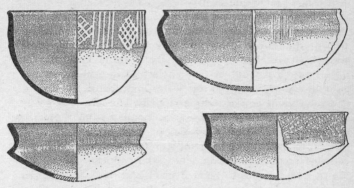

Figure 45. White-painted black-and-red ware from Ahar. 1:5

and it is therefore a matter of great interest to speculate on the origins of the Banas culture and its relations with Indo-Iranian tribal groups.

The early occupation at Ahar is divided into three phases, IA, B and C. Radiocarbon dates indicate that IB extended from *c.* 1650 to 1400 B.C., and IC continued down to the twelfth century B.C. We may expect the early occupation to date back to *c.* 1800 B.C. One of the special features is the complete absence of any stone tools, either axes or blades; copper axes and objects of copper were correspondingly numerous, and indeed copper is locally available as a raw material. The houses were of stone and mud and showed no development during the occupation. Much of the pottery is also rather different from that of the Saurashtran sites, but one of the dominant wares throughout is black-and-red ware, with white-painted decoration; another important ware present in the earliest phases only is a cream-slipped pottery with black-painted decoration. Red-slipped ware is present from the beginning, and in the third phase (IC) Lustrous Red ware makes its appearance. Grey ware with incised or appliqué decorations is found and some of these vessels had surface roughening on the lower part of the exterior, recalling examples from both Baluchistan and south India. A noteworthy form, the dish-on-stand, was present throughout. The large numbers of rubbing stones and saddle querns may be taken as indicating some sort of grain production, and deer were evidently hunted. Terra-cotta figurines included humped cattle. Professor Sankalia has drawn attention to the remarkable similarity of clay spindle whorls with incised designs to whorls from Troy, but it is not as yet clear whether this single trait indicates any direct cultural contact – indeed this seems improbable.

The remains at Gilund are similar. The site is large, and interesting structural details were revealed from the earliest occupation, including a system of mud-brick walls which seemed to have formed part of a great platform, a feature recalling Harappan planning. The pottery appears to have been much as at Ahar, with painted black-and-red ware appearing throughout. In the upper levels only, painted cream-slipped ware was found. Terracotta figurines of humped cattle were again present, but in contrast to Ahar a stone-blade industry was recorded. More precise correlation will be possible when the publication of these interesting excavations is completed. Little is known as yet of this period on the northern fringes of the Rajasthan desert, and although sites in the now dry bed of the Chautang river (Drishadvatī) are reported to have produced a painted cream-slipped ware, their relation to the Sothi culture is not established. In view of the association of this area with the Rigveda, careful exploration is obviously needed.

Directly to the east of Kathiawar and the Aravalli hills lies the fertile Malwa plateau. Drained by the river Chambal and sloping gently away toward the north, the region is bounded

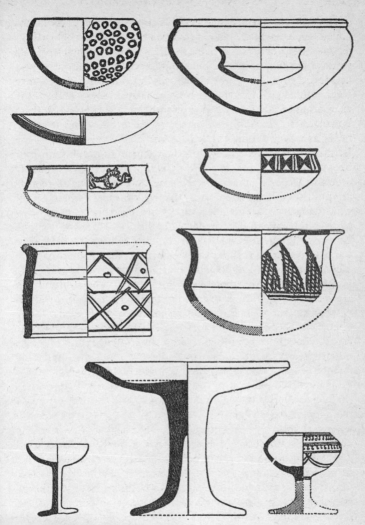

Figure 46. Pottery from Navdatoli, Malwa. 1:6

on the south by the valley of the river Narbada. Two sites have been excavated, Nagda towards the north and Navdatoli on the banks of the Narbada in the south. The first season's work at the latter site has been published in full and provides important evidence of the sequence, but only summaries have been published of the later season's work there and .of the excavation at Nagda. A series of eight radiocarbon dates from Navdatoli so far published is somewhat erratic, and it seems necessary to discount at least one. They suggest that the Chalcolithic settlement, which the excavators divide into four phases, may be dated as follows: IIIA, 1660–1530 B.C.; IIID around 1440 B.C. This being the case, and until the full reports are published, the sequence in this region must remain somewhat tentative. Nevertheless the general outline is clear. The earliest settlement at Navdatoli is Period IIIA, two Stone Age horizons in the vicinity of the site being named Periods I and II.* During this period both round and square huts were built of wattle and daub with plastered floors. A stone-blade industry and copper tools were both made. The stone blades are particularly numerous and often very beautiful. As in Karnataka, there is a regular minority of retouched blades, giving backed or geometric forms. The people kept cattle, sheep, goat and pig, and cultivated wheat, lentils and oilseeds. Their pottery, which again provides the chief distinguishing feature in the culture, included painted black-and-red ware, a distinctive red-slipped pottery with black-painted decoration (known as Malwa ware), and a creamy-white slipped ware with black-painted decoration, also closely related to the Malwa ware in point of manufacture (Plate 29). A grey ware recalling that of Maharashtra and Karnataka was present throughout. This phase would appear to coincide with the earliest phase in southern Rajputana (Ahar IA). Among distinctive pottery forms are many handmade bowls. The painted decoration is rather fussily applied, and gives the impression that its authors had a good deal of time on their hands.

In the second phase at Navdatoli (IIIB), which in parts of

---

* Some confusion has been caused by the renaming in later publications of the four Chalcolithic phases as I–IV. Thus the original IIIA apparently becomes I, IIIB becomes II, etc.

the site followed a minor burning, the first evidence of rice cultivation is encountered. The chief change in the pottery is the absence of the black-and-red painted ware, while a series of small goblets on solid pedestals are distinctive. The third phase (IIIC) followed a more extensive burning and seems to have coincided with the arrival of new traits and perhaps also new elements of population from the west. Among the new traits is a fine red pottery, frequently wheel-thrown, with black-painted decoration (Plate 28 c). This has been named

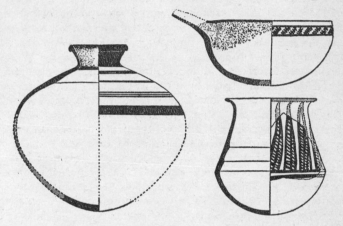

Figure 47. Pottery from Navdatoli, Malwa. 1:10

Jorwe ware. Characteristically it is unburnished, but some of its forms seem related to those of the Lustrous Red ware of Kathiawar. Along with the Jorwe ware came a new vogue for spouted vessels, and distinctive forms which recall those from the second phase of the Neolithic of the Karnataka region. Copper fish-hooks from the surface collection probably belong to this phase. The final stage of the Chalcolithic at Navdatoli (IIID) saw the addition of channel-spouted bowls and of further pottery recalling the Lustrous Red ware.

The sequence at Nagda is not analysed in the brief published note, although the excavator records a Chalcolithic deposit of 22 feet in thickness. The published illustrations of the pottery leave little doubt that the parallels with Saurashtra are particularly close, and lead one to expect a series of phases paralleling those of Rangpur IIB, IIC and III. Painted decoration includes peacocks (as at Rangpur), cattle with wavy or decorated horns, and antelopes with bodies filled with dots. In general the Nagda pottery lacks the individual character of that from Navdatoli, but it may be expected to cover a similar period of occupation. Among the special features of Nagda I we may note grey ware with unburnt ochre-painted decoration as in the Southern Neolithic, an incised grey ware reminiscent of that found at Navdatoli, stemmed goblets and channel-spouted bowls. First reports suggest that considerable interest may be attached to the preliminary excavations at Kayatha, a site some fifteen miles east of Ujjain discovered by V. S. Wakankar. There appear to be three periods preceding the arrival of iron and dated by a run of C14 samples. Period I, dated to *c.* 2015 B.C., yielded painted red ware reputed to have Harappan affinities; a thin buff ware perhaps related to the pre-Harappan ceramic tradition of Sothi and Kalibangan; and a coarse red ware. Period II is dated by two samples to between 1965 and 1675 B.C., and yielded painted black-and-red ware recalling that of Ahar. This level is also reported to have produced a Harappan seal. Period III witnessed the arrival of pottery of the Malwa and Jorwe traditions, and is dated by three samples to between 1675 and 1380 B.C.

The regions we have considered so far, Saurashtra, Rajputana, and Malwa, all belong to the low rainfall zone of western India and West Pakistan. Together they probably represent the areas in which the first synthesis of the Harappan with exotic cultures took place, and from which the first waves of post-Harappan expansion developed. It becomes possible at least to speculate about the identification of archaeological cultures and tribal groups whose names and geographical positions are known from the early Vedic literature, and from later historical traditions such as those of the Puranas. This kind of research is bound to play an increasingly important role as our knowledge advances.

The further archaeological expansion of the post-Harappan cultures now proceeds in three broad directions. Firstly, they

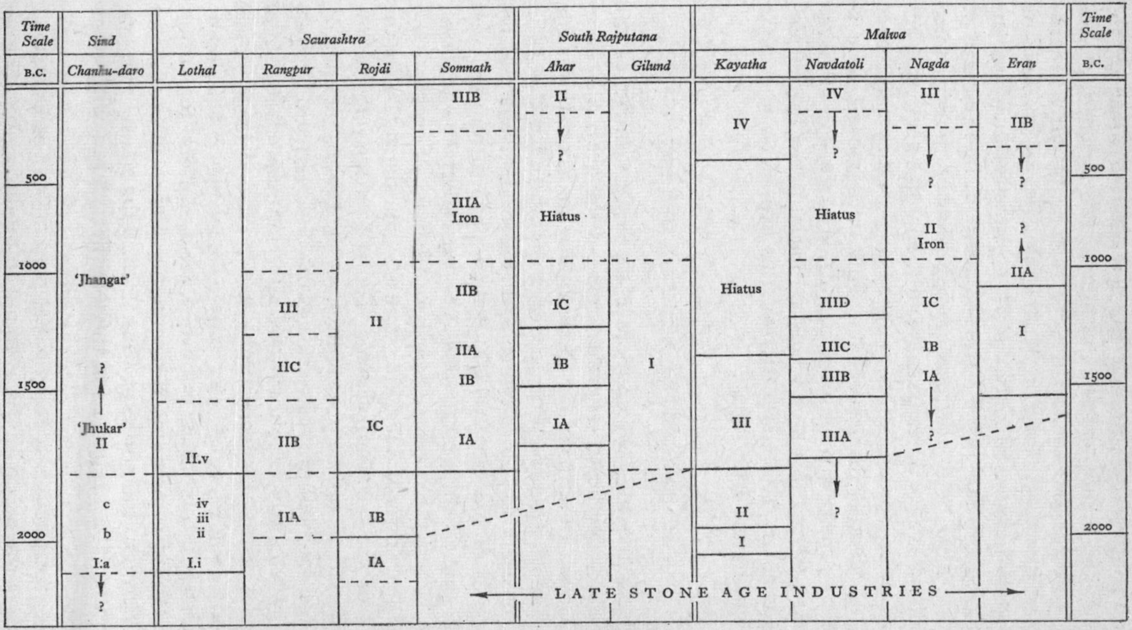

Time Scale B.C.	Sind	Saurashtra				South Rajputana		Malwa				Time Scale B.C.
	Chanhu-daro	Lothal	Rangpur	Rojdi	Somnath	Ahar	Gilund	Kayatha	Navdatoli	Nagda	Eran	
500	'Jhangar'		III	II	IIIB	II ← ?		IV	IV ← ?	III ← ?	IIB → ?	500
1000	? ← 'Jhukar' II	II.v	IIC	IC	IIIA Iron	Hiatus		Hiatus	Hiatus	? ← II Iron	? → IIA	1000
1500	c / b / Ia → ?	iv / iii / ii / Li	IIB / IIA	IB / IA	IIB / IIA / IB / IA	IC / IB / IA	I	III / II / I	IIID / IIIC / IIIB / IIIA → ?	IC / IB / IA → ?	I	1500
2000												2000

LATE STONE AGE INDUSTRIES

Figure 48. Chalcolithic sequence of west and Central India (chart 3)

spread southwards, through the low rainfall areas of the
Deccan, and thence, coming in contact with the existing Neolithic cultures and coalescing with them, eastwards towards
the east coast on a broad front from Bengal to Andhra.
Secondly, they moved more directly eastwards along the Narbada valley to the hills of Central India, and into the heavier
rainfall areas with correspondingly thicker forest cover.
Thirdly, from north Rajputana and the Punjab there was another easterly spread into the upper Ganges valley and thence
into the Central Ganges region. This third movement corresponds or overlaps with the postulated expansion of Aryan
settlements into this area which we encountered in the previous chapter. The completion of this expansion took place
only during the Iron Age.

MAHARASHTRA AND THE DECCAN

South of the hills which border the lower course of the
Narbada valley lies the northern part of the great plateau of
the Deccan. In terms of the Chalcolithic expansion, this is one
of the most extensively excavated parts of India, thanks in
large measure to the activities of Professor Sankalia and his
colleagues of Deccan College, Poona. Thus during the past
decade and a half excavations have been undertaken at Jorwe,
Prakash, Bahal, Nevasa, Daimabad, Chandoli, Sonegaon and
Bahurupa. Two of the sites, Prakash and Bahal, lie in the
valley of the westward-flowing Tapi (Tapti) river; the remainder are all on the plateau itself, in the country drained by
the headwaters of the eastward-flowing Godavari and Krishna
river systems which abut to the south upon Karnataka or the
central Deccan. A special problem is presented because, apparently, out of eight sites only Daimabad, which is unfortunately incompletely published, yields cultural remains of
an antiquity comparable to the earlier phases in Saurashtra
and Malwa to the north, or Karnataka to the south. Thus we
must treat the evidence for these earlier phases with some
caution.

The first phase is represented at present only at Daimabad
(I). Here the occupation was found to produce ground stone

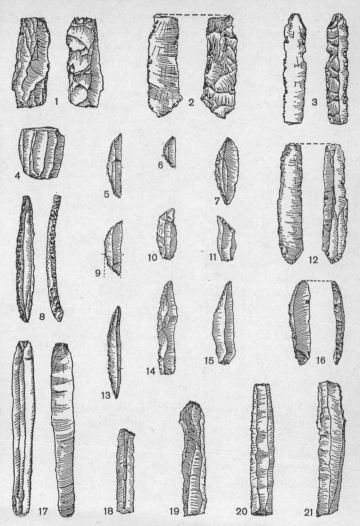

Figure 49. Nevasa and Chandoli, Chalcolithic stone-blade
industry. 2:3

1, prepared blade core; 2, primary guide flake; 3, secondary guide flake; 4, blade core;
5–7, 9 and 13, lunates; 8, awl or borer (?); 10 and 11, truncated blades; 12 and 17–21,
blades; 14 and 16, backed blades; 15, point.

axes, a perforated ringstone and stone-blade industry. The pottery was mainly coarse grey or black, frequently burnished, and sometimes with unburned ochre paint. A second ware was again unburnished, but with a buff surface sometimes painted in black or brown. Fingertip decoration and appliqué bands occur, and it is claimed that at least one painted spout was recovered from this period. Comparatively speaking, this as-

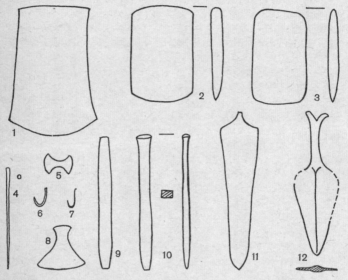

Figure 50. Copper and bronze tools from peninsular India. 1:4
1, Navdatoli; 2, Tekkalakota; 3, 6 and 12, Chandoli; 4 and 9, Nevasa; 5, 7 and 8, Hallur; 10, Piklihal; 11, Daimabad.

semblage is closer to the second or upper Neolithic phase of the Karnataka sites to the south than to the first phase; but its more immediate affinities are with Navdatoli and Malwa. Several extended burials were discovered among the houses. The second phase is reported at Daimabad (II) and Prakash IA. At the former the stone-blade industry proliferates and the first copper occurs. Among the copper objects was a knife blade (Figure 50, No 11), reminiscent of Harappan types. The grey ware continues, but a fine reddish-brown ware with painting is now common. Spouts and a channel spout are found, once again comparable to the Malwa ware. The painted decoration includes a remarkable series of small animals, mainly bulls and a (?) peacock. An unusually fine example of this painting (Plate 28 A) may be assigned to this phase. The first instances of this distinctive style are already present in phase 1, and it continues into phase 3; it is also nearly related to the adjacent Malwa style. The excavator of Prakash divides period I into earlier and later parts. The earlier sub-period IA produced painted red ware akin to Malwa ware, a distinctive black-and-grey ware with white-painted decoration (apparently related to the painted black-and-red ware tradition), and a coarse grey burnished ware, occasionally with unburnt ochre decoration. No C14 dates are available from this site, but the pottery suggests that this sub-period is contemporary with Navdatoli IIIB and IIIC, and may therefore be assigned to *c.* 1700–1400 B.C.

The third phase may be named after the type-site, Jorwe. It represents a great expansion of settlements and hence of population, and it may be dated with some confidence from runs of radiocarbon datings at Nevasa, Chandoli and Sonegaon, to between 1375 and 1050 B.C. Thanks to the publications of the reports on Nevasa and Chandoli there is a great deal of cultural information regarding the way of life of the Jorwe communities. The houses, like those of Malwa, were of wattle and daub on a wooden frame, and the floors were often mud-plastered, or finished with mixed sand and gravel. The stone-blade industry dominated the material equipment, but copper played an important part, flat axes of rectangular form being found at Jorwe and Chandoli, and copper chisels at the latter site (Figure 50). A copper spearhead with faint midrib and antennae hilt was found at Chandoli, as was a copper fish-hook. The people used a variety of stone tools. A small stone-axe factory was discovered at Nevasa, and stone axes at Chandoli. Once again, as at Navdatoli, and the Karnataka sites, the stone-blade industry demands our admiration (Plate 27 A). The predominant raw materials are chalcedony and other semi-precious stones; and because of their gem-like quality and the technical excellence of their manufacture, the finished tools

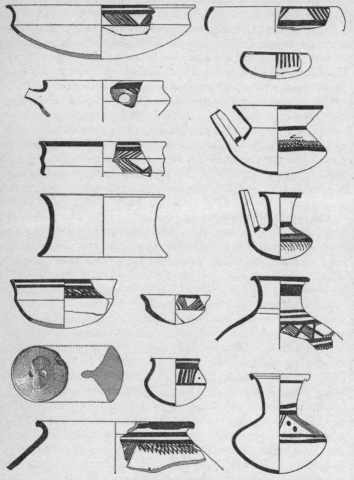

Figure 51. Nevasa and Jorwe, pottery. 1 : 6

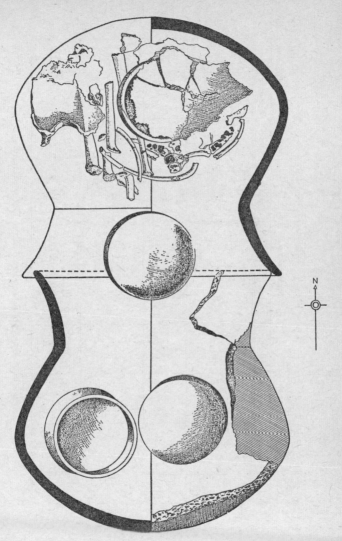

Figure 52. Nevasa III, urn burial. 1 : 6

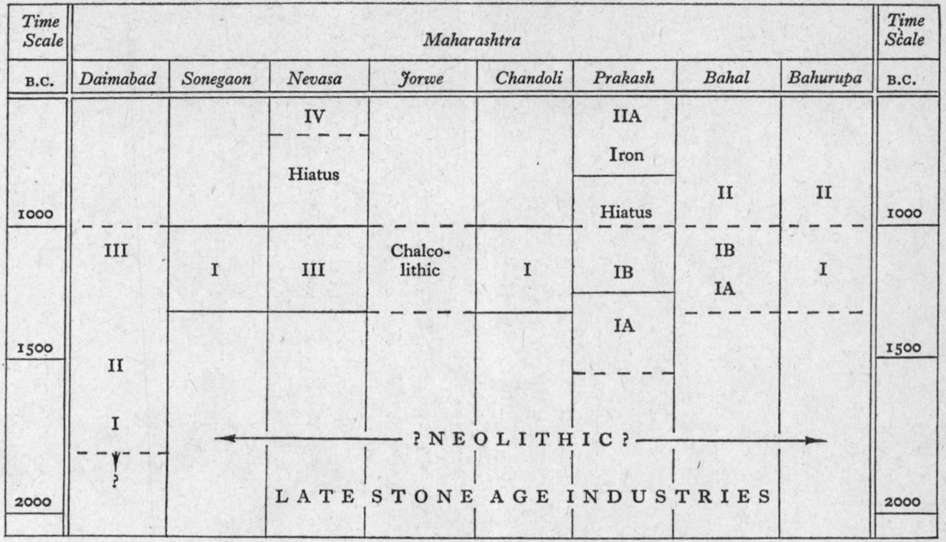

Figure 53. Chalcolithic sequence of the Deccan (chart 4)

are often things of great beauty. Used and unused blades, without retouch, predominate, but backed blades, and various geometric forms, as well as serrated blades, are regular occurrences.

The domestic animals included cattle, sheep, goat and buffalo. Another exciting discovery at Nevasa and Chandoli was of fragments of thread or fibres including cotton, flax and raw silk. The pottery included a continuing coarse grey ware, and the painted red Jorwe ware with its characteristic long-spouted vessels and shallow carinated food bowls. There is a tendency for the painted decoration to become more slapdash, often giving the impression of wheel application, while burnishing becomes correspondingly more rare. At Prakash sub-period IB is clearly differentiated from IA. The Malwa ware continues in decreased quantity, being augmented by a small proportion of Jorwe ware. Also noteworthy is the presence of a small quantity of Lustrous Red ware, suggesting some sort of contact with Rangpur IIC and III. To the east in the Tapi valley another distinctive form of painted pottery, named after the type site of Sawalda, appears to belong to this phase, but its stratigraphic context has not yet been established. At several of the sites there is evidence of the burial customs: skeletal remains of infants or children were found buried in double urns of grey ware beneath the house floors, together with other grave goods. This form of burial recalls phases 2 and 3 of the Karnataka region. The continuing southward extension of these phases, into Karnataka and beyond, has already been discussed.

CENTRAL AND EASTERN COASTAL INDIA

The eastward extension of Chalcolithic cultures from Malwa is soon told. Geographically and culturally, the regions of Central India are to this day somewhat complex, presenting a picture of islands of settled agricultural life amid an ocean of hills and forests. No doubt in ancient times the forest was far more prevalent than it is today, but fundamentally the pattern is ancient. At Eran, some 200 miles north-east of Navdatoli, on a tributary of the Betwa river, and at Tripuri, near Jabalpur, on the Narbada river itself, excavations have revealed Chalco-lithic settlements below those of a later period; and in both cases the material culture suggests an expansion of that of Malwa. A series of radiocarbon dates from Eran have recently been published, but they do not seem to bear a uniform re-lationship to their reported stratified provenances. The indica-tion they provide is that the Chalcolithic culture at this site extended from *c.* 1500 to 1280 B.C., and probably gave way to the Iron Age around 1040 B.C. but the published evidence from both these sites at the moment is too slight to present a very definite picture. There is a suggestion at Eran that the final phase of the Chalcolithic (IIA) may be associated with black-and-red ware; this phase appears to date between about 1270 and 1040 B.C.

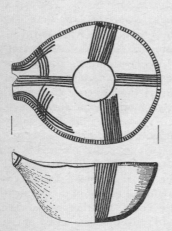

Figure 54. Patpad, painted chan-nel-spouted bowl

1 : 8

The sparse evidence from parts of eastern India of the farthest limits of this post-Harappan Chalcolithic spread can be briefly put forward. At Pandu Rajar Dhibi in the Burdwan district of West Bengal the excavation of a mound has produced a culture sequence with two pre-iron periods, characterized by a stone-blade industry, apparently of debased form, ground stone axes, and a number of copper objects including fish-hooks. The pottery included painted red ware and black-and-red ware, and channel-spouted bowls are of common occur-rence. Taking this assemblage as a whole, we would expect it to belong to something equivalent to the Jorwe phase at earliest, but more probably slightly later than that phase in the west. A single radiocarbon sample gives a date of 1012 ± 120 B.C. and seems plausible. At Mahisadal in the adjacent Birbhum district another recent excavation has yielded confirmation of this sequence. Period I was Chalcolithic, with simple huts of plastered reed. The finds included a typical blade industry and a flat copper celt; pottery included black-and-red ware, sometimes white painted, and red ware, some with black-painted decoration. The forms of pottery recall those of Pandu Rajar Dhibi, channel spouts being prominent. A quantity of charred rice was discovered. This period is dated by three C14 samples to between 1380 and 855 B.C. The succeeding period II saw a continuation of the now somewhat coarser pottery and the arrival of iron, and a single radiocarbon sample suggests that this event took place before 690 B.C.

Far to the south, in the Kurnool district of Andhra Pradesh, a large group of sites, first identified by Bruce Foote, produces a distinctive painted red ware which we may name after the type site, Patpad ware. The culture which produced this pottery at Patpad (Pattupadu) and elsewhere flourished within a few scores of miles of the sites of the Karnataka region, and yet it shows a remarkable difference in the style of painting, and in other details. The channel-spouted bowl is here again a special feature. While evidence of the age of this culture is even less clear than in the case of Bengal, we are inclined to assign it to a somewhat similar chronological horizon. Another site of perhaps about the same age is reported to have been excavated in 1961 at Kesarapalli in the Krishna district, revealing a considerable deposit of late pre-iron materials. Yet farther south in Pondicherry, Casal discovered and excavated a number of urn burials at Gaurimedu and Mangalam. The predominant red pottery associated with them, the pot forms, and the absence of any metal objects other than copper or bronze, all indicate that these belong to a cultural phase anterior to the Iron Age. There is of course no inherent improbability that further, earlier stages of Chalcolithic or Neolithic settlement may be found in all these eastern areas, but in our view those so far reported are more likely to belong to a late Chalcolithic phase chronologically akin to the Jorwe phase of Maharashtra.

THE GANGES VALLEY

The third and northernmost of the eastward thrusts of post-Harappan Chalcolithic settlements may be inferred to have derived both from Rajputana and the Punjab, and to have spread into the *Doab* (or 'two rivers') country of the Ganges and Jamuna. We have already noted the late Harappan sites at Rupar in the Punjab and Alamgirpur in the *Doāb*. Both these settlements appear to have been deserted for some time before their subsequent reoccupation in the early Iron Age. The intervening centuries remain something of a mystery and appear to be filled by the little known 'Copper Hoard culture'. Ever since 1822 hoards of copper implements have come to light from time to time in the Ganges–Jamuna *Doab*, the hills of Chota Nagpur and Orissa, and at odd places in Central India and the Deccan. In 1951 Shri B. B. Lal listed thirty-seven such hoards. We may consider them as divided, culturally, into two main groups, those of the *Doab* and those of the eastern province, the former comprising about half of the total. Until fifteen years ago there was no indication of the cultural context of the copper hoards, but since that date, due largely to the percipience of B. B. Lal, their associations have become slightly clearer. At Bisauli and at Rajpur Parsu exploration and trial excavation in the vicinity of the find spots of hoards revealed a thick, red, rolled and waterlogged pottery, nicknamed 'Ochre-washed' or Ochre Coloured pottery (sometimes abbreviated to OCP) from its distinctive quality. A third hoard site at Bahadarabad in Saharanpur district yielded similar evidence. Excavation at Hastinapura revealed the Ochre Coloured pottery below the Early Iron Age (Painted Grey ware) levels, but in so small a quantity as to give no indication of complete forms. Recent exploration in the Saharanpur district, carried out by M.N. Deshpande of the Archaeological Survey, has revealed a number of sites, some producing late-Harappan elements, such as stone blades, and even a copper bracelet, in association with this pottery. All the sites at which the elusive Ochre Coloured ware has so far been recorded are on the alluvial plains of the Ganges river system, and frequently finds have been reported as having been sub-

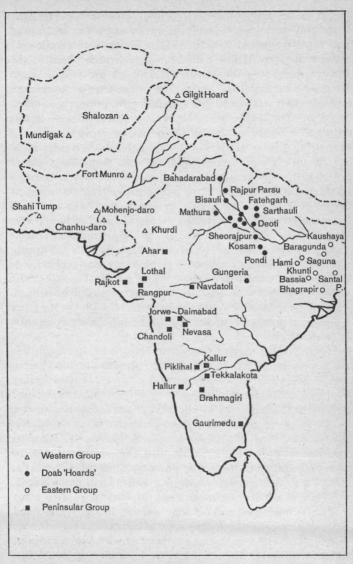

Figure 55. Map of finds of copper and bronze implements

jected to flooding, or as redeposited. This may explain the
worn and waterlogged condition of so much of the pottery
and its disintegrated surface. Similar deposits of waterlogged
pottery of Early Historic date are found farther east in the
districts bordering the Nepal Tarai which are also liable to
constant flooding. Trial excavations at the sites of Ambakheri
and Bargaon have revealed quantities of pottery including
many late-Harappan forms. It seems probable that when this
material is published it will show two or more phases, the
first being a full – if late – Harappan and the second a post-
Harappan. Possible confirmation of this hypothesis comes
from the recent excavations of Aligarh University at Atranjikhera in Etah district. Here a deposit of red pottery was
found stratified below Iron Age levels, and was identified
by its excavator as equivalent to the Ochre Coloured ware
(period IA). A subsequent period, IB, produced black-
and-red pottery, along with a stone-blade industry. No iron
is reported and the excavator is probably correct in asso-
ciating it with the black-and-red ware of the Banas culture.
Ochre Coloured ware has also been found stratified beneath
Painted Grey at Ahicchatra, while at Noh in Bharatpur State
a sequence closely parallel to that of Atranjikhera has recently
been excavated.

Discoveries of copper artifacts in stratified contexts outside
the region seem to belong to a generally comparable chronological horizon. From the end of Lothal I comes a broken
copper ('anthropomorphic') axe of a form otherwise found
only in the Doab hoards. The dominant flat axes are reminiscent
of examples not only from Harappan contexts, but also from
the Jorwe phase in Maharashtra and Malwa. The copper
antennae swords of Fatehgarh may now be paralleled by
the spearhead from the Jorwe phase at Chandoli (Plate 21 A,
Figure 50). A fragment of a dagger with midrib from Navdatoli III also recalls specimens from the hoards.

The chronological and cultural horizons being thus defined,
we may now consider the typology of the objects found in the
hoards. The common flat axes sometimes with slightly splayed
blades require no discussion: as we have already noted they
are common in the Indus civilization and in several post-

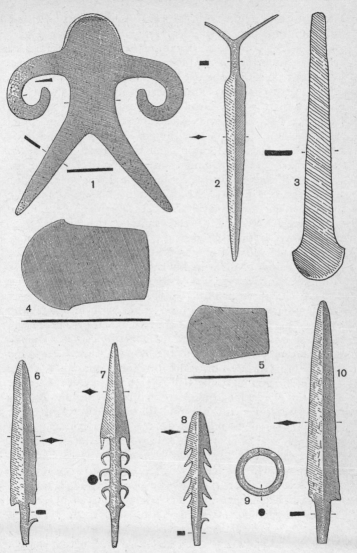

Figure 56. Tools from the Doab copper hoards. 1:8

Harappan Chalcolithic sites. A second type of flat axe has a semi-circular cutting edge and a pronounced shoulder (Figure 56, No. 4). A third type of flat axe has the cutting edge extended to form two wings, as in the modern *Parasū*. The most elaborate type is that often referred to as an anthropomorphic figure (Figure 56, No. 1). These curious pieces have sharpening on the rear of the 'arms' while the inner sides of the 'legs' are left blunt. They bear some resemblance to 'anthropomorphic' sacrificial axes of iron or steel used by the Santals and other tribal people of Chota Nagpur, but their actual function was more probably as some kind of ritual figures. Next there are heavy spearheads or swords having a solid tang, often with a single barb, presumably for hafting, and a blade with mid-rib, ranging in length up to over 28 inches (Figure 56, Nos. 6 and 10). There is no doubt that the examples with antennae hilts were swords or dirks (Figure 56, No. 2), of which a small hoard already referred to was discovered as far south as the Raichur district in the neighbourhood of Kallur (Plate 21 A). Another distinctive type is the barbed harpoon, with triangular tip and with three pairs of barbs below. In some instances these are hafted with a tang and single barb, in others with a pierced lug and tang (Figure 56, Nos. 7 and 8). These again have a stout mid-rib and were undoubtedly cast in a mould. Both the antennae swords and the harpoons have been found to be of bronze with a tin content ranging from 6 per cent to 9·5 per cent. Among these tool types some are characteristic of the earlier Harappan industry, while others show definite external features such as the mid-rib on the swords, daggers, spears and harpoons, and the pierced lug for hafting, which could well have originated in Iran, or the Caucasus region. A third group of traits however is peculiar to India, and may be taken as having evolved locally.

The second distributional group of copper implements is still less easy to fix culturally. It lies south and east of the first, in the hills and forests south of the Ganges in Bihar and Bengal. It includes flat axes, long bar celts, often of 18 inches in length, and shouldered axes. An outlier of this group is from Gungeria, in the Balaghat district of Madhya Pradesh south of Jabalpur, where along with over 400 copper objects about 100

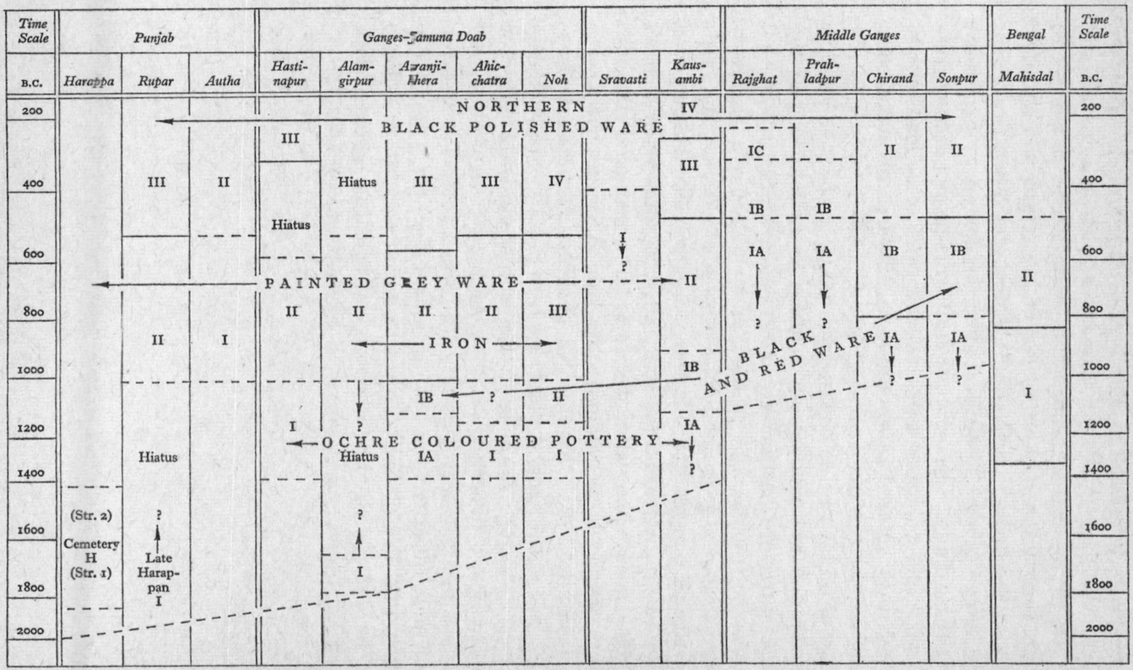

Figure 57. Post-Harappan and Iron Age sequence of Punjab, Doab and Middle Ganges regions (chart 5)

silver plates in the form of a bull's head with down-turned horns were discovered. All this area is rich in minerals and copper was mined there anciently. It thus seems reasonable to expect that the eastern extension of post-Harappan cultures, both up the line of the Narbada valley, and down the line of the Ganges valley, should have been in some way connected with these finds. The absence from this group of such distinctive types as harpoons, antennae swords, etc., leads one to expect that some factors unknown at present must have separated the two main areas of copper finds.

It will be interesting as our knowledge increases to attempt to relate the archaeological evidence with that afforded by the Vedic and more particularly late-Vedic literature. It is well known that by the time of the Yajur and Atharva *Samhitas*, the geographical focus had shifted from the Punjab eastwards towards the Ganges–Jamuna Doab, and in the latest texts even as far east as Magadha (Bihar). But it is noteworthy that all this later Vedic literature appears to know iron, and therefore may be expected to belong to the Iron Age, rather than the Chalcolithic. Where therefore Chalcolithic cultures are found to the east of the geographical region of the Rigveda, they may either indicate pre-Aryan settlements, or settlements of Aryans who had arrived and dispersed before the arrival of those who brought the Rigveda. There is still much room for research upon such questions, and as our knowledge increases a more tangible picture of the cultures to which these texts belong, and more especially of the aboriginal or earlier peoples with whom the Aryans had contact, is likely to emerge.

CHAPTER 8

THE IRON AGE AND THE BEGINNINGS OF HISTORY

THERE seems to be general agreement that the smelting of iron ore was first discovered in Asia Minor or the Caucasus, and that between 1800 and 1200 B.C. it remained virtually a monopoly of the Hittites. These centuries may be regarded as a period of transition leading by about 1000 B.C. to the full Iron Age of that area. Moreover, the breakdown of the Hittite empire has been held to have constituted a stimulus to the earliest diffusion of iron-working. Be this as it may the eastward spread of iron into Iran is well exemplified by the two Necropoles (A and B) at Sialk. In the former iron is a rare commodity, while in the latter, dated by Schaeffer to 1200–1000 B.C., it vies with bronze in frequency of occurrence. The people who buried their dead in Necropolis B were horsemen: they left paintings of horses and riders on their pottery and on cylinder seals, and in the grave with the dead they buried horse-furniture including bits, horse-bells and pectorals. Moreover, they used chariots. They may no doubt be associated in a general way with the horse-centred culture represented by the Late Bronze and Early Iron Age graves of the Caucasus and Luristan, and must therefore indicate movements of turbulent, partly nomadic, peoples, who may be inferred to have been Indo-Iranian speaking.

On the western borders of the Indian subcontinent, in southern and central Baluchistan, a whole chain of cairn cemeteries has been discovered, producing, in the words of Gordon, identical pottery, especially characterized by the squat, spouted flask with lugs pierced for carrying, and representing a people who had a uniform cultural level which manifested itself in horse riding, the use of iron and handmade pottery. Three-flanged arrow-heads in bronze and iron come from this group of sites. A related pottery with black paint on a red slip, known as Londo ware, has been found at sites in southern and central

Baluchistan. A characteristic feature of the cairn pottery is the use of bands of continuous spirals as a painted design – a suggestively Caucasian detail. At present all these sites can only be vaguely dated: it is probable that they cover several centuries, and range from *c.* 1100 to 750 B.C. or even later. Farther north, in north Baluchistan and the former North West Frontier Province, we have already referred to foreign objects of bronze in the graves of transitional or early Iron Age settlers in Swat and nearby valleys (page 152). The question may now be raised whether, or when, these horsemen penetrated farther into India, and if so what contact did they have with the local population? Views on this topic have been considerably revised in the past decade. As recently as 1950 Colonel Gordon could find no evidence of the use of iron in India or Pakistan prior to about 250 B.C.; while in 1959 Sir Mortimer Wheeler put forward the view that the iron industries of both north and south India could be traced back to Achaemenid sources in the sixth century B.C. New evidence has now come to light which necessitates a fundamental revision of both these views, and which incidentally obviates the need of explaining why iron-working should have spread so quickly across Iran, but been held up at the frontiers of India. We shall treat the evidence of north India and Pakistan separately from that of south and Central India.

NORTH INDIA

Although the period we are discussing is narrowly speaking 'prehistoric', there is in the later Vedic literature a considerable volume of material which approaches the historic. This literature is still not strictly datable, but its general age may be determined with reference to the termini provided by the Vedic Samhitas, particularly that of the Rigveda, on the one hand, and such historical events as the life of the Buddha on the other. Thus the later Vedic texts may be said to fall between approximately 1000 B.C. and 500 B.C., and even within this framework may be sequentially arranged. The most striking feature of the literature is the eastward expansion of its horizons. The focus of attention, which in the Rigveda was the Punjab, moves to the Doab of the Ganges and Jamuna rivers, the ancient *Kurukshetra*, the kingdom of the Kuru and Pāncāla tribes. The Punjab seems gradually to fade into the background until by the latest texts of the period, such as the *Śatapatha Brāhmana*, it is regarded even with disapproval. To the east we hear more of such tribes, or states, as Kosala (Avadh, Oudh), Kāśī – whose capital was at Banaras – and even Magadha in southern Bihar. There is another general expansion of horizons towards the south. Even before archaeology could supply any basis against which these data might be evaluated, it was already accepted that they referred to an eastward expansion of the Aryan tribes. A key passage in the *Śatapatha Brāhmana* tells how a certain king who formerly resided in the Punjab on the banks of the river Sarasvatī carried fire (sacrificial or otherwise) eastwards to Videha (in northern Bihar) as far as the Sadānīra (modern Gandak) river. In those days, we are told, there were no Brahmans to the east of this river, but already by the time of the text the expansion had continued and Brahmans were to be found beyond it.

The later Vedic literature provides a mass of information on the life and culture of the times. A wide range of crops is mentioned, including wheat, barley, millet and rice. There are repeated references to iron, as well as to copper, bronze, lead and tin. The plough was used for cultivation, and it must be inferred that there was a progressive clearance of the flat, often swampy, forests of the Ganges plains, in preparation for their adoption for agriculture. There are indications of the growing complexity of society and of the formation of 'castes'. The old tribal groups must have disappeared as population increased and the size and number of settlements multiplied. We find considerable detail on agricultural operations, ploughing, cattle-keeping, etc. We read of numerous trades and crafts. The texts further supply information on those topics on which archaeology is most reticent, such as religious beliefs and political ideas. Thus in a very real sense, for the regions to which these texts apply, we may regard the archaeological cultures as protohistoric.

At present there is very little evidence, besides that already quoted, for the Early Iron Age occupation of West Pakistan. At nearly all the principal sites in Sind and the Punjab the Chalcolithic mounds seem to have been abandoned. In 1947 this was also true of north India, but since then a whole new sequence has been discovered. The earliest Iron Age occupation is associated with a fine, well-fired Painted Grey ware which may

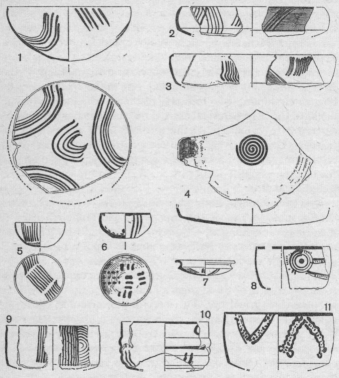

Figure 58. Hastinapur, painted grey ware pottery. 1:6

well be used as a hallmark of this cultural period. This pottery was first isolated in a stratified context in 1946 in an analysis of the finds from Ahicchatra, but its full significance only became apparent in 1950–52 with B. B. Lal's excavations at Hastinapura. The distribution of the Painted Grey ware extends from Harappa in the Punjab, where it is represented by stray surface finds, and a line of sites on the dry bed of the Ghaggar in north Rajasthan, eastwards across the watershed of the Ganges and the Indus to the Ganges–Jamuna Doab. At Rupar in the Punjab it is stratified between Harappan and Early Historic remains. In the Doab, the ancient Kurukshetra of the *Mahābhārata*, it has been found in excavations or on the surface at such historically important sites as Panipat, Indraprastha (the Old Qila mound at Delhi), Mathura, Bairat and Sonpat. Further it has been found in excavations of the vast mounds at Atranjikhera and at Alamgirpur. Many smaller sites have also been recorded. Thus the grey ware culture occupied almost the same area as the late or post-Harappan cultures of this part of India. Its eastern limits are at present at Sravasti, high on the northern plains of the Ganges. Nearer the river it gives way, from about the junction of the Ganges and Jamuna, to another – central Ganges – cultural zone which we shall discuss below. The chronological horizons of the culture which had been proposed on inferential grounds were from about 1100 to 600 B.C.; but a number of radiocarbon dates for this and the subsequent period suggest a slight modification. A sample from an early level of Atranjikhera II gives a date of 1025 ± 110 B.C.; another from the same site gives 535 B.C. for the end of the period. At Noh in Bharatpur state two radiocarbon dates for this period give 821 and 604 B.C. The beginning of the subsequent period, or the transitional phase, is represented at Ahicchatra by a radiocarbon date of 475 B.C. Taking all things into consideration a time span of 1050–450 B.C. may cover the Iron Age in this region.

Most of the excavations of these sites have been exploratory and have not investigated the Iron Age occupation to any great extent as yet. Moreover, only Hastinapura has so far been fully published. Hence when one comes to consider broader aspects of the culture, information is sadly lacking. Another reason for this is that at almost every one of the sites there was subsequent continuity of settlement so that the early levels are now buried under many metres of later deposits. Enough has been recovered to make it clear that the equipment stands in marked contrast to that of all earlier periods. A stone-blade industry is totally absent. Iron is a fairly constant find from the earliest levels, but few illustrations of any objects have yet appeared. The most frequently reported finds are of arrow-heads, both barbed and leaf-shaped, in one case with a socketed tang, and spearheads. Axes, probably shaft-hole but this is not specified, are reported from Noh and Atranjikhera; and from the latter site a pair of iron tongs from a late level of the period. Bone points, most probably arrow-heads, are frequently referred to. Copper is less common but objects made from it include small leaf-shaped arrow-heads with solid tang from Hastinapura, pins and unguent rods. Glass beads and bangles are found, as well as stone, (?) frit and terracotta discs which are probably ear ornaments, and bone dice, which play so important a part in the *Mahābhārata*. The pottery is predominately wheel-thrown and shows a remarkable degree of standardization. The Painted Grey ware is dominated by bowls of two shapes, a shallow tray and a deeper bowl, often with a sharp angle between the walls and base. The range of decoration is limited, vertical, oblique or criss-cross lines, rows of dots, spiral chains, and concentric circles being common. The same forms occur again in plain and slipped red ware, along with larger water pots, showing the combination of wheel-throwing for the upper parts and beating for the lower that so typifies Indian pottery of the Early Historic period. Very little is known of the houses: they apparently had mud floors and were constructed of wattle and daub upon a wooden frame. The diet included rice; and bones of cattle, pig and (latterly) horse are reported.

We have dwelt on this culture in some detail because it played so important a part in the formation of what we may call the second or Gangetic civilization of India. Lal has drawn attention to the fact that many of the places mentioned in the *Mahābhārata* have been found to have settlements of this period. Whether and how far there may have been even earlier settlements of the final post-Harappan phases – those associated with the red, 'Ochre Coloured' and black-and-red wares – has still to be established. But by the end of the Painted Grey ware period a more or less uniform culture, whose hallmark is the black lustrous pottery known as N.B.P. or Northern Black Polished ware, extended from the lower Ganges to the Punjab. This culture provided the milieu for the life of Gautama the Buddha, and Mahāvīra, the founder of the Jain sect, no less than for such dynasties as the Śaiśunāgas, the Nandas and the Mauryas; and for the development of the characteristic Indian script, the *Brāhmī lipi*, and of Indian coinage.

To the east of the junction of the Ganges and Jamuna rivers lies the central region of the Ganges valley, comprising eastern Uttar Pradesh and parts of Bihar. Kausambi stands at the boundary between the two regions, sharing features of each. The distinctive eastern sequence, in which a black-and-red ware plays a prominent role, was first recognized in excavations at Sonepur (Sonpur) in Gaya district in 1956. The sequence at this site has now been refined by further work, and a related sequence revealed by excavations at a number of other sites, some of great historical renown, among them Rajghat (old Banaras), Buxar, Chirand and Prahladpur. At all these sites Painted Grey ware is absent, the black-and-red giving way directly to the Northern Black Polished ware around 500 B.C. This part of the Ganges valley, enjoying as it does a rainfall of over 40 inches per annum, must anciently have been more densely forested than the Doab, and for this reason if for no other the expansion of settlements must probably have depended upon the availability of effective methods of forest clearance. There is at present no indication from which direction the first settlers came. It is possible that they moved in from the hills and forests to the south of the Ganges; but the more likely direction seems to have been from the west, in which event they would have moved eastwards down the river valley before the pressure of the expanding population associated with the iron-using Painted Grey ware culture. It is thus probable that the movement will ultimately be amenable to some sort of proto-historic documentation. The sequence revealed at these Central Ganges sites is as follows:

1. The earliest period is represented by Sonepur IA, Chirand IA and Kausambi I. A radiocarbon date of 845 B.C. from Chirand IA suggests its approximate date. In this period tools of copper are found, but so far no iron. Stone tools include a blade industry (whose raw materials must have been imported into these alluvial areas). Arrow-heads of bone, horn and ivory were common. They included both tanged and socketed vari-

eties, and one variety with a triangular section reminiscent of the triple-flanged arrow-heads of metal encountered in the north-west (Plate 31 A). Houses were apparently made of bamboo or other perishable materials. Diet included fish and fowls, and many bones were discovered. The pottery was generally crudely made and was characterized by black-and-red ware, often with white-painted decoration. Among the forms of pot the dish-on-stand (with corrugated stem recalling Rangpur III), the lipped bowl, and the perforated bowl are noteworthy.

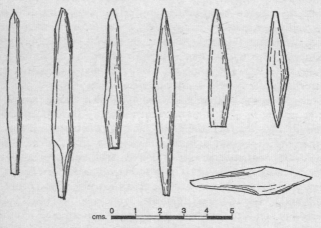

Figure 59. Bone and ivory points, Kausambi II and III

At Kausambi this period may be further subdivided and the lowest strata lacking the black-and-red ware may be compared with the 'Ochre Coloured pottery' phase in the Doab.

2. The second period is found at Rajghat IA, Sonepur IB, Chirand IB, Prahladpur IA and Kausambi II. It is dated at present by a single radiocarbon sample from Chirand, giving 765 B.C., but inferentially its end may be gauged by the beginning of the succeeding period, that of the Northern Black Polished ware, around 500 B.C. This latter date is now supported by a number of radiocarbon determinations. The main innovation in this period in this area is the introduction of iron.

The other items of the material culture continued very much as in the previous period. Charred rice grains from Sonepur provide additional evidence of diet. Another feature at this site was the discovery of urns containing cremated ashes buried in small pits.

Shortly after 500 B.C. at all these sites, no less than those of the Doab and Punjab, a new and striking pottery, the black gloss ware commonly known as N.B.P. or Northern Black Polished ware, makes its appearance. With it the cultural unification of Gangetic India becomes apparent in the material record. The black ware adopted the two major forms of the Painted Grey, a shallow tray-bowl and a deeper, often sharply carinated bowl. The technique of the black gloss surface was apparently very similar to that of the Greek black ware, both cases depending upon the unusually fine particle size of the clay employed for the dressing. The full understanding of this surface-dressing technique has still to be worked out.

The age that follows is one which may in all ways be regarded as a civilization. Coins, both of cast copper and punch-marked silver make their appearance. Writing, although not attested by inscriptions until over two centuries later, may be inferred to have come into use early in this period. Politically the sixth century saw the emergence of Magadha as the dominant state in the Ganges valley and the break-up of the old tribal society which the Indo-Europeans must have brought with them when they entered India. One of the first indications of these developments is the construction of great new mud or mud-brick ramparts as defences for the cities. By contrast the settlements at Hastinapura and most of the early Painted Grey ware sites are really villages rather than cities. But at Rajgir, already before the time of the Buddha a great stone perimeter wall was constructed. At Kausambi the excavator claims for the brick defences even greater antiquity, going back to the tenth century B.C., though this may need some modification when absolute dating is available. At Eran, as we shall see below, and at Ujjain, the first ramparts can claim comparable antiquity. Many other great cities of classical India have such ramparts, but in most cases their age has not yet been established, or appears to be

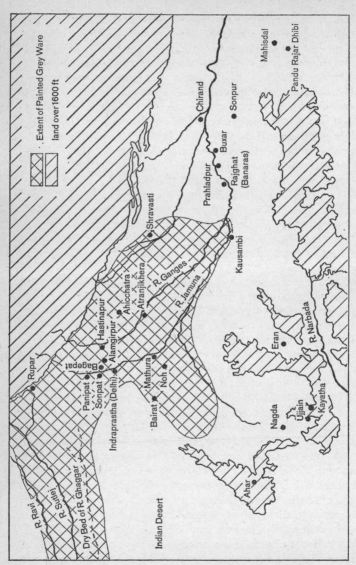

Figure 60. Map of north Indian Iron Age sites

somewhat later. The spread of city life into the ancient Gand-hara region, the former North West Frontier Province, probably took place during the sixth century B.C. when Cyrus conquered the area and made it a province of the Achaemenid empire. The foundation of the twin capital cities of Charsada (Bala Hissar) and Taxila may date from about this time. The former was traditionally the capital city of Pukkusāti, the contem-porary of Bimbisāra of Magadha. The pottery from the lowest levels of the Bala Hissar is closer to that of Mundigak VII than to any of the contemporary wares of the Ganges valley, and thus leads us to expect material contacts with Iran at this stage.

WEST AND CENTRAL INDIA

From the previous chapter it emerged that there were two main paths by which influences from the west entered the Indian subcontinent. The northern path followed the rivers of the Punjab before turning to the south-east and thence to the Ganges–Jamuna Doab. Thus it skirted around the northern edge of the great Indian desert. The southern path crossed the flat arid country between the Indus river and the Aravallis, passing between the marshes of Cutch on the one side and the desert on the other. Thence the way was open to follow three further directions: north-east across the Malwa plateau towards the Doab; eastwards through the hills and lightly forested uplands of the Central belt; or southwards through the low rainfall areas of the Deccan plateau.

For whatever reasons, the sequence at this point in Sind, Kathiawar and south Rajputana is not at present very well documented, and until further excavation has been carried out and better dating evidence is available it remains rather un-certain. The date of the introduction of iron in all these areas is indicated, in a rather negative way, by the dates relating to the end of the preceding Chalcolithic period. Thus at Ahar a date of 1275 ± 105 B.C. marks the topmost layers of period I. The only site to show an unbroken sequence is Somnath, where Period IIIA contains black-and-red ware and iron. In the succeeding phase IIIB, sherds of imported N.B.P. were found, probably here indicative of Mauryan influence. In coastal Gujarat a number of sites have yielded occupation in their lower levels which may be assigned to the Iron Age. Thus at Broach and Nagal, on the north and south of the Narbada estuary respectively, and at Nagara, the old Cambay, excavations have revealed a period of black-and-red ware preceding the importation of sherds of N.B.P. The black-and-red ware at Nagal often bears scratched graffiti or decoration, suggesting its earliness, and a stone-blade industry was found in association. Iron came from all levels except the lowest; while bone arrowheads and points, and beads of carnelian and semi-precious stones were found throughout.

The picture from Malwa and the Central Indian sites is slightly clearer. At Nagda period II appears to have been a direct continuation of the earlier settlement; it produced black-and-red ware, some iron objects, and a continuation of the blade industry. At the neighbouring Ujjain, period I produced black-and-red and plain red ware. At both these sites a considerable depth of occupation ensued before the importation of stray pieces of N.B.P. The Ujjain I assemblage is reported to have included a sherd of Painted Grey ware, along with the more common pottery. Iron arrow- and spearheads and bone arrow-heads were also found. As period II can be reasonably associated with the Mauryan occupation, its forerunner may well extend back to *c.* 600 B.C. The latest recorded radiocarbon dates for the Chalcolithic periods at Navdatoli and Eran are 1440 and 1280 respectively, but as a whole sub-period of the Chalcolithic, IIID, follows at the former site this date has only indirect bearing. At Eran, period IIA coincides with the appearance of black-and-red ware, a copper object is reported, but it is not clear if iron occurs. The period is dated by a radiocarbon sample, said to derive from its commencement, to 1040 B.C. It is noteworthy that at Eran as at Kausambi, the excavator claims that the fortifications were anterior even to the Iron Age, going back to the Chalcolithic period.

Farther east, on the western fringes of the Ganges delta there is every sign that iron working spread to the existing areas of Chalcolithic settlement at an early date. Thus at Mahisadal period II commences before 700 B.C. The main elements of the material culture continue from the previous period, suggesting that the arrival of iron involved no profound change in population. The pottery becomes somewhat coarser and is augmented by a grey or buff ware. Iron appears to have been plentiful and quantities of slag occurred. Whether this culture had closer links with the Central Ganges region, or with settlements in the forests to the south of the Ganges, has yet to be seen and must await further publication. The radio-carbon date is certainly close to that of Chirand IB.

PENINSULAR INDIA

Turning southward into Maharashtra the situation is no more definite. Nevasa and Chandoli provide convincing dates of 1250 and 1042 B.C. respectively for the continuation of the Chalco-lithic; and at several sites there appears to be continuous occupation through into the Iron Age. There is still, however, a perplexing absence of radiocarbon dates relating to early Iron Age levels. At Prakash in the Tapi valley, there was a short hiatus before Period II. This latter was represented by some fourteen to fifteen feet of black-and-red ware deposits below the first occurrence of N.B.P. and therefore testifies to a fairly protracted occupation. Iron appears at the beginning of the period and continues alongside the black-and-red ware. Among iron tools we may note the flat celt-like axes, recalling the forms of copper axes of Harappan and post-Harappan times; shaft-hole axes appear at Prakash only in the sub-sequent period. Although the duration of the period must have been considerable, there is little apparent indication of any significant changes in the material culture throughout. At Bahal, period II produced similar evidence. At Tekwada on the opposite bank of the Girna river an important related burial site was discovered. Here M. N. Deshpande excavated three urn burials and one pit burial. The burial-pit had a floor lined with stone slabs. The pottery from these burials is a compound of elements belonging to the Jorwe phase and elements of the earliest phase of the Iron Age. Hence we are inclined to assign them to the transitional period heralding the arrival of iron. No iron was discovered, but the black-and-red ware was in some cases marked or rather scratched with owners' marks. These graffiti recall those commonly found on pots of Rangpur III, and also on black-and-red grave pottery from many sites in the south. The pit burial and pottery recall certain early Iron Age burials from Brahmagiri (to be considered below). The excavator assigned the Tekwada graves to Bahal IB, but we may not be incorrect in placing them at the junction of IB and II. Another grave site at Ranjala in West Khandesh also produced typical Iron Age black-and-red ware with scratched graffiti.

In the Karnataka region the position at the settlements so far excavated is little clearer. At Brahmagiri, Piklihal, Sanganakallu and Maski, the depth of Iron Age occupation is generally less than four feet. More recent excavations at Hallur in south Dharwar district, and Paiyampalli in North Arcot district yield rather similar evidence. The introduction of iron takes place at the close of the Neolithic–Chalcolithic period. The earliest phase of the Iron Age is represented in the excavation at Piklihal (Site VI, layer 3) and Hallur (layers 4–7). It is probably to be identified in burial-pits with stone-slab floors excavated by Wheeler in the Iron Age burial ground at Brahmagiri, but antedating the later cist graves. These burials produced a combination of black-and-red ware, and a distinctive mat painted buff and red ware, somewhat akin to the Jorwe ware, along with the first iron objects, therefore recalling the Tekwada burials. Another diagnostic trait which appears in the region at this time is white-painted black-and-red ware. In the settlements stone-axe and blade industries apparently continue. Radiocarbon dates from Hallur suggests that the opening of the period may be as early as 1020–950 B.C.

The succeeding phase is dominated by burnished but unpainted black-and-red ware with accompanying red or black wares. This is represented by the 'Megalithic' period at Brahmagiri, Piklihal Iron Age, Sanganakallu 'overlap' and Maski II. Iron is now a fairly regular occurrence, both in graves and habitations, while copper, bronze and gold are also found. The stone-blade industry continues but on a diminished scale, and stone axes are rarely present. There are indications that this period may ultimately be amenable to some sort of further division on the basis of grave and pottery types, but more

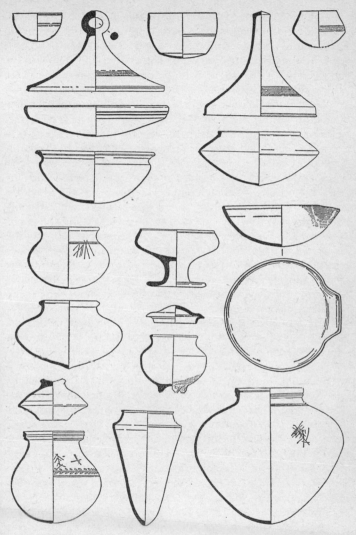

Figure 61. Brahmagiri, black-and-red ware pottery. 1:8

research is called for before this can be achieved. The excavations hitherto have not been very helpful, in terms of purely stratigraphic differentiation.

At Brahmagiri, Maski and Piklihal, the period is followed by one in which a distinctive white-painted black-and-red or plain red ware with russet dressing (the 'Russet coated' or 'Andhra' ware) appears. With it are tray bowls recalling north Indian forms appearing in the N.B.P. ware, but bearing a rouletted pattern on the inside of the base. From the coincidence of this ware on the Tamil coast at Arikamedu with Roman imports, including inscribed or stamped sherds of Arretine ware, the commencement of the period as a whole cannot be much earlier than the opening of the Christian era. However, the rouletted ware pre-dated the Arretine at Arikamedu, and there is a likelihood that in the western parts of the peninsula it may be found to occur at a somewhat earlier date. As the principal form of the rouletted ware is the tray-bowl characteristic of the Ganges valley, and as this form more or less disappears from pottery in the north before the opening of the Christian era, some considerable revision of chronology may be necessary when further evidence comes to light.

The sequence of the eastern coastal plain or Tamilnad is revealed by the excavations of Wheeler and Casal at Arikamedu, and the more recent excavations at Kunnattur, Alagarai and Tirukkambuliyur in Trichinopoly district. At all these sites, a period coinciding with Roman trade imports and producing a predominantly red pottery is preceded by one in which the characteristic pottery is black-and-red, similar to that of the graves. It is obviously of great interest to discover how this sequence relates to the introduction of such elements as writing, and to the flowering of the early south Indian civilization which finds its echoes in the poetry of the 'Sangam' period. In this region, as in Karnataka, there are indications of several sequential phases of the Iron Age, although as yet excavation has scarcely demonstrated this. For example, from T. Kalluppatti, about thirty miles west-south-west of Madurai, a surface collection has been made of fine white-painted black-and-red ware of a kind which may well date from the very beginnings of the Iron Age and indicate a rapid movement from far to the north-west in Malwa or beyond. Certainly it demands comparison with that from Hallur in Karnataka. This type of painted decoration is comparatively rare at present. The russet dressed and painted black-and-red ware, from Coimbatore, Jadigenahalli, Tirukkambuliyur, etc., probably indicates a late phase of the Iron Age, coinciding with the centuries around the turn of the Christian era and also echoing the third phase of Karnataka.

BURIAL COMPLEX OF THE SOUTH INDIAN IRON AGE

From the preceding paragraphs it will have seemed that the Iron Age of the southern peninsula is in some respects curiously neglected, and indeed little understood. But there is another large body of evidence relating to it, which derives from the great complex of Iron Age burials, frequently known as 'megaliths'. The term has been rather widely interpreted and has on occasion been used for urn burials lacking the presence of small, let alone great stones! We have associated an important change from burial among the settlements to burial in separate graveyards with the first appearance of iron in the south. The subsequent centuries saw an enormous proliferation of varied practices of disposing of the dead, and as modern observation has revealed a corresponding variety still in vogue in south India, it seems reasonable to infer that the burial complex has continued as a part of south Indian culture for a very long period.

The distribution of these Iron Age graves is far wider than any one culture region: they are reported in great numbers from the extreme south and coastal Ceylon, throughout most parts of the peninsula in which granites and gneisses are the predominant rocks, and as far north as Khandesh and Nagpur. A few isolated sites from the hills south of the Ganges valley (such as Kotia in Allahabad district) may also be regarded as outliers both in time and space.

Among the graves certain main types regularly recur, of which we note the following:

(*a*) Large urns, often piriform, containing collected bones previously excarnated, and buried in a small pit, marked in

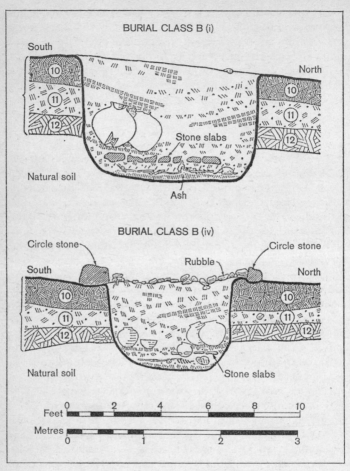

Figure 62. Maski, section of pit graves

some cases by a stone circle or small capstone or both. The pits, and sometimes the urn itself, often contain grave goods. Urn burials of this sort are common on the eastern coastal plains, and have a wide distribution elsewhere.

(b) Legged urns and legged pottery sarcophagi, the latter

sometimes with an animal's head, are less frequently found but
have a fairly wide distribution.

(*c*) Pit circle graves, of which several examples were excavated at Brahmagiri, in which the body had evidently been placed
on a wooden bier in a large open pit and exposed, perhaps to
allow for excarnation. Grave goods are found in the pits, and a
stone circle is erected round the circumference.

(*d*) Cist graves (Plate 32 A). Of these there is a great variety.
The stone cists are usually of granite slabs, sometimes with
portholes, variously oriented. The cists may be deeply buried
in pits, partly buried, or erected upon the bare rock surface.
Some cists are compartmented and have several separate
chambers: in some instances a separate slab resting on four
stones suggests a bed. The capstones may be single or multiple.
Many different arrangements of burial – both single and multiple – are found, and grave goods were placed both within and
around the cists. In some cases a ramp below ground level leads
down to the porthole entrance and this has been covered by a
slab door. The cist is usually marked by a stone circle or on
occasion by a double or treble circle (Figure 63).

(*e*) In the Malabar coastal laterites small rock-cut chambers
are found, sometimes approached by an entrance from above
and covered with a capstone. Some of these chambers have
vaulted roofs.

(*f*) One further monument associated with the graves and
belonging to the Iron Age is the stone alignment, comprising
carefully oriented rows of standing stones set in a square or
diagonal plan. The standing stones are generally from 5 to 8
feet in height but occasionally examples of over 20 feet are
recorded. Small alignments have been reported with as few as
three rows of three stones, four rows of four, five rows of five,
etc. but large diagonal alignments with sometimes many hundreds of standing stones are reported from Gulbarga district.
These monuments are so far mainly distributed in the central
Deccan, in the districts to the south of Hyderabad.

A century and a half have elapsed since the first excavation
of one of these burial sites, and during this period many hundreds of graves have been excavated. A recent bibliography
lists more than 250 published books or articles on the subject.

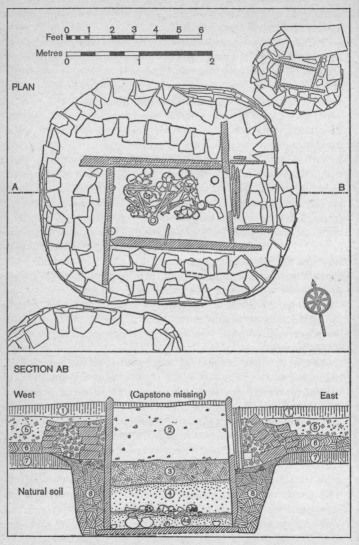

PLAN

A ——————— B

SECTION AB

West   (Capstone missing)   East

Natural soil

Figure 63. Brahmagiri, plan and section of stone cist grave

Among them a few outstanding examples may be mentioned: between 1851 and 1862 Colonel Meadows Taylor published accounts of his excavations in Shorapur; Alexander Rea between 1899 and 1904 excavated many urn burials at Adichanallur in Tinnevelly district (Plate 30 B); in 1916 and 1924 Dr Hunt published accounts of graves he had excavated at Raigir and Bhongir, east of Hyderabad. Since 1945 several sites have been excavated including Brahmagiri, Sanurin Chingleput district, Porkalam in Trichur district, and many graves around Nagarjunakonda and Yelleshwaram, Maski, Jadigenahalli in Mysore, Souttoukeny and Mouttrapaleon in Pondicherry.

Although there is a wide diversity of burial customs, other factors give this whole series a general uniformity. In all the graves pottery, and particularly black-and-red ware, is found, often in quantity (Plate 32 B). In almost every excavated grave some objects of iron, of surprisingly uniform types, occur (Figure 64). The pottery from the graves is patently that of the Iron Age levels in the settlements, although certain special forms are found in the graves. Distinctive types include a shallow tray-bowl and a deeper bowl, both with a rounded base, conical lids with knobs or loops on the apex, pottery ring stands, larger waterpots, invariably with rounded bases, and so on (Figure 61). Other commonly found grave goods include etched carnelian and other beads, small gold ornaments, and occasional objects of copper, bronze or stone. But iron is almost universal, and the range of identical tool types, repeated many times, at sites as far apart as Nagpur and Adichanallur – that is to say some 900 miles apart – must testify to the diffusion of a fairly tightly knit group of iron-workers. Among the most common tools are flat iron axes often with crossed iron bands for hafting. The shaft-hole axe, which appears at a very early date in north India and spreads to south India during the first millennium A.D. to become today almost the universal axe type, is unknown in the Iron Age graves of south India. A second common type includes varieties of flanged spade, hoe, spud or pick axe, and a third includes sickles or bill-hooks. Iron wedges and crowbars, or perhaps spears, of up to seven feet in length are found. A variety of knives, chisels or adzes, iron tripods or pot rests, saucer hook-lamps and many-armed lamp-pendants,

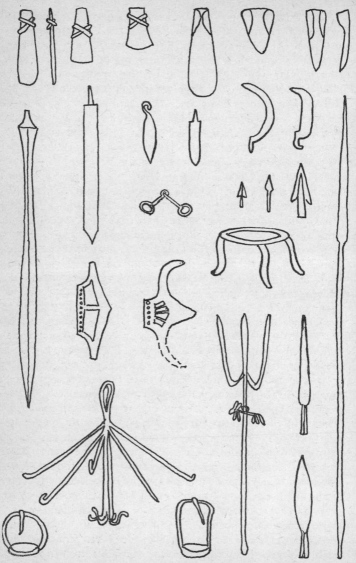

Figure 64. Iron objects from south Indian graves. 1:18 (approx.)

are perhaps for domestic use. Daggers and swords, sometimes with ornamented bronze hilts, arrow- and spearheads usually with hollow sockets and ceremonial scalloped axes are probably for military purposes. Iron tridents, in one case with a wrought iron buffalo attached to the shaft, were probably of ritual significance. Another special group of objects includes horse-furniture. In one instance a snaffle bit was found at Junapani near Nagpur and two simple bar-bits with looped ends came from the same site. From Sanur and at least five other sites in south India a different type of bar-bit with a looped nose- and mouthpiece is known. Among metal objects bells of copper or bronze are particularly numerous and may have served either as horse- or cattle-bells. One specimen from Raigir has a bronze band to fit the animal's neck.

There has been a great deal of often quite unwarranted discussion of the origin and external affinities of the Indian megalithic graves. Over a century ago Meadows Taylor wrote of them as the works of 'the great Aryan nomadic tribes of the Eastern Celts or Scythians', and since that time numerous other often extravagant claims have been made for them. In particular Sir Elliot Smith, W. J. Perry and other Diffusionists have sought to show that the graves were traits of a great Megalithic or 'Heliolithic' civilization which spread through the ancient world from its centre in Egypt, bringing with it to India the working of iron, the black-and-red pottery, gold mining and even alphabetic writing! A more sober view, based upon archaeological data, does not substantiate such generalizations. The south Indian graves appear as a developing complex with several streams of influence combining in them. First, some grave types are reminiscent of those of Central Asia, Iran or the Caucasus, and could well represent traits brought from these areas by Indo-European speaking immigrants. Next, some appear as developments of the indigenous Neolithic–Chalcolithic burial customs of the Deccan. A third series points to influences from outside India, and comparable types may indicate the source of the influences. Thus, stone cist graves, with and without port-holes, are found in the Levant, and on the coasts of south Arabia. Pottery sarcophagi occur in Mesopotamia and the Persian Gulf region during the late centuries B.C., and legged urns identical to Indian types are reported from the Yemen. The same regions provide evidence of rock-cut graves with shaft-like entrances, in forms strikingly reminiscent of those of the Malabar coast. Strictly speaking not all these examples are dated with any precision, and therefore they can scarcely provide a firm basis for comparisons; but they suggest that during the first millennium B.C. India received them as influences by dint of maritime contacts with the Middle East. A fourth stream also cannot be excluded, being the possibility of local development in peninsular India itself: the stone alignments appear to belong to this class. In our view the need of the present moment is to find ways of dating individual graves, and to attempt to work out the history and development of the several types in India by empirical means. Only when a more satisfactory framework is obtained will it become possible to consider the nature and direction of these external influences with greater assurance.

It will be seen that our discussion of the Iron Age of Central India, Maharashtra and the south raises a number of unanswered problems. The late stage of the Neolithic–Chalcolithic cultures in all these regions is indicated by a series of dates between 1000 and 1200 B.C. One pair of dates from Hallur suggests that the introduction of iron followed between 1050 and 950 B.C., a date which corresponds surprisingly with that obtained for the beginning of the Iron Age in the north. Archaeology can supply some cross-datings to support this date. Aiyappan excavated two graves in the Perumal hills, far to the south in the Madura district, which produced jugs with long raised channel spouts, channel-spouted bowls and a small bowl-on-stand with vertical cuts in the stand. These forms have analogies in Sialk Necropolis B, and more locally the bowl-on-stand occurs in one of the earliest Iron Age graves at Maski. The horse-bits and bells in the graves suggest that at least one part of the cultural equipment of the makers derived from outside India, and one is forcibly reminded of the Late Bronze and Early Iron Age graves of the Caucasus and Sialk Necropolis B. The discovery of horse bones in the transitional Chalcolithic–Iron Age levels of Hallur is suggestive. A third clue is contained in the 'transitional' burials from such

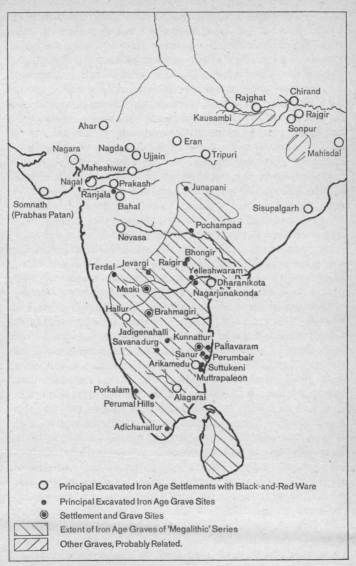

Figure 65. Map of south Indian Iron Age sites and graves

sites as Tekwada, Tekkalakota and Brahmagiri, with the mix-
ture of Jorwe-like painted ware and black-and-red ware along
with iron objects. All these features would support the earlier
date for the Iron Age which we have postulated. The cultural
implications of so great a duration of the south Indian Iron
Age have still to be investigated. The thinness of the occupation
levels in the settlements so far excavated is perplexing and leads
one to expect that the period saw a steady increase in population
and hence a need to extend the area under cultivation. In the
earlier phase agriculture was probably of the 'shifting' kind,
and it may be that there were few permanent settlements. The
horse-furniture, if it could be assigned to graves early in the
series, might indicate that the first users of iron in south India
were at least in part nomadic. Certainly the excavated settlements do not give much indication of any major change in the
way of life accompanying the arrival of iron. One is left with a
feeling of a remarkable conservatism among the population of
south India throughout the period. There can be little doubt
that many of the traits already established in the Neolithic
period persisted right through the Iron Age.

Outside the Ganges – Jamuna Doab, the diffusion of iron-
working seems to have been accompanied by a diffusion of the
mainly plain black-and-red pottery. The presence of a nodal
black-and-red ware tradition in south-east Rajputana in pre-
iron times may suggest a focus for the inception of the spread
of the new metal. It is perhaps significant that a black-and-red
pottery tradition is found beneath the Painted Grey ware in the
Doab, though whether associated with iron is not yet clear:
certainly when the early development of the great city sites in
the central Ganges valley began, iron had already been adopted
by the black-and-red ware users. A special feature of both the
black-and-red ware of the Early Iron Age and the Painted Grey
ware is the predominance of two forms, the shallow tray-bowl
and the deeper cup-like bowl. In our view these two must have
had some special cultural significance to do with eating habits,
and therefore would suggest that a broad cultural unification
went along with the spread of iron. How this can be related to
the spread of Indo-Iranian speech or Brahmanical caste and
customs, is a fascinating problem which demands attention.

CHAPTER 9

PATTERNS OF SETTLEMENT

THROUGH the earlier chapters of this book we have been
following the development of Indian society from its beginnings in the Early Stone Age. Through the long periods of the
Early and Middle Stone Age it probably consisted of little more
than extended family groups living by hunting and gathering
in their own loosely defined territories. With the Late Stone
Age we see indications of what is probably a wider network of
social contacts reflected in the large factory sites and the rock
shelters with paintings which illustrate a varied range of activities and concepts. The first permanent agricultural settlements clearly indicate a more highly organized, if still relatively
simple society, demanding a considerable degree of social dis-
cipline and conformity. From these we progress by comparatively rapid stages, represented by settlements of steadily increasing size and magnificence, to the Harappan cities. There
can be no doubt that these represent a sophisticated and highly
complex society. Thereafter, society as a whole, however much
depressed during unsettled periods of its development, could
never return to the uncomplicated barbarian simplicity of
earlier times.

Much of this development can be inferred from the excavation of individual sites of different periods, of which there are
now quite an impressive body. But the information yielded by
single sites tends to be somewhat two-dimensional – a series of
snapshots taken at different times and places. The study of
patterns of settlement, and leading on from that, of interregional
relationships, which is now only beginning in India, provides
the third dimension necessary to put all this information into
perspective, and to show as a dynamic process what otherwise
appears as a series of tableaux. It is worth stressing once more
that in the past, as today, in addition to the normal range of
sites of different size and importance by which any particular
cultural phase is always represented, throughout the Indian

subcontinent distinct cultural groups at very different levels are to be found living in more or less close proximity to one another. The inhibitions and the stimuli provided by the inter-relationship of these groups are factors which the archaeologist can never afford to lose sight of and to which we must return again and again.

As we have pointed out in an earlier chapter, with the exception of Sanghao in the former North West Frontier Province, no settlement of the Early or Middle Stone Age is known in the Indian subcontinent. A few factory sites such as Kondapur in the Deccan, or some of those in the Narbada valley in Central India, for example, the frequent occurrence of stone tools in gravels of most of the major rivers, and their remarkable absence from cave deposits, all indicate a nomadic life in the open, centring upon the banks of the great rivers and the better-watered parts of the country. The considerable size of certain of these Middle Stone Age factory sites suggests continuity of population and local tradition over a considerable period of time, as indeed does the material from Sanghao. With the Late Stone Age the number and variety of sites, particularly in some regions, greatly increases. Wherever they occur they include small open-air sites, almost always on the summits of hills or ridges, at which a fairly representative range of tools is usually found. The same sort of position is frequently chosen for their rather impermanent settlements by modern aboriginal peoples such as the Chenchu of south-eastern India and various groups in Central India. Here a family or a small group of families build their huts with low walls of wattle and daub and roofs thatched with palm leaves. They may spend the greater part of the year there, or only a few weeks or months, and occasionally move the huts to a different position. When this happens, few traces of the settlement remain, except for any indestructible oddments they may have dropped. Late Stone Age sites of this kind therefore would appear to represent temporary living places where huts or shelters of a rather flimsy nature were probably built.

Frequently one also comes across a small scatter of Late Stone Age tools on the surface of the ground, which include only a limited range of tool types. In these cases it seems likely that a certain piece of work such as cutting down a tree, making wooden tools or vessels, or skinning and disembowelling an animal was carried out there. This situation is clearly demonstrated by ethnographic accounts of hunting people using stone tools in regions as far apart as South Africa and Australia. Large factory sites of the Late Stone Age are also found in certain regions, notably in Central India, North Mysore and Ceylon, and like corresponding sites of the Middle Stone Age suggest continuity of local tradition. It is highly probable that huts were erected at these larger factory sites. Post-holes noticed at Birbhanpur in the extreme eastern extension of the Central Indian hills strongly suggest this, and so does a quantity of charcoal found by the excavators at Bandarawela in Ceylon. The charcoal may however have resulted from fires used to heat pieces of quartz before shattering them, in the process of making tools. Tools of the same Late Stone Age industrial tradition, but varying somewhat in the range and relative proportion of the different types, are found at all open-air sites and also in caves and rock shelters where these occur.

Apparently it was only with the Late Stone Age that people began to inhabit caves and rock shelters regularly (Plate 1). We have very few records of tribal people living in caves for any length of time in India or Pakistan, although herd boys may shelter or even camp in them, and religious mendicants or Sadhus sometimes establish themselves in them for many years together. In Ceylon early in this century the Veddas are described as living in caves during the wet season, and erecting screens of sticks and animal skins as additional protection from the weather. This probably provides an analogy for Late Stone Age practice elsewhere in the subcontinent. Clearly we have here the material for a study of settlement patterns in the Late Stone Age, such as we have tentatively suggested in the case of the Late Stone Age sites of West and Central India or Ceylon in an earlier chapter.

At any stage the essential features of a living site are its proximity to water, and to land suitable for hunting, agriculture, or other essential activities. At different periods other factors, such as a view of the surrounding countryside, freedom from insects, accessibility, defence and communications may take on increasing importance. Factory sites, or for that matter the sites of any special activity, are obviously selected for different but related reasons. Once the archaeologist is aware of the factors which influenced the choice at any period he can more easily locate further sites, and a sufficient number of sites will indicate the pattern of settlement and hence the range of activities of a society. The settlement sites of the earliest agriculturalists are very different from those of the Late Stone Age – selected initially for very different reasons, they are larger and more permanent. The more elaborate structures of houses, compounds and cattle-pens have left comparatively massive deposits and many were clearly inhabited over several centuries or even millennia. As a result, more detailed plans of living become clear.

The choice of habitations for communities of the Neolithic–Chalcolithic period must have depended primarily upon their suitability for varying pastoral and agricultural requirements. Water for men and animals was obviously a prime necessity, and perhaps too proximity of land suitable for cultivation. As we have seen, the earliest Neolithic sites within the subcontinent are in Baluchistan, where in the fourth millennium groups of nomadic pastoralists encamped at such places as Kili Ghul Mohammad, Anjira and Rana Ghundai. Probably such groups would have carried around with them temporary huts of matting or wattle, much as the semi-nomadic castes do to this day in many parts of India and Pakistan. Whether these people were already cultivating any cereal crops is not yet clear, but the continued occupation into later periods at each of these sites suggests that they were suited for such a purpose. This same general continuity of settlements is notable throughout Baluchistan, and even extends in a general kind of way to the present day, suggesting as Fairservis remarks a similar dependence upon identical water and soil resources. Whether the continuity is unbroken, or whether the correspondence between the prehistoric and modern patterns of settlement is determined simply by geography remains to be seen; unfortunately much less is known about the settlements of Baluchistan in later prehistoric or early historic times, as archaeologists have concentrated mainly upon the earliest period of settlement there.

The earliest houses so far discovered at Kili Ghul Mohammad are of packed earth or perhaps mud-brick, but no complete plan has yet been excavated. Better evidence comes from Mundigak where the earliest houses (in period I.4) were tiny oblong cells with pressed earth walls. In the following layer (I.5) larger houses appear, with several square or oblong rooms, built of sun-dried bricks, and these, as the excavator remarks, set the style of construction which is followed in all the subsequent periods at the site. Later the houses tend to become larger and the number of rooms greater. Domestic hearths are found from the beginning, and ovens, presumably for bread, are situated at first outside the houses and later possibly in courtyards. Wells are found among the houses. Where stone was locally available, it was used with mud for house-walls, as at Anjira. Throughout Baluchistan water is scarce and consequently settlements are never large, unless they coincide with a good permanent spring or source of water.

The initial settlement of the Indus plains, when viewed from the Indian subcontinent, marks an event of great cultural significance. Its importance centres on the vast possibilities of agricultural productivity which are opened up by exploiting the flood-plains of the rivers, and the corresponding population expansion. For this reason settlements were placed either on the flood-plain itself, or else on high ground immediately beside it. This may be sufficient to explain the presence of great walls around Kot Diji and Kalibangan, or it may be that they served another function, to discourage human or animal intrusion. The tradition thus established continues into the Harappan civilization. The evidence published to date does not permit us to say much regarding the house-plans at these sites. Both dried brick and stone were used, domestically and for town walls. At Kalibangan there appears already to have been a standardization of brick sizes, and although the ratio (3:2:1) differs from that of the Harappan period, it clearly suggests the way in which the pre-Harappan anticipates what follows (Plate 9). It is probable that house-plans will be found to have much in common with those of contemporary Baluchistan.

If comparatively little is yet known of the settlements and

dwellings of the pre-Harappan phase in the Indus Valley and Punjab, far more information is available concerning the civilization which succeeded them. The basic geographical determinants remained constant, and therefore in almost every case the earlier sites remained in occupation. But there must also have been a great increase in population and as a result not only did the size of settlements increase, but many new sites were founded. We have already remarked upon the extraordinary uniformity of culture found at all the Harappan sites, and this uniformity permits us to infer from the larger and better-known sites the common features of architecture and planning of the smaller and less well known. We have also noticed something of the relationship of the cities to towns, trading-posts or ports, and smaller settlements. Unfortunately very little attention has hitherto been paid to the last category, and much remains to be learnt of the village communities which may be expected to have formed the basis of the Harappan system. Indeed at the present moment we have no idea how much of the population was centred upon the cities and how much was dispersed through villages. Harappan uniformity begins with the basic conception of the city plan (Figure 66). At Harappa, Mohenjo-daro and Kalibangan this consists of two distinct elements: on the west a 'citadel' mound built on a high podium of mud brick, with a long axis running north–south, and to the east – apparently broadly centred upon the citadel – a 'lower city', consisting of what must have been the main residential areas. The citadel certainly, and probably also the lower town, was further surrounded by a massive brick wall. The principal streets at best were laid out with controlled skill (although at Mohenjo-daro they are not in precise alignment), and the widest streets appear to have run across the lower city from north to south. At Kalibangan the roads on the east–west axis only partly run across the whole town, some being staggered from block to block; and the same feature, at least in part, is repeated at Mohenjo-daro (Plate 10 A and Figure 70). There appears too to have been a general coordination of measurements of the streets, the largest being twice the width of the smaller, and three or four times that of the side lanes. Within the blocks thus formed were the dwellings of the general popu-

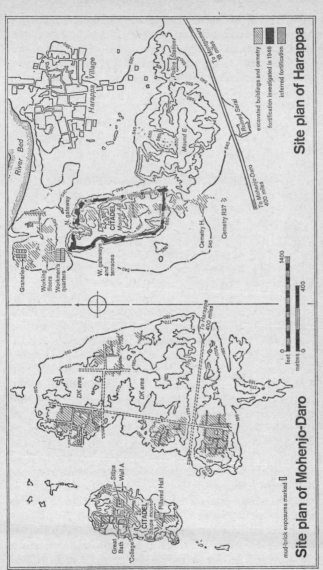

Figure 66. Outline plans of Indus Valley cities

lation, while on or beside the citadel mound were buildings of
a civic, religious or administrative status, including granaries.
At Kalibangan traces have been discovered of the remains of
massive brick walls around both the citadel and lower town.
The citadel in particular had square towers and bastions. An

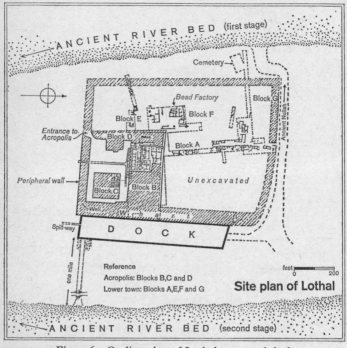

Figure 67. Outline plan of Lothal town and dock

entrance was set into the main line of the north wall, and there
was another from the south.

The layout of the somewhat smaller settlement at Lothal
was in some respects different, perhaps because of the different
role that it played, as a Harappan trading station. The site was
nearly rectangular with the longer axis running from north to
south (Figure 67). It was surrounded by a massive brick wall
probably as flood protection, as it is situated on low-lying

ground near a tributary of the Sabarmati river. Along the east side of the settlement was a dockyard, connected in ancient times to the river by artificial channels, one of which was traced over 2·5 kilometres. Beside the dockyard was a massive brick wharf which ran along the entire eastern side of the town. The south-eastern quadrant abuts this wharf, and takes the form of a platform of brick and earth filling, rising to a height of about 4 metres, and serving a similar function to the citadels of the cities, either as simple flood defence, or to provide added security for the food and materials stored there, or even perhaps to provide added prestige for the ruling group. An important part of the raised platform contained further brick platforms intersected by ventilating channels, representing no doubt the foundations of warehouses or granaries comparable to those of the other sites. The overall dimensions of this block were 48·5 by 42·5 metres. Evidently there were other buildings on the platform, for a row of twelve bathrooms and drains were discovered there. The remaining three-quarters of the town seem to have been the principal living area, divided by streets of 4 to 6 metres in width and narrower lanes of 2 to 3 metres. The main street ran from north to south. In this area numerous traces of specialists' workshops were found, including copper and goldsmiths' shops, a bead factory, etc. The brick dock basin deserves special comment. It was 219 by 37 metres in length, with extant brick walls of 4·5 metres in height. A spill-way and locking device were installed to control the inflow of tidal water and permit the automatic desilting of the channels. On its edge the excavator discovered several heavy pierced stones, similar to the modern anchor stones employed by traditional seafaring communities of west India. Near by was a modern shrine of a goddess still worshipped particularly by sailors, although Lothal is now several miles from the sea.

The entire body of structures in the lower city at Harappan sites shows an almost monotonous uniformity. The most common material throughout was brick, both burnt and sun-dried. The latter was used at Mohenjo-daro mainly for fillings, but at Harappa it sometimes alternated with burnt-brick course by course, and at Kalibangan it seems to have been if anything more common, burnt-brick being almost exclusively reserved for wells, drains and bathrooms. The predominant brick size was 11 by 5·5 by 2·75 inches, that is a ratio of 4:2:1. The bricks were mainly made in an open mould, but for special purposes, such as bathrooms, sawn bricks were invariably used, and wells were constructed with wedge-shaped moulded bricks. The flooring of houses was either beaten earth, or sun-dried or burnt-brick. In some bathrooms a sort of plaster of brick dust and lime was reported. Worked stone was rarely employed structurally, and the true arch was not used, but the corbelled arch in brick is frequent. Certain pieces of worked stone suggest segments of pillars, but it is not clear whether these were ever employed structurally. Timber was used for the universal flat roofs, and in some cases the sockets indicate square-cut beams with spans of as much as 14 feet. In certain rare instances timber also seems to have formed a semi-structural frame or lacing for brickwork.

Considerable variation is seen in the size of dwellings, which range from single-roomed tenements to houses with court-yards and upward of a dozen rooms of varying sizes, and to great houses with several dozen rooms and several courtyards. Nearly all the larger houses had private wells. In very many cases brick stairways led up to what must have been upper storeys or flat roofs. Hearths are commonly found in the rooms. Almost every house had a bathroom, and in some cases there is evidence of bathrooms on the first floor. The bathroom is indicated by a fine sawn brick pavement, often with surround-ing curb, and its connexion by a drainage channel to chutes built in the thickness of the wall, giving access to the main street drains. A number of pottery drainpipes were also found. Mackay has shown that many of the smaller examples of these fine brick pavements in fact represented privies, and that the chutes for these are vertical as against the sloping chutes of the baths.

The entrances to the houses were from the narrow lanes which were set at right-angles to the main streets. A distinctive feature of the construction was thus that the roadward side of a block presented a plain blank façade broken only where drainage chutes discharged. The houses seem often to have been built with an oblong perimeter wall, and adjacent houses

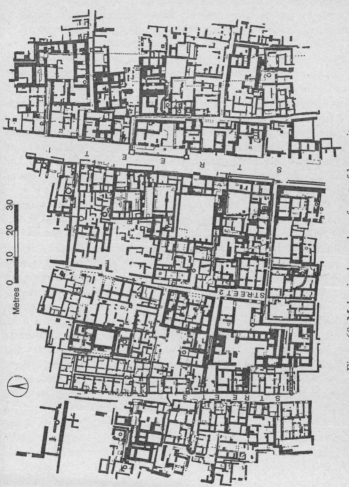

Metres 0 10 20 30

Figure 68. Mohenjo-daro, plan of part of lower city

were separated by a narrow space of 'no man's land'. If the general batter of the brickwork in the walls be allowed for, this interstice would grow wider with the height of the walls.

One other feature of the lower city deserves comment. Many of the lanes and streets had brick drains, covered over by bricks or sometimes stone slabs, into which the house drains flowed, while others led directly into large soak pits or jars. The street drains were equipped with manholes, and sometimes flowed into soakage pits, but nothing is known of their final discharge on the edge of the city. Altogether the extent of the drainage system and the quality of the domestic bathing structures and drains are remarkable, and give the city a character of its own. It may be noted in passing that privies and drains of identical kind may be found in many modern towns of north India and Pakistan, and were also built in cities of the early centuries of the Christian era.

As far as our evidence goes, the lower city must have included houses of many different kinds. There are some barrack-like groups of single-roomed tenements at Mohenjo-daro which forcibly recall the rows of tenements beside the granary at Harappa. These must belong to a much poorer class than the houses with a courtyard and many rooms. The lower town must also have contained a wide range of shops and craft work-shops: among these potters' kilns, dyers' vats, metal-workers', shell-ornament-makers' and bead-makers' shops have been recognized, and it is probable that had the earlier excavators approached their task more thoughtfully, much more informa-tion would have been obtained about the way in which these specialists' shops were distributed through the settlement. Another class of building to be expected in the lower city is the temple. Wheeler has argued convincingly that one building in the HR area of Mohenjo-daro which comprised a monumental entrance and double stairway, leading to a raised platform, and in which was found one of the rare stone sculptures of a seated figure, may be identified as a temple. Several other buildings of unusually massive character, or unusual plan, have also been tentatively identified in this way. We may well wonder what would have been the population of these cities. Lambrick has made a convincing case for a figure of 35,000 at Mohenjo-

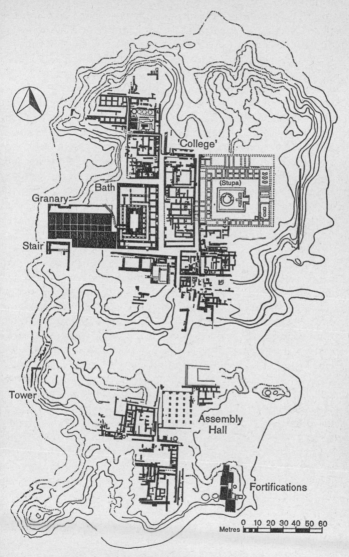

Granary

Bath

'College'

(Stupa)

Stair

Tower

Assembly Hall

Fortifications

0 10 20 30 40 50 60
Metres

Figure 69. Plan of the citadel at Mohenjo-daro

daro, based upon comparison with the population of a city of comparable area in Sind in 1841. As Harappa appears to have been of roughly equivalent size, its population may well have been more or less the same.

Turning to the buildings of the citadel mounds, or their vicinity, we encounter a series of remarkable structures of a very different character. Their special nature is emphasized by the great podiums of brick or mud-brick and earth filling upon which they stood. The floods which at Mohenjo-daro devastated the lower city several times probably provide the *raison d'être* for the citadel mounds. The great brick embankment, some 43 feet in height, which ran round the platform at Mohenjo-daro must also have served the same purpose, and is no doubt the counterpart of the massive defensive wall which surrounded the Harappan citadel.

Perhaps the most remarkable feature of the citadel mound at Mohenjo-daro is the Great Bath (Plate 11). This finely built brick structure measures 39 feet by 23 feet, and is 8 feet deep from the surrounding pavement. It is approached at either end by flights of steps, originally finished with timber heads set in bitumen. The floor of the bath was constructed of sawn bricks set on edge in gypsum mortar, with a layer of bitumen sealer sandwiched between the inner and outer brick skins. Water was evidently supplied by a large well in an adjacent room, and an outlet from one corner of the bath led to a high corbelled drain disgorging on the west side of the mound. Surrounding the bath were porticos and sets of rooms, while a stairway led to an upper storey. The significance of this extraordinary structure can only be guessed. It has been generally agreed that it must be linked with some sort of ritual bathing such as has played so important a part in later Indian life, and therefore that it must mean that this part of the citadel was connected with the civic–religious life

Immediately to the west of the bath excavation has revealed an equally remarkable group of twenty-seven blocks of brick-work criss-crossed by narrow ventilation channels. Sir Mortimer Wheeler has shown that this structure is the podium of a great granary (akin to that of Harappa, although of somewhat different design), and that below the granary were the brick loading-bays from which corn was raised into the citadel for storage. Therefore this too is a building of civic importance. Around the bath on the north and east were other large blocks of buildings which may be inferred to be associated with the group of administrators (perhaps priests) who controlled not only the city but the great empire which it dominated. Further excavation on the south of the citadel mound may corroborate this view. Here an oblong assembly hall was unearthed having four rows of five brick plinths upon which no doubt wooden columns were erected. The floor between these plinths was of finely sawn brickwork, recalling that of the bath. In the complex of rooms immediately to the west another seated male statue in stone was discovered, and near by a number of large worked stone rings, possibly pieces of architectural masonry but more probably part of a stone ritual column. These finds recall those supposedly associated with a temple in the lower city, and almost certainly indicate the presence of a temple in this part of the citadel.

The citadel mound at Harappa is comparatively much less well known, both because it has been less excavated, and because it is more disturbed by subsequent occupation and depredation. But immediately to the north, between it and the old river bank lies an area of ground of comparable interest to the citadel at Mohenjo-daro. Here was another series of brick platforms which constituted the basis for two rows of six granaries, each 50 by 20 feet, lying within a few yards of the river's edge. The combined floor space of the twelve units must have been something over 9,000 square feet, approximately the same area as that of Mohenjo-daro. To the south of the granaries was an area of working floors consisting of rows of circular brick platforms, evidently for threshing grain: wheat and barley chaff were found in the crevices of the floors. Immediately below the walls of the citadel were two rows of single-roomed barracks, recalling the smallest dwellings in the lower city at Mohenjo-daro and artisans' or slaves' quarters in such sites as Tel-el-Amarna in Egypt.

The smaller citadel mound at Kalibangan has not yet been fully excavated, but it shows a number of corresponding features. In the southern part are brick platforms, probably for granaries, while the northern, separated by a wall with a single small entrance, contains dwellings. The whole is surrounded by a massive brick wall.

The patterns of settlement in parts of the subcontinent out-

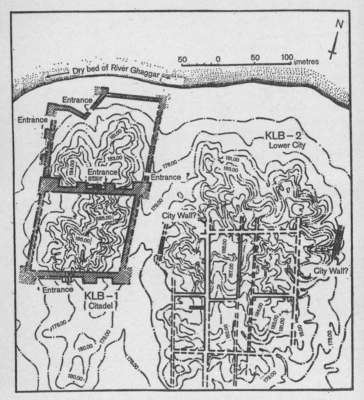

Figure 70. Outline plan of Harappan settlement, Kalibangan

side the Indus system and Baluchistan stand in contrast to what we have just discussed. First there is the northern Neolithic area in Kashmir: here excavation at Burzahom has revealed a series of pit-dwellings cut deeply into the Karewa soil, narrow at the top and widening towards the base, with floor and walls occasionally mud-plastered. In the deeper pits steps were cut for part of the depth. Post-holes on the periphery of the mouth suggest a conical roof. The largest of these pits measured 3·96 metres in depth and had a diameter at base of 4·57 metres, while the mouth was only 2·74 metres. The entrance steps extended down to a little more than one metre, suggesting that a ladder was used for the lower part. There were ashes both in the pits and at ground level in stone hearths near the entrance. Storage pits in the same area yielded animal bones. Obviously such 'earth houses' were intended to give protection from the cold, and it is improbable that the custom of making them would survive any excursion on to the plains of the Punjab or beyond, but none the less they form a type of habitation at present without parallel in the subcontinent, and they appear to belong rather to a northern culture zone than to anything Indian.

The settlements of the southern Neolithic present another sort of contrast. In the part of the Deccan plateau where they first developed, the predominant features are residual granite hills rising from a rolling 'sea' of black cotton soil. The hills were favoured for settlement, and wherever they contained suitable caves or rock shelters these were used for habitation, and often enlarged by the construction of a levelled stone terrace in front. Small plateaux on the summits of hills or level areas on hillsides were likewise exploited and artificially levelled or extended. In some cases there seem to have been single large terraces, while in others there were many small ones, rising one behind the other up the slope of a hill (Plate 23 B). At this period sites are only rarely found on the banks of rivers away from hills. There is as yet no evidence for structures associated with the earliest settlements in this area, but when they do occur, slightly later, it is in the form of circular huts with wooden frames interlaced with wattle screens and plastered with mud and cow-dung. The roofs may be inferred to have been conical and thatched. At some sites dry stone walls, rising to a height of only a couple of courses, are found marking the circular outline. Recent excavations at Tekkalakota, Sanganakal and Hallur have all produced evidence of circular huts (Plate 24 B). The floors were coated with mud, or perhaps cow-dung plaster. Hearths, sometimes associated with tripods of small upright slabs of granite, were found either within the house or near by, and so too were grinding stones, some with mullers still in position. A large pot, buried up to the neck, probably served as a storage jar. In the later 'Chalcolithic' phase which covers the transition from the Neolithic to the Iron Age, walls of more massive boulders were built. In many parts of southern India circular huts are still in use among the poorest strata of society and their construction, furniture and utilization, can scarcely have changed since Neolithic times. At Tek-kalakota Dr Nagaraja Rao found several such huts in the modern village at the foot of the hill on which the Neolithic inhabitants first constructed their dwellings some 4,000 years earlier (Plate 24 A). In our excavations at Piklihal fragments of the clay moulding of door frames were discovered in the excavations which were identical with those of huts in the modern village of Mudgal. Even though the settlement as a whole covered a large area, these scattered groups of huts on hill terraces cannot, we believe, have housed a very large population, and certainly its numbers cannot be estimated with reference to modern settlements in the same region in the way that they may be in Sind or Baluchistan.

Another feature of this area during the Neolithic period was the construction of large cattle-pens with stockades of timber posts. An inner stockade provided the area in which the cattle were herded, while an outer provided a space within which the herdsmen lived. Some of these pens are attached to the permanent settlements, but others are in the forest, remote from any settlement, and they provide evidence for a pattern of the seasonal movements of the herds. So far there is only limited evidence available for the form of these structures, derived from our own excavations at Utnur (Plate 26 B). Here the stockade was burnt and rebuilt several times, each burning being associated with the conflagration of great accumulations of cow-dung. This is what gave rise to the Deccan ash-mounds which for so long mystified archaeologists.

The regions which lie between the Indus Valley and Karnataka offer a series of intermediary styles of house building and settlement. In Saurashtra the influence of Harappan building construction appears to have persisted. At Rangpur, in the earliest occupation, houses and drains were constructed of both mud-brick and burnt-brick. In the second sub-period huts appear to have consisted mainly of wooden frames which supported some non-durable material such as thatch or matting, but by the end of period II and the beginning of III mud-brick was once again in common use, although floors were still of rammed earth and post-holes, perhaps for the timbers to support the roofs, are found. No complete house-plans are available. At Ahar in southern Rajasthan the picture is rather different. Houses were oblong and often of fair size; one completely excavated measured 30 feet by 15 feet. The walls were of stone and mud, or mud-brick, and perhaps also of wattle and daub. Apparently the roofs were flat, made of bamboo and matting, and covered with earth. No indication is recorded of any development or change during the Chalcolithic occupation at this site.

Going eastwards to Malwa, we encounter at Navdatoli a marked change. Here the huts of the Chalcolithic period were both round and oblong, but all seem to have employed a wooden frame and wattle and daub walls. The floors were made of clay and cow-dung, and sometimes given a lime-plastered surface. The oblong houses were the larger and one measured 40 feet by 20 feet, while the round huts did not exceed 8 feet in diameter, clearly indicative of their subordinate status. The smallest of these round huts must have been used for no more than the storage of grains or other materials. There is no evidence of roof tiles, and the probability is that roofs were thatched. Every house had its own hearth, of a pattern identical to those of Ahar, with three compartments, side by side, made of clay and lime plaster; the store-rooms within the houses contained lines of jars, the larger standing on raised earth stands. The settlements of Maharashtra, as represented in the excavations of Nevasa, Daimabad, Chandoli, etc., appear to have been very similar to those of Malwa. In Malwa and Maharashtra the settlements reflect the geography of the trap regions; they are invariably sited on the edge of rivers or streams, and usually on a high and solid part of the bank. The present evidence therefore suggests that the building styles of the Harappan period never reached beyond Saurashtra, and that thence eastwards into Central India and southwards into the peninsula, another set of building customs prevailed, with the use of round or oblong houses of wood and wattle and daub, with thatched roofs.

If the hypothesis of continuity linking the Harappan, post-Harappan and 'Ochre' ware culture phases in the Punjab and western Uttar Pradesh is correct, it is likely to follow that much of the Harappan building tradition would have been passed on, albeit in attenuated form, in these areas. Unfortunately the current state of research does not permit any clear picture to be drawn. Nor for that matter is the picture much clearer for the Early Iron Age of these areas. At Hastinapur the excavator reported fragmentary walls of mud or mud-brick, but the scale of the work did not permit the discovery of complete house-plans. From the more recent and as yet incompletely published reports of such sites as Noh, Atranjikhera, etc., it appears that Painted Grey ware is rarely found associated with very solid structures: mud or mud-brick and post-holes suggestive of wooden frameworks are found, and the floors are usually of rammed earth. It is really not until the subsequent period (that associated with the Northern Black Polished pottery) that substantial evidence is available for the house and settlement pattern of the Ganges valley, and this is largely beyond the time limits of the present book. It is possible that the vogue for burnt brick began again in the Ganges valley during the first half of the first millennium B.C. This is certainly suggested by the dates proposed for Kausambi, although mud-brick continued in general use until some centuries later. It is interesting to consider the constituent parts of the cities of the Ganges valley, but while their chronology remains so much in doubt we are hesitant to do so. From the recent excavations at Kausambi, Rajgir, Ujjain, Eran, etc., it would seem that the need to protect the growing cities by great brick ramparts and moats or ditches was felt from early in the first millennium, if not before, and during the course of the millennium the same features are found at many of the great cities.

The picture from peninsular India too is not at present very clear. We may infer that where regional house and settlement patterns had already established themselves, they continued with little change during the Iron Age, but as we have already seen the archaeology of these settlements is still in an unsatisfactory condition and must await further, more extensive excavations. The relatively greater frequency of grave sites, often of considerable size, suggests that a substantial element of the population must have been nomadic. Altogether, archaeological research, both exploration and excavation, offers great potential interest in the study of the development of the patterns of house and settlement, and the relationship of town, city and village. This sort of palae-demography, as we may call it, leading through to estimations of, for example, the size and density of settlements, and ultimately to estimates of population of a given area during a particular period, is a study for which the Indian subcontinent seems to be peculiarly suited.

CHAPTER 10

ECONOMY AND AGRICULTURE

THE Harappan culture and the later Neolithic and Chalcolithic cultures of India clearly depended to some extent upon trade to maintain their elaborate social structure and their standard of living. How far they depended upon it for basic essentials such as food, and how far it was simply a means of obtaining luxury goods is a question we shall examine as we go on. The economy of the earlier Neolithic cultures on the other hand was apparently a simple one of subsistence agriculture, but in some cases they also may have received considerable stimuli from outside contacts, both with more advanced peoples and with neighbouring hunting tribes. In an archaeological context hunting people are commonly assumed to be ignorant of all forms of trade and commerce; an assumption which is supported by the ease with which unscrupulous traders have frequently managed to exploit illiterate hunters in modern times. This assumption is not always supported either by archaeological or by modern ethnographic evidence. In India communities with very different standards of living have for long coexisted at very close quarters, and have in fact depended upon one another economically, as we have already had occasion to point out. The whole question of the effect of trade upon the economy of India is a complex one which needs to be considered in terms of the internal evidence, as European parallels and accepted stereotypes seldom seem to apply. Both hunting and agricultural communities could clearly maintain themselves for long periods, and in many cases can still do so, with only the most superficial contact with the outside world. On the other hand trade and traders, and the part they play in linking the city and the countryside together have long been important factors in Indian life and culture, and they form an integral part of both, as does the interdependence of neighbouring communities.

Of the economy of the Early Stone Age we can only say that

it was probably of the simplest hunting and gathering kind, with little forethought, and provision for future needs almost nonexistent. How far man had begun at this time to attempt to insure his future by propitiating the forces of nature by magic and ritual, or to consider the possibility of an afterlife we do not know. At present there is also little comparative material from other parts of the world to which we can refer. Tools of the Middle Stone Age suggest, as we have seen, an increasing degree of forethought and variety in cultural equipment, but as far as India is concerned they are still virtually the only available evidence of their makers' mental activities. Elsewhere this period appears to be one of adaptation to varying local needs, and in parts of Europe and Central Asia this is when we see the first evidence of concern for the dead, exemplified by deliberate burials in occupied caves.

Initially the economy of the Late Stone Age cultures must have been based primarily upon hunting and gathering. Actual hunting methods were probably more efficient than those of earlier times. Late Stone Age tools take over from those of the Middle Stone Age in all the drier parts of western and Central India, and in much of the peninsula, with a completeness that suggests that they represented a marked improvement. But in regions of higher rainfall and in the extreme south, continuity of Middle Stone Age techniques suggests a somewhat different state of affairs. Late Stone Age coastal sites both on the west coast, and in Madras and Ceylon, show by their situation, and by modern analogy, that fishing must have formed an important, if not a staple part of the economy of the people who used them: they are chosen for proximity to the coast and to lagoons and inlets rather than for access to good hunting grounds. For the inland peoples of the Late Stone Age in areas of moderate and low rainfall hunting must have taken on a greater importance, as new methods meant that it could provide a higher proportion of their food, thus swinging the balance away from the collection of vegetable foods which must have continued to be of primary importance in regions of higher rainfall. Two sites, Langhnaj and Adamgarh, which we mentioned earlier, and which are among the few systematically excavated sites of this period, both show clear evidence of contemporaneity for a considerable period with Neolithic or later settlements in adjacent regions. The presence of bones of both wild and domestic animals here suggests that the economy of the hunters was augmented by pastoralism, or perhaps by trading with settled neighbours, or preying upon their herds. The bones identified include cattle, pig and buffalo at both sites, and sheep and goat at Adamgarh only, along with several species of deer and smaller wild animals. Birbhanpur and other sites on the other hand give no indication of anything except hunting and gathering.

The size of the larger factory sites of this period, which have been found in parts of Central India, north Mysore and Ceylon, is such that they must have served the needs of more than a single extended family group or band. Either many groups may have visited them, or those who lived near such sources of good-quality raw material must have exchanged tools or pieces of stone with people from other, surrounding groups. There are many cases of such exchanges between hunting groups recorded in Australia, where objects sometimes passed from hand to hand over distances of several hundred, or even thousand miles. Dancing scenes in the caves of Central India depict gatherings which must have included quite a number of families or bands, on some occasions at any rate. Occasions such as these are known to have provided the means of exchanging objects of interest and value, and also of strengthening wider social ties, beyond the immediate family or local group, among the South African bushmen and the Australian aborigines, and it seems highly probable that they did so in the case of the Late Stone Age inhabitants of many parts of India also. Such gatherings would facilitate the passing on of stone working and other techniques. One or two larger sites of the later Middle Stone Age (see pages 80–81) indicate that such practices may in fact antedate the Late Stone Age in certain places.

If Late Stone Age groups were already in the habit of exchanging objects with one another when the first settled agriculturalists appeared on their horizon, it cannot have been very difficult for them to establish some sort of economic link with the newcomers. The most direct evidence for this comes from north Mysore. Here the stone industries of the Late Stone Age sites and those of the Neolithic settlements are identical in raw material and in techniques, and they can only be distinguished by comparing the proportions of different tool types present. The Late Stone Age industries include more geometric microliths, and those of the Neolithic more unretouched, utilized blades. This and a good deal of other evidence point to mutual exploitation of certain large factory sites by hunters and settlers alike. More probably in the Indian milieu, the hunters exchanged stone tools for other goods, perhaps food, with the Neolithic settlers. In any case, such exchanges would only have occurred during the final stages of the Late Stone Age, when Neolithic settlers moved into any region. Baskets, honey, venison and Mohua flowers, which tribal people still barter with their village neighbours for food and cloth, may also have begun to change hands at this early stage. The large factory sites of Central India are suggestive of some form of external trade of this kind. Barasimla is not many miles from the Chalcolithic site of Tripuri, and Barkaccha and Siddhpur, at the former of which a butt of a Neolithic axe was found, are both on the edge of the Ganges plains where these meet the hills of Central India. This position alone suggests some contact during part of the life of the site with the people of the plains as well as with the Late Stone Age hunters of the hills.

The late Professor Childe defined the Neolithic Chalcolithic cultures as enjoying a 'self-sufficing, food-producing economy'. In recognizing that this definition coincides admirably with the picture archaeology permits us to reconstruct in India and Pakistan, we must not forget the diversity of economic patterns surviving even in the twentieth century. Therefore we must refrain from superimposing upon our evidence any over-simplified or dogmatic scheme, or looking for a series of unilinear stages developing from pastoralism to agriculture. As with the sketch of settlement patterns in the previous chapter, the evidence at present available is often incomplete and the picture we draw must be correspondingly uneven. But a great deal of work has now been done, particularly in India during the past two decades, and the attempt seems to us worthwhile, if only because it may help to focus attention on the lacunae.

Bearing in mind the climate of the subcontinent and the markedly seasonal nature of even the little rainfall received in most of the areas of early settlement, it comes as no surprise to find that water and its supply are prime determinants of the economy. In much of Baluchistan, Sind and southern Afghanistan the scarcity of water must at all times have set strict limits upon the production of crops, and a pastoral element in the economy has consequently predominated. There are signs that in Baluchistan in prehistoric times attempts were made to retain rainwater in surface drainage tanks, behind earth or stone embankments. There are divergent views upon the age of these so-called 'Gabarbands', but it seems likely that they may belong to the Neolithic–Chalcolithic period. The actual evidence of food grains from pre-Harappan cultures in Baluchistan is still very slender. From Mundigak, period II, come grains of club wheat (*Triticum compactum*), one of the three ancient varieties probably native to this region. The same site produced the Indian jujube (*Zizyphus jujuba* or *ber*). Of animal remains three species are reported at nearly every site so far excavated; they are sheep, goat and cattle. It is not as yet possible to determine from skeletal remains whether the earliest domestic cattle of Baluchistan were of the Indian humped variety (*Bos indicus*), but as both terracotta models and painted pottery figurines depict this variety almost exclusively at a slightly later date, it may be fairly certainly inferred. At Mundigak humped bull figurines occur from period I onwards, and therefore provide the earliest evidence so far for the domestication of *Bos indicus* (Plate 7 A).

There is not much information regarding the pre-Harappan culture-phase in the Indus valley and the Punjab. At Amri the animal remains from period I were largely the same as those of contemporary Baluchistan, with the addition of the ass (?*Equus hydrontinus*). With the Harappan civilization there is suddenly much more information. Wheat is frequently recorded, apparently of two varieties, the club wheat (*Triticum compactum*) and the Indian dwarf wheat (*Triticum sphaerococcum*). Barley (*Hordeum vulgare*), probably of a small-seeded six-rowed variety, is also found at both Harappa and Mohenjo-daro. Other crops include dates, sessamum, and varieties of leguminous plants, such as field peas. Of particular interest is the discovery at Lothal and at Rangpur (period II A) of rice husks and spikelets embedded in clay and pottery. Their presence in these outlying Harappan contexts, and apparent absence in the Indus valley, calls for a fresh study to be made at the city sites. Another find of great interest was a fragment of woven cotton cloth at Mohenjo-daro. The plant belonged to one of the coarser Indian varieties closely related to *Gossypium arboreum*, and the fibre had been dyed with madder, which is indigenous in India.

The range of domesticated animals, or of wild animals used for food, is quite large. In addition to sheep and goats, there is, as we have seen, repeated evidence of Indian humped cattle. One strain of these is depicted on the Harappan seals (along with a more commonly represented humpless bull of a *Bos primigenius* variety), and is beyond doubt the ancestor of a strain still bred in parts of western India and Sind (Plate 13, No 1). Zeuner has suggested that the zebu may be descended from *Bos namadicus*, a wild cattle which occurs throughout the Indian Pleistocene, and in this case it is probable that the centre of its domestication may have been in South Asia, just as that of *Bos primigenius* was probably in western Asia or Europe. Whether the humpless bull of the seals was actually present in the Indus cities, and if so whether it was imported from the Middle East, are interesting matters which deserve attention. Another species whose bones are of frequent occurrence at more than one site is the Indian boar, *Sus cristatus*, which must have been either domesticated or regularly hunted. The buffalo (*Bos bubalis*) is another such species, but its bones are less common, and at Mohenjo-daro only appeared in the upper levels. Yet more rare are bones of both elephant and camel, but as the former is a fairly common motif upon seals it may be assumed that the Indian elephant was already domesticated. Among birds, bones of the domestic fowl are noteworthy. There is also a range of wild animals which were undoubtedly hunted for food: these include the Sambar deer (*Rusa unicolor*), the spotted deer and the hog deer, and several varieties of tortoise. From Amri comes a single instance of the Indian rhino-ceros, of interest because it too is depicted on the seals, and remained a native of the lower Indus valley at least until the fourteenth century A.D. It is perhaps worthy of note that the only plausible evidence of the horse comes from a superficial level of Mohenjo-daro. A terracotta figurine from Lothal is scarcely unequivocal. It is not possible to rule out Zeuner's cautious appraisal of the supposed equine teeth from Rana Ghundai as those of hemiones, and indeed with the present state of evidence it would be unwise to conclude that there is any proof of the regular use of the horse in pre-Harappan or Harappan times.

Lambrick, from his intimate personal knowledge of Sind, has been able to suggest the way in which the various crops would have been grown, and how they exploited the flooding of the Indus. The principal food grains, that is wheat and barley, would have been grown as spring (*rabi*) crops: that is to say sown at the end of the inundation upon land which had been submerged by spill from the river or one of its natural flood channels, and reaped in March or April. In modern prac-tice such land is neither ploughed nor manured, nor does it require additional water. Lambrick remarks that 'the whole operation involves an absolute minimum of skill, labour and aid of implements'. Other crops including cotton and sessa-mum would be sown as autumnal (*kharif*): that means they would be sown at the beginning of the inundation and har-vested at its close, in the autumn. For this fields surrounded by earth embankments would be required, most probably along the banks of natural flood channels. Although this method is more precarious than the former, both exploit the natural fertility of the alluvium, and the annual inundation. Both systems are still in use, and they provide a very convincing explanation of the means by which the Harappans filled their vast granaries; and yet neither of them would have left any surviving traces for the archaeologist. There is no clear evi-dence of the tools used for agriculture. D. D. Kosambi has ventured the opinion that the plough was not employed in Harappan times, but only a light, toothed harrow. This view is based upon the identification of one of the ideograms of the

Harappan script as either a rake or a harrow. Kosambi may
well be right, but the hard fact is that up to this time archaeology can supply no tangible evidence.

In Chapter 7 we saw that Neolithic cultures had appeared
in various parts of India to the east and south of the Indus
river system. Those of east, east-central and central India are
not as yet well enough known to allow any inferences regarding their economy. The Northern Neolithic of Kashmir is
becoming better known as the reports on the excavations at
Burzahom are published, but it is too early to say what relative
part hunting, stock-raising and agriculture played in the
economy. Present showing suggests that hunting was of para-
mount importance. We are left with the Southern Neolithic
which flourished in north Mysore. Here considerably more
evidence is available. The culture seems to have flourished
particularly in those parts of the Deccan in which rainfall is
lowest – below 25 inches per annum at the present time. Today
north Mysore is an area of low population density. Before
modern irrigation schemes were introduced its land produced
little besides millets, and small quantities of cotton and oilseeds. It is not as yet certain what crops were produced by the
earliest settlers, but from later phases of the Neolithic there
are several indications. At Tekkalakota I grains of horse-gram
(*Dolichos biflorus*) are reported, and the same grain is again
reported at Paiyampalli, along with green gram (*Phaseolus
radiatus*), and *rāgi* (*Eleusine coracana*). *Rāgi* was also found in
the excavations at Hallur. *Rāgi* is to this day one of the most
important millets grown by the poorest groups in all parts of
peninsular India; and the two pulses are still grown throughout the region. Wood of the date palm is reported from Tekkalakota and probably also Utnur. We have seen that the terracing of hills was an important feature of the settlements of the
Neolithic period, and it is probable that it was also employed
for making tiny fields for growing crops. Such terraces, behind
a stone retaining wall, would help incidentally to conserve both
soil and moisture after the monsoon. Terracing would further
provide a logical first step towards the earth or stone embankments which from the Iron Age, at least, served as surface
drainage tanks throughout the areas of impervious granite

rocks. Field-terraces are still widely constructed by the villagers throughout this region, and even by such tribal groups as the Badaga of the Nilgiris. It is therefore highly likely that Neolithic cultivation was restricted to terraced fields and that it never spread on to the black cotton soil, which at the first rain becomes sticky and too heavy to work without a plough.

There is more abundant evidence respecting the animal husbandry of the Southern Neolithic groups. Bones of humped cattle are most numerous at all sites, from the earliest period onwards. Next, among domestic species come goat and sheep, though these are far less common. Rock paintings and terracotta figurines also depict humped cattle, the earliest almost always having long curling horns (Plates 25 A and B). The buffalo is far less common, and indeed it seems uncertain whether it was domesticated or hunted in this region. Bones and terracotta figurines of fowls are reported. Among other animals there are references to deer, tortoise, and a unique bone of an Indian elephant, and from the final phase of the Chalcolithic at Hallur comes a bone of a horse (*Equus cabalus*). It is evident that the cattle were used for food, and split and cut bones commonly occur.

The frequency of cattle bones and of cattle as art motifs suggests that the people attached great importance to them. This is borne out by a further remarkable source of evidence revealed by excavation at the ash-mounds. Two of these, at Utnur and at Kupgal, which have been excavated in recent years, have shown that Bruce Foote was correct when he deduced, many years ago, that these mounds were the sites of Neolithic cattle-pens (Plate 26). The recent evidence suggests that the dung dropped while the cattle were kept in the pens at nighttime was allowed to lie on the floor and accumulate, and that from time to time it was burned, either by design or accident. What were the intervals between the burnings is not clear, but the presence of cattle-pens both in habitation areas, and in areas remote from any Neolithic habitations, may be taken as an indication of seasonal migration to forest grazing grounds. The size of the larger pens has been inferred to represent herds of between 600 and 1,000 beasts, assuming traditional densities of herding. This whole pastoral cycle survives among

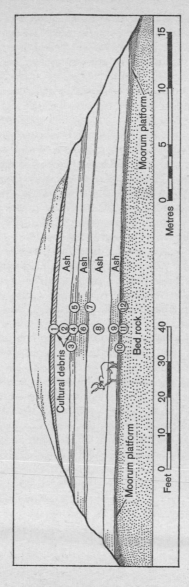

Figure 71. Sketch section of Kudatini ash-mound

cattle-keeping castes in many parts of southern India, the pens providing night-time protection from wild beasts; the animals being driven by day into the forest grazing grounds; and seasonal migrations linked to the dry season being a regular feature.

In Saurashtra and Maharashtra, we find some evidence relating to the agriculture of the areas which lay between the Indus Valley and Mysore, and which witnessed important developments in the post-Harappan period. It will be recalled that at Lothal and Rangpur IIA rice husks were reported during the later stages of the Harappan civilization. From the post-Harappan period III at the latter site comes a millet, identified as possibly *bājrā* (*Pennisetum typhoides*). The domestic species at Rangpur are similar to those of the Indus, cattle, sheep and goat being augmented by the Indian pig (*Sus cristatus*), and the buffalo. That the cultivation of wheat spread into Malwa and Maharashtra during this period is suggested by its occurrence at Navdatoli and Sonegaon. The finds from the former site are of particular interest and represent one of the most comprehensive series of specimens from any archaeological context in the subcontinent. Wheat grains are of the *Triticum compactum* and *Triticum vulgare* types. Rice is found in period IIIB, and so are several pulses including the lentil (*Lens culinaris*), black gram (*Phaseolus mungo*), green gram (*Phaseolus radiatus*) and grass pea. It is interesting that linseed appears, as well as two fruits, the Indian jujube or *ber* as at Mundigak, and the Myrobalan (*Phyllanthus emblica*). This picture again is remarkable for the sense of continuity which it affords; almost all the crops are still grown in the region. The domesticated animals as usual included cattle, sheep, goat and pig; and the hunted, deer. Another discovery of peculiar interest is of beads strung upon a thread of silk with a cotton nep from a Chalcolithic burial at Nevasa; and of a second such string from a similar context at Chandoli with a thread of flax. These finds, taken with the presence of linseed at Navdatoli, show that during the second millennium B.C. cotton was already being spun in Maharashtra, which in later centuries has always been famous for this commodity, and that at this time at any rate flax was also used.

It will be of great interest, as research advances and publication proceeds, to study the agriculture and economy of the Ganges valley during the first millennium B.C. Unfortunately the archaeological materials so far to hand are scanty, the best evidence being that of Hastinapur. In recent centuries the staple crops of the western part of the region, the Doab, have been rice and wheat, but to the east of Banaras rice becomes the main food grain. Irrigation, either by canal or by wells, is very widespread. It has been suggested that references in later Vedic literature relate to the clearance by burning of the thick forests which originally covered much of the region, and also that the Iron Age spread was connected with the development of the plough as an agricultural tool. The *Taittiriya Samhita* of the *Yajur Veda* provides considerable information regarding agriculture, and specifically mentions the use of the plough. But archaeology has as yet nothing to say, either to confirm or refute these suggestions. At Hastinapur the period of the Painted Grey ware produced only one food grain – rice, and bones of cattle, buffalo, sheep, goat and pig. It also produced a few bones of a horse, from a late level, and among wild animals deer are reported. From the same period Noh again produced rice. At Sonepur in Bihar rice is reported from period IB, while from Mahisadal in the Ganges delta, rice occurs during period I, probably well before 700 B.C. We may add here our own observation of the frequency of rice husk additions to clay for pottery both in the Iron Age and subsequent Early Historic periods in the sites of the Ganges. Thus the archaeological record suggests that the cultivation of rice was a feature of the rise of the Ganges civilization, not only in the Central Ganges region but also as far west as the Doab. It is evident that the cultivation of rice spread through the peninsula during the Iron Age, and grains are reported at Hallur from the beginning of the period.

From the evidence we have reviewed in the foregoing paragraphs it will be seen that a picture, even a coherent picture, is beginning to emerge. It appears that the subcontinent may be divided into several major regions, in terms of its ancient agriculture. The earliest region to develop was in the west, comprising a major part of West Pakistan in Baluchistan and the Indus valley. Here the ancient crops so far reported include wheat and barley, field peas, lentils and flax. These plants are all found in a wild condition in West Asia and evidence from Jarmo and other Mesopotamian sites would indicate that they were first cultivated there and spread towards India with the early spread of settled life. The southern part of the Deccan plateau forms a second province, in which evidence of cultivation becomes available during the first half of the second millennium B.C. Here a different range of plants was cultivated including the finger millet (*rāgi*), possibly the bulrush millet (*bājrā*), and varieties of pulses such as green gram and horse-gram. The two millets would seem to be particularly interesting as both are considered to have been first cultivated in Africa and wild varieties are not known in India. How they were imported is therefore a matter of considerable interest. Between these two provinces lies the intermediate area of the north Deccan and western India. Here we find the earliest evidence so far for the cultivation of rice during Harappan times. Rice appears to be an indigenous crop. Otherwise the region witnesses an expansion of wheat, flax and lentils from the west during post-Harappan times, and shares some of the legumes and millets with the south. Rice seems to have spread into the peninsula at an early date and is recorded from far to the south by early Iron Age times. A fourth region would include the Ganges valley. Here the available evidence indicates that rice cultivation spread eastwards around the close of the second millennium with the advance of settled life. One or two other points deserve mention. It will be seen that there are as yet no finds of the great millet (*javār*, *Sorghum vulgare*) throughout the period. This is in keeping with the evidence of literature that it was not imported until the opening of the Christian era. The earliest evidence for the cultivation of cotton comes from the Indus civilization. Both cotton and rice appear to be indigenous. Finally archaeology can still give no indication of the date at which that other typically Indian crop, sugar cane, was first cultivated.

We must now discuss the evidence – such as it is – relating to economic organization and to trade between groups. We recalled above Childe's dictum of the 'self-sufficing, food-producing economy' of the Neolithic–Chalcolithic societies. In a strict sense our evidence from the start seems to controvert this view. Already in the earliest stages of settled life in the subcontinent there are suggestions of some sorts of craft specialization and even of trade. For example, it has been observed that in the Southern Neolithic sites there are tools of a distinctive kind of chert which in some cases has been carried upwards of fifty miles from its source. This stone made tools larger and superior to those made from the more locally available river gravels. Again, from the same culture region, a certain distinctive green rock, pistacite, was chosen, among others, for the manufacture of a single tool type, the spheroid hammer or rubber. Tools of this rock, which is by no means common in its occurrence, are found at well over a dozen sites, many miles apart. From this we infer their manufacture at one particular factory, and dissemination among the settlements by a specialist group. Thus there are at least indications that during this period in this region there was a certain degree of internal specialization and hence trade.

There is more evidence, as we shall see, of trade between different culture regions, and in this light we should perhaps qualify Childe's definition of the economy as being 'relatively' self-sufficing. We may recall the suggestion already noticed of trade relations between the settled peoples and their Late Stone Age hunting neighbours, and of its material expression in the trading of stone blades, and following from this the probable exchange of forest produce and other commodities. Throughout central and southern, and indeed all parts of India there are numerous seasonal or annual fairs and markets, frequently linked with religious festivals. These are often held at a temple, or sometimes far from any settlement beside some natural feature such as a hill or a spring. Many scholars have been impressed by their evident antiquity. Whole families will travel many miles in order to attend the largest fairs, and they form important social occasions. Moreover, they frequently serve as cattle markets at which breeders sell their young oxen to the agriculturalists. Such fairs would provide a suitable mechanism for the sort of economic relations between groups which we have postulated, and may well have continued with little change since Neolithic times. Their roots may in some instances be even more ancient.

Research is only now beginning to show evidence of the extent to which such craftsmen as stone-, copper- or bronze-workers were organized on a basis of trade. For example, a petrological examination of granite axes from the Deccan College excavations at Sonegaon in Maharashtra reveals that they almost certainly originated in the neighbouring Karnataka region. Another class of object which deserves careful scrutiny is the glazed steatite disc bead. These occur from the second phase of the Southern Neolithic and the excellence of their manufacture is only one of the characters they share with their counterparts of the Indus region and Baluchistan. We believe that they were probably imported as items of trade between the two regions, but positive proof of this assumption is still wanting. We find much wider evidence of interregional trade when we consider the economy of the Harappan civilization.

'One of the most striking facts revealed by the excavations at Mohenjo-daro and Harappa (and to these we may now add Kalibangan, Lothal, etc.) is the complete uniformity of their culture.' So wrote Sir John Marshall, and this uniformity cannot fail to impress any observer. Quite apart from its implications of a degree of administrative control undreamt of elsewhere in the ancient world, it carried with it clear evidence of a highly organized system of craft production and distribution. A glance at the finds from Mohenjo-daro will suffice to recognize the presence of specialized groups of potters, copper- and bronze-workers, stone-workers, builders, brick-makers, seal-cutters, bead-makers, faience-workers and so on; while that of scribes and priests, administrators, traders and caravan leaders, farmers, and such menial groups as sweepers is implicit. A single example will suffice to show how common products were distributed throughout the empire. From the limestone hills at Rohri and Sukkur (Sakhar) come nodules of fine flint which were worked at vast factory sites nearby. Thence they were imported, no doubt by river wherever possible, to form a uniform item of equipment at Harappa, Mohenjo-daro, Lothal and Rangpur, Kot-Diji and Kalibangan (Figure 26). At Rangpur they are present only in period IIA and are replaced by tools of inferior local stones in the subsequent period. It may be confidently assumed that many other specialist products, such as weights, beads, seals, etc., were equally much the work of craft groups in the cities, and were disseminated in similar fashion throughout the Harappan state.

This trade implies, as in Mesopotamia, a regulation of exchange and of weights and measures. Sir John Marshall remarks upon the extraordinary profusion of stone weights at Mohenjo-daro, and the system of weights has been analysed in some detail by Hemmy. The use of writing must also have been essential. There can be little doubt that the Harappan seals were (at least as one of their functions) necessary elements in the mechanism of trade. The seals carry two principal kinds of information: first there is an animal, often before a manger or standard, and second there is an inscription varying from one or two to a dozen or more ideograms (Plates 13 and 14). The script has unfortunately still to be deciphered, but it has recently been proven that it was written from right to left. Many of the seals appear to carry numerals as a part of their information. An interesting context is established for their use in applying clay sealings to bales of merchandise. Impressions of cords or matting are not infrequently found on the backs of such sealings. Further proof of this use is derived from the discovery of several such sealings lying among ashes in the ventilation shafts of the brick platform of what is considered to have been a granary or warehouse beside the 'dockyard' at Lothal (Plate 12 c). How the exchange was regulated is not yet apparent, but it is easy to picture Lothal as being an outlying trading post of the Harappan state. To reach it there would doubtless have been a journey by sea down the Indus and around the coast of Saurashtra. The ships which unloaded at the Lothal dockyard must have brought not only such objects for internal consumption as the stone blades, and perhaps even seals, but may also have carried beads and other items for trade or exchange with the barbarian people who lay outside the empire. Again they must have carried back with them to Mohenjo-daro and the centre of the empire objects of trade or raw materials derived from the coastal province or from neighbouring territories.

There is plentiful evidence that the Indus merchants or caravan leaders carried their trade far beyond the frontiers of the empire, and established contacts with other peoples, either still in a state of barbarism, or belonging to contemporary civilizations. Of the former we can form some impression by a study of the raw materials imported into Mohenjo-daro. Gold was almost certainly an import, and the presence of clusters of Neolithic settlements contemporary with the Harappan civilization around the goldfields of north Mysore suggests an important source. Silver was imported, probably from Afghanistan or Iran. The sources of copper may have been several, in Rajputana and perhaps south India towards the east, and in Baluchistan and Arabia towards the west. Lead may have been derived from either east or south India. Lapis lazuli, though rare, can only have come from the region of Badakshan in north-east Afghanistan; turquoise from Iran; fuchsite from north Mysore; alabaster could have come from a number of sources both east and west; amethyst probably came from Maharashtra; agates, chalcedonies and carnelians from Saurashtra and west India; jade from Central Asia.

Of trade with other civilized states, notably with the cities of Mesopotamia, there are two kinds of evidence, archaeological and literary. Of the former we may list objects imported from the Indus and exported in return. The most convincing sign of the presence of Indus merchants is the discovery of some two dozen seals, either actually Harappan, or copying Harappan, or of intermediate 'Persian gulf' types, from Susa and the cities of Mesopotamia (see above, pages 139 and 141). Of actual imports, the certain origin is often not easy to determine, but carnelian and etched carnelian beads, shell and bone inlays, including some of the distinctly Indian 'kidney-shape', leave little room for doubt. From the Indus the reciprocal evidence is even less sure: only three cylinder seals of Mesopotamian type from Mohenjo-daro, all probably of Indian workmanship, and a small number of metal objects suggesting Mesopotamian origin. It is probable therefore that the trade included many objects of less durable kind, cotton, spices, timber, etc. A more definite indication of foreign trade comes from Lothal where a circular button seal of a distinctive kind was discovered (Plate 18 A). This belongs to a class of 'Persian Gulf' seals known otherwise from excavations at the port of Bahrain, and also found occasionally in the cities of Mesopotamia, notably at Ur. The Persian Gulf sites such as Bahrain and Failaka near Kuwait were beyond doubt entrepôts for sea trade between Mesopotamia and outlying regions, and these seals therefore provide very convincing evidence of some sort of trade activities. Also from Lothal come bun-shaped copper ingots, suggestive of a foreign source, and they too may be compared with ingots found on the Persian Gulf islands.

The literary evidence from Mesopotamia helps to fill in the gaps in the archaeological record. It shows that in the time of Sargon of Agade and during the succeeding centuries, merchants particularly from Ur carried on trade with various foreign countries. Among those mentioned most frequently are Tilmun, Magan and Meluhha. The first is now fairly confidently identified with Bahrain and must have served largely as an entrepôt. The second, reputed as a source of copper, has been sometimes identified with Oman or some other part of South Arabia, although the similarity of its name to the modern Makran coast certainly tempts one to locate it in Baluchistan; and the third is now generally identified with India, the region of the Indus river, Mohenjo-daro or Saurashtra. Comparison of the name with the Sanskrit word *mleccha*, barbarian, is suggestive. We learn of Tilmun merchants residing in Ur, and once at least we hear of an official interpreter of the Meluhhan language in the period of the empire of Akkad. We hear also of boats of Meluhha. Among the imports from Meluhha are various kinds of timber, including a black wood identified as ebony, copper of a different quality from that of Oman, gold, a red stone identified as carnelian, of which were made monkey- and kidney-shaped beads, and ivory, of which were made multi-coloured birds and combs. Pearls are often mentioned but their Meluhhan source is not specified. It can be argued that these imports could have originated in Africa, and that the absence of cotton, although this seems to have been

known as an import at Ur, is significant. But we feel that probability favours India as the source of all these items.

The discussion of trade focuses attention upon methods of
transport. There is a growing body of evidence to support a
considerable extent of sea and river traffic. Several representations of ships are found on seals or as graffiti at Harappa,
Mohenjo-daro (Plate 12 A and B), etc., and a terracotta model
of a ship, with a stick-impressed socket for the mast and eye-
holes for fixing rigging, comes from Lothal. Then at Lothal is
the great brick dockyard with its elaborate channel and spill-
way (Plate 12 c). By the side of the dockyard several heavy
pierced stones which the excavator has convincingly identified
as anchors were discovered. Both the form of the dockyard and
of these anchors can be paralleled in west Indian shipping
practice of recent times.

Of inland travel on the plains there is plentiful evidence
from terracotta models of bullock-carts, to all intents and
purposes identical with those of modern times (Plate 18 c).
Further, cart-tracks were found on the roads of the cities
which indicated that the wheelspan of the Indus carts was also
little different from that of their modern descendants. From
Harappa and Chanhu-daro come copper or bronze models of
carts with seated drivers, and also nearly identical models of
little carts of the modern 'ikka' or 'ekka' type, still common in
the Punjab. These have a framed canopy over the body in
which the passenger sits. For longer journeys and through
rougher and more wooded country there can be little doubt
that the chief means of transport would have been by caravans
of pack-oxen. Such caravans continued to be the principal
means of carriage in large parts of the subcontinent until the
advent of the railways and motor traffic. The more recent historical and anthropological evidence is of particular interest
because we learn that the caravan trade was largely conducted
by the same communities as the breeders of cattle and the
organizers of the cattle trade. Moreover, Saurashtra and the
north Mysore region are often interlinked among the surviving caravan communities and this leads one to speculate that
already cattle may have been one of the links between the
Southern Neolithic and the Indus valley. Traditional methods

of transport and their organization, as they have been observed and recorded during the past century and a half, leave little doubt of their extreme antiquity. One may question whether other aspects of the trade which was carried on both within India, and by Arab dhows or country boats around the coasts, and westwards to the Hadramaut, may not also have followed equally ancient patterns which time had done little to disturb.

CHAPTER 11

CRAFT AND TECHNOLOGY

TECHNOLOGY has always played an important part in the attempts of any human group or society to control the resources of its environment, by means for example of more effective methods of hunting, house building, agriculture, or transport. The appearance of new technological processes such as the utilization of metal, or the wheel for transport and potting, can frequently be observed directly from finds made in a particular level or cultural horizon. The same processes may also be reflected in changes in the nature of settlements, and in the settlement pattern of a region as a whole. Naturally such changes often coincide with others of a more broadly cultural or political nature, such as the domination of one group of people by another. On the other hand, craft traditions and technological processes may survive many major cultural, economic or political upheavals. Local tradition is tenacious everywhere, and especially so in the Indian subcontinent. Those crafts and techniques which relate to the peculiar conditions of a region, by utilizing its natural products in the form of stone, metal, pottery, textiles, etc., always tend to survive. Others which are intimately connected with religious and social concepts, or with the basic attitudes of a people, often show a tenacity far beyond their apparent economic significance. The last point is perhaps most clearly illustrated by terracotta figurines, whether they served as objects of religion, as presents and mementoes at fairs and pilgrimages, or as toys, and also by decorative motifs in general; all these incidentally overlap the fields of art and religion. Traditional tools and methods of carrying out all kinds of everyday tasks which are passed on by precept, and perhaps never completely verbalized, are also very persistent. They are closely bound up with the mental processes of those who use them, and form part of the same folk tradition as the terracotta figurines, etc. The digging tools used by workmen all over the subcontinent for moving earth are obvious examples of this, and so are the vessels used for cooking and serving food.

The techniques employed in working stone during Early and Middle Stone Age times in the Indian subcontinent are basically very similar to those found in western Asia, Europe and Africa at corresponding periods. They consist essentially in chipping or flaking stone to certain more or less regular and often repeated forms. Types of stone were chosen which would fracture in a predictable manner. By a steady, but extremely slow, refinement in the methods used to remove the flakes, an increasing variety of tools were made, and they also became smaller and more delicate. There are already many excellent accounts of the various methods of making stone tools, so we shall not describe them here, but simply indicate what appear to be the most important developments. The tools of the Early Stone Age include as we have seen handaxes, cleavers, chopping tools and bifacial ovoid and discoid forms. They were all made by removing flakes from a block or core of stone until it reached the required size and shape. The flakes which were struck off also show signs of use in some cases, but the core tools were clearly the principal objectives of their makers, and they too are characteristic of this immensely long period. There can be little doubt that these tools, with the possible exception of some of the latest and most refined examples, were used directly in the hand. They must have been used for a wide variety of purposes, including cutting down trees and making wooden tools such as spears, digging sticks and clubs, and as time went on wooden vessels. Chopping tools and flakes are still used for these purposes in Australia. They were probably also employed for skinning and dismembering game, splitting bones to obtain the marrow, chopping honey out of trees and clefts in rocks, and for many other purposes.

The stone-working techniques of the Middle Stone Age develop slowly out of those of the Early Stone Age. The emphasis changes from the core to the flake which has been struck from it. Heavy core tools are still used, but the efforts of the tool-makers are now directed towards obtaining flakes which are comparatively much lighter, thinner in section and more regular. Several could be struck from a carefully prepared core. Although some flake tools were no doubt held directly in the hand, as scrapers were in both South Africa and Australia within living memory, others must have been intended for hafting. The reduction in size alone suggests this and so do the tanged flakes recorded in some collections of Middle Stone Age tools. No examples of hafted tools of this period have been found in India, but it is always possible that they may be found preserved in exceptional conditions, as very occasionally objects of a corresponding or even greater antiquity have been found in Europe and Africa. Analogies from prehistoric Europe and sub-Saharan Africa, and from Andamanese and Australian aboriginal usage all suggest that scrapers, knives or missile points might be mounted on wooden handles or shafts with the aid of mastics. Australian aboriginal practice further suggests that many tools normally classified as scrapers may have been used as adze blades, mounted by these means. Resin of various kinds, and lac were no doubt available, and these could be heated once people knew how to manage fire, and worked round the wood to form a base to hold the stone point or edge tool.

Middle Stone Age techniques continued into the Late Stone Age industries of almost every part of India, and especially those of the extreme south and Ceylon. This must indicate a continuity of population. The significant technological developments which we can see in assemblages of stone tools of the Late Stone Age are the methods of making parallel-sided blades, and microlithic tools of various shapes fashioned from these blades and also from small flakes and chips of stone. The method of making parallel-sided blades (see page 79) makes it possible to produce large numbers of blades from a relatively small core of good quality stone in a short space of time. The blades themselves could then be used for various purposes, or converted into the component parts of composite tools. The same component parts could also be made from flakes and chips of stone produced by other methods, which included producing flakes from prepared cores as in Middle Stone Age industries but on a smaller scale, and also by heating suitable pieces of certain kinds of stone and then shattering them with one or two carefully directed blows. The last method was only applied to quartz, the crystalline nature of which lent itself to shattering in this way. The microliths or component parts produced by all these methods could be used together with mastics and wood to make a whole range of cutting tools and missile points. Some idea of the possible range of variation can be gained from contemporary rock paintings, archaeological finds and ethnographic parallels from many parts of the world (see page 95). The new techniques in stone working must have accompanied technological developments in other fields. It seems most probable that the bow and arrow was one of these, and that improved methods of snaring and trapping, of fishing and perhaps of canoe or boat building, the making of baskets, and mats for shelter, and other crafts were all introduced or developed in the Indian subcontinent as part of the Late Stone Age culture.

The technique of making parallel-sided blades which is so characteristic of the Late Stone Age is also an important feature of the Neolithic and Chalcolithic cultures of certain regions. We have already discussed in the previous chapter the evidence for trade between the Southern Neolithic peoples and the Late Stone Age hunters of the same region, and for trade in stone blades within the Harappan culture. The fine blade industries of the Late Stone Age, Neolithic and Chalcolithic cultures of Karnataka, Maharashtra, western India and the Indus plains are a notable feature (Plate 27 A). Their technical uniformity raises many questions of culture contact both in time and space. The same technique, in a somewhat modified form, has persisted into modern times in the hands of stone bead-makers, who frequently collect their material – semi-precious stones such as agate, carnelian and so on – from the same sources as the Late Stone Age tool-makers. During the Neolithic and Chalcolithic period, an increasing number of semi-precious stones and other materials were used for making beads, an industry which reached its apogee in the cities of the Indus valley. Here several bead-makers' shops and their equipment were excavated. Less than a century ago, the Andaman islanders were recorded as shattering quartz with the aid of fire to make tools, but this method does not appear to have sur-

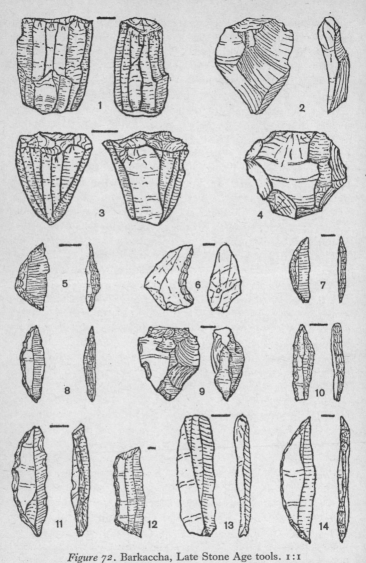

Figure 72. Barkaccha, Late Stone Age tools. 1:1

1, 3 and 4, cores; 2 and 9, flakes; 5, 7, 8, 11 and 14 lunates; 6, hollow scraper; 10, awl or borer; 12, trapezoid; 13, blade.

vived as an integral part of any craft tradition, as the blade tradition does in bead-making. One related technique is still widely practised in southern India however: this is fire-setting as a means of detaching large slabs of crystalline rock such as granite from the parent rock. The evidence of the frequent use of this technique today, in the regions where we are postulating that a similar method was employed in Late Stone Age times to produce quartz tools, cannot be without some significance.

The manufacture of ground stone axes seems to have come into the Indian subcontinent with the first Neolithic settlers. There were several processes involved, and each axe must have taken a considerable time to complete. Rocks, such as dolerite, basalt and chert, which could be relied upon to fracture in a predictable manner, were first brought to the required shape by flaking. Rough-outs for Neolithic axes abandoned at this stage have a superficial resemblance to hand-axes of the Early Stone Age. The blade, and sometimes the whole or part of the body of the axe, was then ground and perhaps also polished. Crystalline rocks such as granite or gneiss which would not flake regularly were hammered or pecked into shape, and then treated like the first group. The grinding process must have taken a long time. In Australia, in recent years, we know that the manufacture of a flaked and ground axe took an experienced man two to four days. In south India and also at Sukkur on the Indus there were regular axe factories. At Sukkur the axes were only flaked and not ground, but in Mysore, where they were ground, at several sites there are deep grooves in the rocks, some feet in length, which fit the width and curve of the local axe blades. The manufacture of stone axes does not seem to have survived long into the Iron Age, probably because it was tedious and relatively expensive. Stone axes do appear however to have continued to be made in Mysore and south India when copper was in regular use in Maharashtra and the north-west. The techniques of pecking and grinding stone may be regarded as Neolithic innovations. By these means, tougher and less brittle rocks could be used for cutting and chopping than was previously possible; an axe once made would outlast many flaked tools. The same techniques were also used in making hammer-stones, querns and grinding-stones. The number, variety and perfection of the stone axes found in southern, central and eastern India clearly differentiates this tradition from that of western Asia. The general question of their relationship to the stone axes of Southeast Asia on the one hand and of Central Asia on the other must await further elucidation.

Among the special uses of fine soft stones such as alabaster we may note the manufacture of stone bowls and other vessels. This is more or less restricted to Baluchistan and the Indus valley, and scarcely appears to have spread into the south or east of the subcontinent.

The quarrying and handling of larger blocks of stone calls for special techniques. In the Indus civilization slabs of hammer-dressed limestone are occasionally found covering brick drains. Probably such blocks would have been quarried with the assistance of copper chisels and stone hammers, as in Egypt. In the granite regions of the south, already by the end of the Chalcolithic period, and increasingly during the Iron Age, we find slabs of granite detached with considerable skill, used for cist graves and occasionally the embankments of small surface drainage dams (Plate 32 A). These slabs can only have been obtained by using fire-setting, and as the technique is still common throughout south India, it may well be that the ancient craft survives with little change. With the use of iron and steel, wedges, crowbars and even cold-chisels are found, and these must have augmented fire-setting and the use of heavy hammers. In the gold bearing regions of Karnataka fire-setting was also used, probably from the Iron Age onwards, in connexion with the deep shafts of gold mines sunk in the quartz veins. At Hatti such mines have been recorded at frequent intervals along several miles of reefs, reaching by the first centuries of the Christian era to depths of over 600 feet. At Kolar and other localities in the same region similar ancient shafts are reported.

The use of copper for making tools and ornaments is attested in Baluchistan from the earliest period of settlements. At Mundigak several finds are reported in period I and at Kili Ghul Mohammad the first copper is recorded in III.

From the pre-Harappan period in the Indus valley and Punjab objects of copper are reported at Amri (IA), Kot Diji and Kalibangan. From the latter site comes a flat axe recalling the form of the succeeding Harappan axes. Present evidence suggests that some of these finds may include bronze, but so far analyses are published only for specimens from Mundigak, and it is not possible to state certainly when bronze first occurs in the Indian subcontinent, nor what alloys were first used.

There is far more evidence in the cities of the Indus. From the outset there seems to have been a plentiful supply of copper, though the general standard of workmanship is fairly elementary. Nearly all the basic tool types, flat axes, chisels, knives, spear- and arrow-heads, small saws, etc., could have been made by simple casting, and/or chiselling and hammering. Daggers, knives or dirks with mid-ribs and flat tangs begin to appear in the upper levels of Mohenjo-daro (Figure 25). Although they may show foreign influence, we concur with Childe's remark that they are 'technically very Indian'. Bronze appears to have been present from the lowest levels at Mohenjo-daro, but is noticeably more common in the upper levels. Four main varieties of metal were present: crude copper lumps, in the state in which they left the smelting furnace, with a considerable quantity of sulphur; refined copper containing trace elements of arsenic and antimony, doubtless deriving from the original ore; an alloy of copper and arsenic having from 2 to 5 per cent of the latter substance, probably present as a natural constituent of the ore; and bronze, having a tin alloy content often as high as 11–13 per cent. The copper-arsenic would have been harder than the pure copper. The presence of this alloy in ancient Egypt may indicate a common source, or common technical method; but the presence of traces of nickel and arsenic in so many of the Harappan specimens almost certainly indicates the source of the ore as being in Rajputana. Indeed we need to know much more about the ancient copper-mining localities of that region.

The splendid copper and bronze vessels which are among the outstanding examples of the Harappan metal-workers' craft were either raised or sunken by hammering (Figure 73). In the late-Harappan period an additional technique, that of lapping

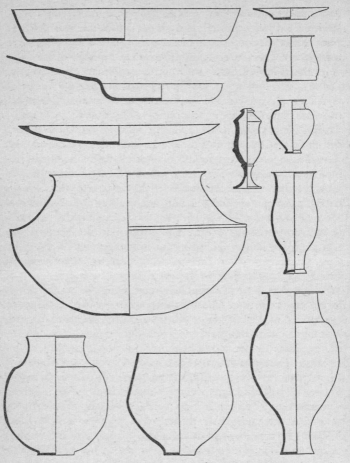

Figure 73. Mohenjo-daro, Harappan copper and bronze vessels. 1:4

or joining two parts to make a composite jar, appears. Casting of copper and bronze was understood and employed, apparently throughout the Harappan period. Copper bun-shaped ingots are among the regular finds. Apart from simple casting in a mould, the method known as *cire perdue* or lost-wax was also employed with great skill, particularly in making the bronze figurines of human beings, animals, etc. (Plate 16 B). Kilns of brick have been discovered at a number of places and some of them were fairly definitely associated with copper-working, as for example in Block 1 of the DK area of Mohenjo-daro.

We have noticed in Chapters 6 and 7 the finds of copper and bronze tools and weapons, including shaft-hole axes, adze-axes, daggers with mid-rib, trunnion axes, the Fort Munro dirk, etc., in late-Harappan or definitely post-Harappan contexts in West Pakistan (Figures 30 and 31); and we have taken these as indications of the movement of peoples, rather than trade, from the direction of Iran, during the second millennium B.C. Apart from the new designs and probably greater efficiency of some of these weapons, we can say little regarding their composition or methods of manufacture. Nor indeed do these things represent any significant additions of technical knowledge of metal working beyond that of the Harappans. At the time of writing no metal objects are known from Neolithic sites in the northern or southern groups belonging to a pre-Harappan or even early Harappan period. The indications are that at Brahmagiri, Piklihal, Maski or Hallur, it was not before the end of the Harappan period that the working of both copper and bronze became at all common. When it did so the forms of the predominant tools, chisels, flat axes, fish-hooks, etc. (Figure 50) are all reminiscent of those of the Indus valley. Probably in the third phase of the Neolithic–Chalcolithic of Karnataka and Maharashtra this repertoire was augmented by certain new and exotic types, such as the antennae swords of Kallur (Plate 21 B) and the antennae spearhead of Chandoli (Figure 50). The copper hoards of Uttar Pradesh and Central India again lead us to expect them to belong to a comparable post-Harappan period (Figure 56). It is interesting to note that the bronze alloy found in these regions often repeats the high tin content of the Indus bronze: thus 9·0 per cent tin is recorded at Brahmagiri; and 15·81 per cent tin in one Brahmagiri Iron Age grave. The most extensive collection of bronze vessels from any part of south India comes from the Adicha-nallur urn fields dating from the Iron Age. Here were found

a remarkable series of vessels, some with lids, these being frequently decorated with figures of rams, cocks, buffaloes or
birds, and in one instance, a dog (Plates 30 B and 31 B). Bells of
bronze are common in Iron Age graves from many parts of the
peninsula. Analysis of a bronze sample from Adichanallur
showed a 23 per cent tin alloy.

Doubtless gold, because of its attractive native appearance,
was one of the first metals to be sought after by man. Doubtless
too the panning or washing of gold-dust was the principal
means employed anciently to obtain gold. There is as yet in-
sufficient evidence in the Indian subcontinent to indicate the
character and use of gold in pre-Harappan times. With the
Indus civilization there is more evidence. Objects of gold are
reasonably common, though by no means prolific. Gold occurs
in the form of beads, some of minute size, pendants, armlets,
brooches, needles, and other small personal ornaments, including small hollow conical caps with interior soldered loops,
doubtless for use as forehead ornaments and identical with
modern examples. Much of the Indus gold is of light colour,
indicating a high silver content, or rather that it is unrefined
'electrum'. This suggests that it originated from the reefs of
Mysore rather than from panning, and the possibility is certainly not discouraged by the numbers of Neolithic settlements which are reported from Mysore, particularly clustering
around the Hatti gold bands. Gold is certainly reported in the
region – although rarely as yet – during the Neolithic–Chalcolithic period at such sites as Tekkalakota (phase I). Even from
the Iron Age graves of south India finds of gold are very
limited, although there can be little doubt that gold was by
this time being extensively mined. A gold pendant of spiral
form was found in Chalcolithic levels at Daimabad in Maharashtra. Of later south Indian finds the diadems from the Adichanallur urn burials are noteworthy. Further investigation
of the Mysore mining localities is obviously needed. The evidence of stray finds in old workings, two radiocarbon samples
from Hatti, and field investigation of settlements associated
with old workings, all indicate that already by the opening of
the Christian era shaft mines through the quartz veins had
reached a considerable depth; and it is probable therefore that

the open-cast beginnings of this mining are very ancient. Whatever the history may have been, we may recall the vast quantities of gold-dust paid by the Indian provinces as tribute to Darius the Achaemenid at the close of our period. The similarity of the ancient gold-working of Mysore to that recorded on the Red Sea coast of Egypt by Agatharcides in the second century B.C. is interesting.

Silver makes its earliest appearance, to date, in the Indus civilization. That it was relatively more common than gold is indicated by the number of larger vessels made of silver, and by the frequency of other finds. Beads and smaller ornaments apart, the forms of the utensils almost always repeat those made in copper. Among examples of finer workmanship is a silver buckle from Harappa with soldered scroll pattern of gold wire and gold-capped beads, and a boss of silver inlaid with conch-shell. Of the manifold possible sources of this metal available to the Indus merchants, it is difficult to determine which were exploited. Objects of silver are almost unknown in later prehistoric or protohistoric contexts in the subcontinent. A rare, indeed almost unique, occurrence is in the copper hoard from Gungeria (see pages 204–6) where about a hundred thin silver plates in the form of (?) bulls' heads were discovered. Their age is still a matter for speculation. The Indus cities also provide testimony that lead was imported in ingot form, and occasionally used for manufacturing objects such as vases or plumbbobs.

The discovery of the smelting of iron ore to produce a spongy bloom, and of the forging of the bloom to make wrought-iron tools, has been supposed to have taken place in Asia Minor and to have spread from this centre at the end of the second millennium B.C. Certainly the Indian evidence we reviewed in Chapter 8 would not controvert such a theory. Until recent years tribal peoples in many parts of the subcontinent continued to smelt their own ores by methods which are not only relatively primitive, but which share much with the techniques observed, for example, among ironsmiths in many parts of Africa. For, once discovered, the techniques involved are relatively simple, and we may expect that the picture of the modern Agaria smiths of Central India recorded two decades ago by Verrier Elwin differs little from that which archaeology may one day reconstruct for the first Indian iron-smiths. The essential elements are a small blast furnace, usu-ally of less than six feet in height, and generally fired with the aid of bellows, and a second hearth for heating during the forging. Tools, including even substitutes for tongs, may be of stone or green withies. We have noticed above the curious range of tools and objects made throughout the southern Iron Age (pages 227–9 and Figure 64). The evidence from the north of the subcontinent is still very fragmentary, but there appears to be a fundamental difference in the type of iron tools found there. Shaft-hole axes occur throughout – in place of the flat axes with iron cross-bands – and other tools also employ shaft-holes for hafting. Arrow-heads in the north include from a very early date the three-fanged varieties which provide a link with Iran and central Asia, and which are absent in the south. The direct process was almost certainly used to produce the iron for both industries. Modern observation suggests that iron-rich earths or nodules of haematite or limonite were pre-ferred to massive ferruginous quartzes, etc., probably because they were fed into the furnace directly, without troublesome crushing.

Ever since Alexander the Great invaded India in the fourth century B.C. she has been renowned for the quality of her steel. How this steel was produced is something about which archaeology has as yet very little to say. The early European travellers in south India recorded a technique employed by the ironsmiths of Mysore to produce 'wootz' steel, and there is some reason to believe that this, in default of any other, was the method employed anciently also. To make this steel, pieces of wrought iron are cut off and put in a crucible to-gether with certain organic substances. The crucible is then sealed and fired in a furnace. The principal result of this firing is to increase the carbon content of the metal and thus produce a low-grade steel. Crucibles which may have been employed for this purpose are reported from a number of sites, but all belong to a later date than our period.

Pottery is so common a find in almost every site of Neolithic or later date, that it is difficult to generalize about the craft which it reveals. Archaeologists, in India no less than other parts of the world, have often been imprecise in the terms they employ in describing pottery, and no single system of description has so far been accepted. In these circumstances we can do little more than provide a few general observations on some key aspects of the potter's craft as our material exemplifies it.

Baluchistan provides a single province in terms of the potter's craft (Figures 13–15). In the earliest levels of Kili Ghul Mohammad and related sites a substantial proportion of the pottery is handmade, including pottery moulded (? and fired) within coiled baskets, and pottery probably made upon some sort of turntable. But wheel-thrown pottery is reported at almost all sites in increasing quantities in the immediately succeeding periods. So too are slips used to provide red or brown colouring, occasionally burnished, and painted decorations in black or red paint. Painted decoration tends to grow more varied with the passing of time, and develops from monochrome to bichrome and even polychrome. There is, throughout, a tendency to abstract geometric or linear designs, although some animal motifs, such as those of the Togau ware, occur. There is not as yet direct evidence of the form of wheel employed, but from the pottery itself it may be inferred that it was some kind of foot-wheel, probably mounted in a pit. The skill exercised in control of firing likewise suggests that already at an early date a kiln with a separate fire-chamber was introduced. Altogether the early Chalcolithic pottery of Baluchistan shows evidence of close affinities with that of Iran and Mesopotamia. The craft traditions once established proved remarkably virile and although fashions of painting and design changed, they persisted at least until the times of turmoil in the second millennium B.C., if not far longer.

The pottery of the pre-Harappan culture of Sind and the Punjab takes over many features from Baluchistan, although it appears as one travels eastwards to Kalibangan to become more and more distinct (Figures 18–20). It may be inferred that the same kinds of wheel and kiln were adopted, and probably too that some of the range of forms and decorative motifs were derived from Baluchistan. For example, the techniques of surface roughening known in Baluchistan are also found in the Indus Valley, and even beyond. At Kalibangan it is interesting to contrast the turntable built pottery of Fabric A with the wheel-thrown pottery of Fabrics B–E (Figures 21 and 22). The latter group has the strongest affinities with the pre-Harappan pottery of Kot Diji; the former the most individualistic appearance. Indeed the A Group may even belong to a pre-Harappan Indian craft tradition of which at present few examples are known. A number of features anticipate the Harappan wares, such as the internal incised decoration upon bowls, and offering stands. The extraordinary self-assurance of the pottery of the Harappan period calls for comparison with the crafts and arts of the Roman empire or of Victorian Britain (Figures 27 and 28). There is extreme standardization, and technical excellence goes hand in hand with a lack of aesthetic sensibility. Even after allowing for the increasing 'Indian-ness' of the craft, its roots in the west, in Baluchistan and Iran are undeniable.

The foot-wheel is still in use in Sind and parts of the Punjab, Saurashtra, and the North West Frontier Province, and may be taken with some degree of certainty to be a legacy of this period. The modern foot-wheel closely resembles those which are found right across Iran and into Mesopotamia, both today and probably in ancient times. The wheel is set in a pit, and an axle connects to a smaller lighter turntable on which the pot is thrown. The potter sits on the side of the pit and regulates the speed and duration of the movement of the wheel with his foot. The majority of the pottery is plain, but a substantial part is treated with a red slip and black-painted decoration. Polychrome pottery is rare. Throughout the whole range of forms, flat bases are dominant, and many show the string-cutting marks of their removal from the wheel.

Leaving the Indus civilization, we find to the east in pre-Harappan and even post-Harappan times a number of fundamentally different potting traditions. From the Eastern Neolithic the single excavation of Daojali Hading produces crude handmade pottery with external cord-marked or striated beaten-impressed decoration. Such pottery immediately and strongly recalls the Neolithic wares of south China, and clearly belongs to such a culture-zone, and we eagerly await more information regarding it. Equally distinctive is the pottery of the Northern Neolithic, as revealed by the excavations at Burzahom (Figure 32). This is a predominantly grey, buff or black burnished ware: heavy in section and ill-fired. The mat-impressions on the bases and the irregular form indicate that it is handmade, and there can be no doubt that it was fired in an open or bonfire kiln. The range of forms includes simple rim-less bowls, and bottle shapes with flared rims. Apart from the burnish the only decoration is crude incised and fingertip decoration. It is difficult to find any relationship of this tradi-tion with that of Baluchistan: the superficial resemblance of mat-impressions fades away when it is remembered that those of Kili Ghul Mohammad are almost entirely from the base-mats of coiled baskets. Certainly it has many features of both form and surface treatment which recall the grey wares of such sites as Shah Tepe, Turang Tepe, or Hissar in north-eastern Iran: features which are shared in many respects also by the Southern Neolithic pottery. We shall leave open the difficult question of its external affinities and consider the Indian re-lationships more closely.

The potter's craft of the third Neolithic group, the South-ern, presents yet another distinctive tradition, somewhat bet-ter known than the others (Figures 34 and 37). When we first encounter it at Utnur or Piklihal it combines several separate wares. First, a frequently burnished grey or buff ware, gener-ally plain, but including an important decorated group usually with simple bands of red ochre apparently applied after firing – in contrast to the painted wares of Baluchistan and the Indus. This pottery is handmade, probably usually built on some simple kind of turntable, and very rarely it has mat-impressions upon the base. The forms include simple lipped bowls, larger pots with flared rims, and, at least in the later phases, spouted pots and basins. Incised decoration occurs only rarely, and at a later time surface roughening is found. The second element is a less well-fired clay, also probably hand-built, but having a red, black or brown dressing applied before firing, and burnished. Some of the vessels of this ware are painted before firing with black or purple paint. The forms in this fabric include a curious sort of offering stand on horn-like legs, and bowls with applied ring bases or hollow stands. If the first of these two elements recalls the pottery of Burzahom and even of north-eastern Iran, the second shows its relations, however remotely, with the traditions of the pre-Harappan Kalibangan Fabric A. Throughout the whole industry the evidence suggests that pottery was handmade upon a turntable, and that it was fired in an open, bonfire kiln.

The pottery of Saurashtra during the Harappan period shows, alongside the typical Harappan ware, a different local tradition, including black-and-red ware. In the post-Harappan period, now well represented by the excavation at Rangpur, the purely Harappan elements of the craft become gradually less prominent, while a new range of forms and craft techniques come into evidence (Figures 43 and 44). One of the hallmarks of this change is the increasing popularity of bowls, water and cooking pots, and so on, with rounded bellies rather than flat bases. Probably this change reflects a giving up of the foot-wheel, in favour of turntable building for smaller vessels, such as the shallow carinated bowls which now become common, and of the Indian spun-wheel for larger vessels. This wheel, which is today found distributed throughout the entire subcontinent, east of the provinces in which the foot-wheel is used, is an ordinary cart wheel, sometimes weighted with clay, balanced on an iron pivot set in a clay core about eight inches above the floor. The wheel is spun by hand with a short staff, and when it gains momentum spins freely for upwards of a minute. The manufacture of any one pot must therefore be completed before it loses momentum and falls off balance. In any case the completion of the forming was almost certainly carried out with the aid of a potter's dabber and anvil.*

* The potter's anvil is generally made of either stone or terracotta in the form of a small bun loaf, the narrower end fitting into the palm of the hand. The dabber or 'paddle' is commonly made of wood, and in form resembles the 'hands' used for making butter pats. The potter beats the plastic clay from without with the dabber, supporting it from within with the anvil. If as was often the case the dabber was decorated with incised patterns, these were naturally transferred to the surface of the pot, and thus form a common mode of decoration. Similar tools are used in parts of India by tribal people for beating bark-cloth.

The new techniques which we find here in evidence for the first time have diffused through most of the central and eastern parts of the subcontinent and continue to this day to form the main determining factors in the range of forms produced by the village potters. The burnished black-and-red ware, sometimes found with the addition of simple linear decorations of white paint (Figure 44), is of particular interest. The technique of production by inverted firing is simple once learnt, and doubtless identical to that used to produce the black-and-red ware of pre-dynastic Egypt or of the modern Sudan. As we have seen the black-and-red ware forms a dominant element of the post-Harappan pottery of Ahar and south Rajputana (Figure 45) and it seems to have spread thence into Malwa and Maharashtra, and then southwards (probably with or before the spread of iron-working) to the extreme south. Also from these centres it spread eastwards across Central India and into the Ganges valley. Thus during the whole of the Iron Age and part of the succeeding centuries in south India (Plate 30 A), and at the opening of the Iron Age in the Ganges region, one or other of the sub-varieties of this black-and-red ware formed an important element of the material culture. Two forms of vessel occur again and again: a wider shallow bowl with rounded belly, and often with carination between the belly and walls; and a deeper narrower bowl, sometimes with a flat base (Figures 58 and 61) .The firing of the black-and-red ware does not call for any special kiln and a simple bonfire or pit kiln would have sufficed.

A new and important forming technique is encountered in the pottery of the Southern Iron Age; this involved the pressing of the clay over a clay form or mould. The technique is obviously only suitable for producing open bowls or forms of a limited range, but it may well be that it was already in use in the Deccan during the Neolithic–Chalcolithic period, and it continues in use to the present day among the potters of Bengal and Assam, and to a lesser extent the Ganges valley.

In Malwa and Maharashtra the pottery shows a parallel development to that of Saurashtra (Figures 46 and 47). In the earlier part of the second millennium the most common pottery is a red or white slipped ware with black or brown painted decoration, known as Malwa ware (Plate 29). There is some doubt whether this was made on the turntable or thrown on the wheel, as is sometimes claimed. Certainly the major part of it is not wheel-thrown. Distinctive forms of this pottery include chalices with solid stems and feet. There is a remarkable range of painted designs, including those of dancing figures and animals (Plate 28 A). Among the animals are bovines with long wavy horns recalling those of Cemetery H, at Harappa, and Rangpur IIC and III. Another very distinctive form of animal has the body hatched with dots. The slip in many cases has been burnished. A further group of pots is decorated with applied bands, zigzags and even figures. Bowls, both with and without carination are common. Black-and-red ware with white-painted decoration is found. Another fabric is a coarse grey ware, manifestly handmade and probably related to the grey ware of Karnataka. In the second half of the millennium a new pottery, the Jorwe ware, both turntable built, wheel-thrown and with beaten rounded belly, comes into prominence (Figure 51). This has a matt red slip with painted decoration, often in the form of simple linear patterns, far less intricate or time-consuming in the production than those of the Malwa ware (Plate 28 B). The grey wares continue, often with incised or fingertip decoration. The presence of unburnt ochre paint on some grey ware vessels from Daimabad and Prakash again suggests some relationship with the region to the south.

On the whole, all the pre-Iron Age pottery of the regions east of the Indus valley presents regularly recurring features. Among these we may comment on the absence of the foot-wheel and probably of the spun-wheel until relatively late times, the predominance of simple pit or bonfire firing and the variety of ancillary forming techniques, including the turntable, the mould or form, and the use of dabbers and anvils. The dabbers and anvils are exemplified by specimens from excavation in several sites, and represent a potter's technique which diffused throughout the entire subcontinent and continues to dominate its pottery down to the present day.

Of the pottery of the Ganges valley prior to the Iron Age too little is as yet known to discuss its craft aspects. The

Painted Grey ware however represents an important stage (Figure 58). Made from fine alluvial clays, its body is uniformly thin and well-fired. There is clear evidence of the use of both the turntable and the spun-wheel, and of the beating of the rounded bellies. Two dominant forms are the shallow carinated bowl, and the deeper, narrower bowl, sometimes with carination. The range of painted design is surprisingly limited. Coarser grey and pink wares occur alongside the fine ware, and a rice husk addition is of common occurrence. Already during this period some vessels have been treated with thick bands of fine black dressing and these provide the forerunners of the Northern Black Polished ware of the following period. The control of firing and temperature throughout bears witness to a more sophisticated kiln than those of the peninsula, and, although archaeological evidence is still wanting, it may be inferred that it involved a separate fire-chamber with a good draught control. The Northern Black Polished ware represents one of the technical high water marks of the Indian potter. It is a black gloss ware with a surface very closely related to that of the Greek Black, but there seems to be no reason to suppose that the Indian potters derived their technique from any external source.

We have dwelt at some length upon the craft aspects of stone- and metal-working and potting, because these cover the most prominent and important categories of archaeological finds. We shall now briefly notice some of the other crafts of the Harappan civilization. In the previous chapter we noticed the discovery of fragments of dyed and woven cotton fabric at Mohenjo-daro. The prehistory of a textile industry is necessarily elusive, as so much of the evidence disappears unless climatic conditions favour its survival. That woven textiles were already common in the Indus civilization, and that the craft for which India has remained famous was already in a mature stage of development, must be inferred from this single find, and from occasional impressions of textiles upon earthenware, pottery and faience from the Harappan sites. A whole class of small vessels of the latter material were evidently formed upon a cloth bag filled with sand or some other suitable substance, leaving the textile impression upon the interior of the pot. The employment of fabric for this and for equally humble tasks in baling goods (evidenced by the cloth impressions upon sealings) surely testifies to its common availability. Whether both cotton and flax were spun, as they were in post-Harappan times in the Narbada valley, is not yet clear.

Comparatively few examples of ivory carving have been found. They include combs, probably the cousins of those imported to Ur, carved cylinders perhaps for use as seals, small sticks and pins. A unique piece of a much-damaged plaque carved with a human figure in low relief is notable. Another craft was that of working and inlaying shell. The shell most commonly used was probably obtainable locally from the coast, being the *fasciolaria trapezium* variety. This was used for several kinds of beads, bracelets, and decorative inlays. The conch shell, more commonly used in later millennia, is only rarely encountered.

The lapidary's craft was of considerable importance, and its products included the range of steatite seals, whose artistic aspect we shall discuss in the next chapter, beads and various ornaments, and numerous weights. Beads were manufactured from a wide variety of semi-precious stones brought to the Indus valley from many different regions, and doubtless some derived from the same sources as the stone blade cores. At Chanhu-daro and Lothal bead-makers' shops were discovered, with their equipment, which included stone borers and drills, anvils, grinding stones and furnaces, and larger numbers of beads in all stages of completion. The beads and the weights were made by flaking techniques similar to those in the preparation of blade cores, and then ground, polished and drilled, with extraordinary skill and accuracy. The seals were intaglios, made of steatite, first cut to shape with a saw; the boss was then shaped with a knife and bored from either end. The carving of the animal motif was done with a burin, probably of copper, and at some stage, generally before carving, the seal was baked to whiten and harden its surface (Plate 13). An alkali was probably applied to the surface before firing to assist in the whitening and to glaze it.

Steatite was used for a wide variety of other objects: beads, bracelets, buttons, vessels, etc., but its use for making faience is of particular interest. In this material numbers of beads, amulets, sealings and even animal models have been found. Several techniques are indicated, using a body paste of either powdered steatite or perhaps sand, and a glaze of some related substance. Minute disc-cylinder beads of this material were apparently extruded in plastic form, fired and then snapped off. Pieces of glazed earthenware and even faience pots, some with coloured decoration, are recorded, and again testify to a remarkable level of technical achievement.

Another related technique which deserves mention is the decoration or etching of carnelian beads. The beads of carnelian were painted with an alkali paste and toasted to whiten them, or further decorated with black lines obtained from metallic oxides. It seems probable that India was anciently a source of carnelian beads, and therefore that etched beads may well have been among the items of export to Mesopotamia. On the other hand disc beads apparently of steatite, and faience barrel beads occur already in Mundigak I, and it seems clear that these techniques were of earlier development in Mesopotamia and Egypt. The technique of making beads of semi-precious stones must long have remained a special feature of Indian craftsmanship. Archaeology is able to supply a mass of evidence from sites from the earliest Neolithic and Chalcolithic settlements in many regions to testify to its longevity. Another, most comprehensive, body of evidence comes from a bead-worker's shop at Ujjain, actually dating from about 200 B.C., which was excavated by N. R. Banerjee.

CHAPTER 12

ART AND RELIGION

WHETHER we consider the past or the present, the boundary between the field of craft and technology and that of art is never very distinct, and they constantly overlap. Where works of art survive, they add greatly to our comprehension of pre-historic cultures, for they provide an insight into the minds of the artists. Not only do they often reflect the spirit and atmosphere of a culture, but in some cases they also give an indication of social values and religious beliefs in a way in which other material remains cannot possibly do. Unfortunately the art of prehistoric cultures does not always survive. Rock art, if it is in a sufficiently well-protected situation, survives for many thousand years, and so to some extent do carvings in stone, bone or ivory, as we see in Europe. On the other hand, wood carving and painting on wood, bark, or even on the bare ground, which form, for example, the major part of Australian aboriginal artistic expression, have no chance of survival whatsoever.

Whether people of Early and Middle Stone Age times found any means of artistic expression other than that shown in the making of tools we do not know. The rock art of Central India, where caves and rock shelters have proved favourable to its survival, all appears to date from Late Stone Age and even later times. At present we have no means of knowing whether the Late Stone Age peoples of other regions practised any comparable form of art which has been lost. In Karnataka in Neolithic times another type of rock art flourished. But these are the only two regional cultures which provide a body of material. Before discussing either of them, however, it is worth considering briefly the stone industries of the Late Stone Age, especially those of western Central India and Ceylon, which often show a technical excellence and precision far surpassing that demanded for purely utilitarian purposes. In Central India great attention was given to the choice of material, and the same range of semi-precious stones – agate, carnelian, jasper, blood stone, and so on – which were employed by Late Stone Age tool-makers were also in use continuously throughout Neo-lithic and Chalcolithic times, and down to the present, by the makers of beads and semi-precious jewellery of all kinds (Plate 27 A). The facets of extremely fine, regular blades produce an effect not unlike that achieved by faceting gem-stones today, causing the tools to reflect the light and sparkle. It seems highly probable that the makers of these tools were guided by aesthetic as well as utilitarian considerations.

The same region, western Central India, in which the micro-lithic blade industry reaches its zenith, is also that in which a remarkable body of rock art survives. Many of the rock shelters which were inhabited during Late Stone Age times, and which have protected rock surfaces, have been decorated with single figures or scenes. Painting is perhaps a misnomer: crayoning might be more accurate. The pieces of haematite found among the Late Stone Age debris of some of these rock shelters, and the pictures themselves, demonstrate this. Animals are the most frequent subjects, either alone on a small flat area of rock, or in larger groups where this is possible (Plate 3 B). They are shown as herds or in hunting scenes, such as the rhinoceros hunt from the Adamgarh group of rock shelters. They are drawn boldly in outline and the bodies are sometimes filled in completely, or partially with cross-hatching. Examples of all three methods can be seen among the drawings of deer on the walls of the Morhana Pahar group of rock shelters near Mir-zapur. The animals most frequently represented are deer or antelope, which are shown with rather bulky bodies and slender legs and horns. It is not always clear to what species they be-long, but sometimes there are suggestive details. Other animals, including tigers, monkeys, etc., are also shown, but not so frequently (see page 86). In spite of the somewhat stylized representation, many of the figures are full of life and action. People are even more stylized than animals, but equally active and lively. They are shown with bows and arrows and spears, and also dancing in lines, this last being reminiscent of decora-tions on the Malwa ware pottery of the Chalcolithic period in western India. Other subjects include animal-headed human figures; squares and oblongs partly filled in with hatched designs which may represent huts or enclosures; and what appear to be pictures of unusual events, such as the chariot waylaid by men armed with spears and bows and arrows at Morhana Pahar (Plate 3 A). The colours used range from purple, through crimson and vermilion to terracotta, light orange and brown. In western Central India, where most of the rock paintings are found, they are usually on Vindhyan sandstone, which provides a pinkish buff or light yellowish brown background.

The granite rocks of North Karnataka and Andhra also provide suitable protected surfaces for rock art at such sites as Kupgal, Maski, Piklihal, etc. Most of this can be attributed – on account of its content – to the Neolithic people who settled on these hills, but it is quite possible that a few can be attributed to the hunting people who preceded then. Others again are certainly later. The pictures are made by crayoning rather than painting, in a similar range of colours to those seen in Central India. The most frequent subjects depicted are cattle: long-horned humped bulls, unmistakably *Bos indicus*. They are shown singly and in groups, some with their horns decorated as though for a festival. Other animals, such as deer and tigers, are occasionally illustrated, and it is these which suggest links with the hunting peoples. There are also elephants, some with riders; and human figures, again like pin-men. Some of the men carry axes or spears, and occasionally they ride horses. The presence of horses in the region in late Neolithic or Chalcolithic times is further suggested by horse bones found at Hallur (page 165). The elephants, the horses and the armed men almost certainly belong to the final phase of the Southern Neolithic, or even to the Iron Age, but the method of representation is the same as in earlier times, although lacking the grace of some of the finest early bulls.

Alongside the rock paintings associated with the Southern Neolithic, there is a whole series of rock bruisings (Plate 25 B). These are done by hammering or pecking the surface of the granite and so changing its colour and producing a pattern. These again show animals, chiefly bulls. The rock bruisings, however, unlike the paintings, continued to be made at certain sites until the present day, the principal subject throughout being cattle. The style changed steadily, until the most recent bulls closely resemble the emblem of the Congress Party. The bulls shown in the earliest rock bruisings on the other hand are similar in style to the early rock paintings, and both are parallel to the terracotta figurines of bulls which are found in the early phases of the Southern Neolithic. All these early representations emphasize the long horns, the hump, and sometimes also the pronounced dewlap of *Bos indicus*. At Piklihal in North Mysore a group of terracotta headrests like those found in excavations of Neolithic levels at T. Narsipur and Hallur are found bruised on the rocks.

It must be confessed that the art of the Stone Age exhibits peculiar limitations, at least in the form in which it survives. Of the Neolithic and Chalcolithic settlements the remaining categories of art are also strictly limited. As we find them in the Indian subcontinent they may be classified under three heads: painting on rock, painting on pottery, and modelling in clay to make terracotta figurines. We have already discussed Neolithic and later survivals of rock art. The painting of pottery appears almost from the beginning of settlement in Baluchistan. The most common elements are linear or simple geometric designs, but occasionally animals are represented as early as in Mundigak I (Figure 13). These decorative designs soon blossom into more complex patterns, including quite elaborate geometric motifs, as in the Quetta ware or the pottery of Mundigak III (Figure 14). Already friezes of cattle and other animals occur in north or central Baluchistan showing a measure of stylistic evolution, as in the Rana Ghundai 'bull' pottery or the Togau ware. Stylized plant motifs, particularly the *pipal* leaf, occur, as well as less obvious plant and bird motifs. The art of pottery painting seems to have reached its peak in these regions in late pre-Harappan or early Harappan times, with the graceful fish or animals of the polychrome Nal ware, the naturalistic friezes of animals or *pipal* leaves of Mundigak IV (Figure 15), the 'Animals in landscape' motifs of Kulli ware, recalling the 'Scarlet' ware of Diyala and Susa in south-west Persia, and many more. The whole of this development shows strong Iranian influence, and many of the patterns and motifs can – in a general rather than a precise way – be paralleled in Iran.

There is a strongly abstract flavour running through the whole pre-Harappan range, with geometric patterns preferred to naturalistic or stylized representations of animals or plants.

As it is known at present the painted pottery of the pre-Harappan settlements of the Indus plains shows a range of common elements and a number of distinguishing features. The pottery of Amri most nearly reflects Baluchistan, with a predominance of geometric patterns, but that of Kot Diji and Harappa stands apart with its austere use of plain bands of colours or wavy lines, and very limited use of linear or other motifs (Figures 18 and 19). Very similar decorated pottery is indeed found in Baluchistan, but it is generally overshadowed by more striking forms of decoration. All the more significant therefore are the coincidences of horn (or 'moustache') and flower-petal motifs, between Kot Diji and Kalibangan. The range of painted designs from this latter site is the farthest removed from that of Baluchistan, although some patterns or motifs recall those of Quetta or the Loralai sites. The frequently repeated arch or arcade, often bisected by wavy or diagonal lines, deserves comment, as do the less common flowers, fish, birds and cattle (Plate 8 A). One of the most interesting anticipations of the Harappan style is found in the 'scale' design which appears to evolve throughout the whole region (Figure 20).

The painted pottery of the Harappan civilization is so well known that it needs little comment. Abstract geometric motifs are comparatively rare, the nearest approach being in 'scale', leaf or petal designs. Natural motifs such as birds, fish, animals, plants, trees, and *pīpal* leaves are not infrequent (Figures 27 and 28). Varieties of the 'animal in landscape' style are by no means rare. As with the monotonous repertoire of forms of the Harappan potter, so the painting has a utilitarian quality and a kind of heavy insensibility. On the other hand many pieces show a remarkable delicacy of line and artistic feeling, as for example the pot from Lothal (Plate 19). The pottery of the Cemetery H phase at Harappa shows overwhelming craft continuity with that of the preceding culture (Figure 29). In the same way the painting, with its continuing use of black upon a red ground, may be said to form a logical development rather than a break.

The star and rosette motifs which are characteristic of the Cemetery H pottery are to be found also in Harappan levels, as are the peacock and the humped bull (Figure 75). It cannot be denied however that the often bare vessels with single friezes of decoration, and the extraordinary painted covers with their bird or *pīpal* leaf themes have no counterparts in the Harappan itself, and seem to take their inspiration rather from styles found in Western Iran, for example in Giyan II or Djamshidi II.

Sherds of the early painted ware of the Southern Neolithic pottery are too fragmentary to say much about their design. We see purple paint on a red or brown burnished slip, simple linear patterns, triangles radiating from the neck of the vessel, and wavy lines. Far more interesting is the Malwa ware of Maharashtra and Malwa which shows a wide variety of animal and human motifs, in addition to simple linear designs and geometric patterns (Plate 29). Some of the Malwa patterns are drawn with a fussy, uncertain line. The style is quite distinct from anything in the Indus region, and forms a distinctive stylistic province. Such geometric patterns as are employed are frequently unsurely drawn, and limited to an elementary range, including crossed-hatched panels or bands of square, triangular or lozenge shapes, wavy lines, and loops. Far more prominent is the range of naturalistic motifs. Cattle and antelope are not uncommon, the horns often swept back in wavy lines, recalling those of Cemetery H at Harappa; sometimes registers of indeterminate animals, perhaps felines or panthers, are found; and birds include the peacock. Humans feature mainly as lines of dancing figures with interlinked arms, strikingly reminiscent of rock paintings from both Central India and the Karnataka; but there are also single figures, some with long wavy hair standing on end and some grasping long staffs. A few special motifs, including stars or rosettes, quite elaborate cross patterns, horn patterns, and curious tufted spirals all deserve comment.

The pottery of the succeeding Jorwe phase has two styles: one a continuation of that of Malwa, and the other a new style whose keynote seems to have been speed and deftness of application. The fussiness disappears and the linear patterns are simplified (Figure 51). The geometric patterns continue, but the number of animal and human motifs diminishes. Among animals there are several which almost certainly represent horses. Continuous spirals and tufted spirals occur regularly. Another interesting stylistic variant, the so-called Sawalda ware, takes the form of hastily drawn stylized fish, arrow-heads, and perhaps flying birds. A new feature is the appearance of a range of symbols used singly as space fillers in the painted design and perhaps serving as owner's marks, although applied by the potter before firing, many of which recall letters of the alphabet (for example T, C, V, +, o, o°, o°o,). The decoration of the Painted Grey ware of the Punjab and the Ganges–Jamuna Doab exemplifies in its own way a rather similar tendency to economic and rapidly applied decoration (Figure 58), with simple linear and curvilinear designs.

Finally with the later stages of the Iron Age and the pottery of the Early Historic period throughout the whole subcontinent, plain unpainted shapes became fashionable. But the older traditions lingered on, to be resuscitated particularly in Sind, Rajasthan and the Punjab, where painted pottery is to be found to this day. Elsewhere it survived mainly among tribal peoples. Exceptions are the Russet Coated black-and-red ware of Mysore which flourished around the turn of the Christian era, and preserved a range of simple linear designs recalling those of the Painted Grey ware, and also those of the post-Harappan pottery of Saurashtra.

The tradition of painting pottery appears to constitute an 'applied' rather than a 'fine' art. This can scarcely be said for the art of modelling in terracotta, but such are the limitations of this medium that it only rarely transcends them. For this reason its timelessness has often attracted attention, and the archaeologist must be aware of the pitfalls of over-facile comparisons which do not also have a basis of cultural or geographic continuity. Terracotta figurines occur in Baluchistan almost from the earliest ceramic levels. The most common subject is *Bos indicus*, often with a heavy and exaggerated hump. In the later pre-Harappan stages sticked modelling for the heads and eyes is found, and painted decoration of heads and bodies. It is remarkable that throughout the region, from Mundigak or

Quetta and Zhob in the north, to Kulli and Shahi-tump in the south, cattle depicted are almost always the humped variety (Plate 7 A). Other cattle are rare, and so are other animal species, although sheep, goats and birds are sometimes found. Human figurines form the second subject, although less common than animals, and their appearance is somewhat later. In the immediately pre-Harappan and even Harappan period a definite type series emerges through the region with the so-called 'Mother Goddesses' (Plate 6, Nos. 1, 2, 4 and 5). They exhibit a minimum of modelling of the body, with heavy applied details, such as breasts, head and neck ornaments, etc., and eyes formed by deep stick incisions. They may be divided into a northern group, including those from such sites as Mundigak IV, Damb Sadaat II–III (Figure 16), Sur Jangal III, Chhalgarhi, etc; and a southern group typified by the Kulli types with more intricate ornamentation and eyes often formed with an incised line around the pupil. A very different style is exhibited by two pieces, one from Chhalgarhi and one from Mundigak IV, both unfortunately fragmentary (Plate 6, No 3). The latter, which is more complete, is evidently a kneeling figure, and in both cases the head is tilted backwards and the eyes are half closed. These two have a far more sculptural quality than the goddesses, and immediately recall Harappan stone sculpture, with which they may well be contemporary.

The Indus civilization produces evidence of the universal popularity of terracotta figurines, whether as toys or cult objects, or more probably as both (Plate 17). Technically they show little to distinguish them from those of Baluchistan, hand-modelling and applied detail being general. A few pieces are certainly made in single moulds. They include a range of birds and animals, including monkeys, dogs, sheep and cattle. Both humped and humpless bulls are found, the pride of place seemingly going to great humpless bulls, clearly of the *primigenius* stock, well modelled and with sticked details of eyes, head and neck. Both male and female human figurines are found, the latter being if anything more common. The head-dress is often quite elaborate, and some figures have heavy appliqué dress or ornament on their bodies. Seated women, and mother and child groups, are often among the most lively modelling. Of especial interest is a group of heads with either horns or horn-like appendages. These appear on both male and female torsos, and may be associated with the horned figures on seals and elsewhere so that with some certainty we may regard them as deities. The male heads sometimes have small goatee beards. One other group of figurines deserves notice; these are models of carts made of terracotta and almost certainly used as toys (Plate 18 c). The various types of cart are recognizably the ancestors of actual vehicles surviving in the modern countryside of India and Pakistan, and once again bear remarkable testimony to the extraordinary continuity of the culture during the past four millennia. With these Harappan terracottas we notice for the first time a general tendency which is repeated many times in later Indian art: the plastic qualities of the animals are as a rule more noteworthy than those of the human beings, and show considerable skill on the part of the artists in representing natural observations.

The terracotta art of the peninsula in Neolithic–Chalcolithic times is less prominent than that of the Indus, but in the Southern Neolithic it is present from an early date: humped cattle, birds and human male figurines are recorded (Plate 25 A). On present evidence there appears to be something of a gap between all these traditions and those of the Early Historic period in the Ganges Valley and North West Frontier regions, when a new series of types began to appear, rapidly developing into the remarkable single and later double moulded figurines of historical times, and some showing clear evidence of Hellenistic influence.

There remain a small group of works of art which appear only in the narrow confines of the Harappan civilization; these are sculpture in stone and metal, and the seal-cutter's art. Stone sculptures are not common: about a dozen pieces only come from Mohenjo-daro and two or three from Harappa. Most are mutilated or fragmentary. The stone employed was usually soft, either steatite, limestone or alabaster. The function, wherever indications are available, seems always to have been as cult icons. The size is never great, and in each case well under life-size. The outstanding pieces are the bearded head and shoulders from the DK area at Mohenjo-daro (Plate 15) and two small figures from Harappa (Plate 16 A and C). The Mohenjo-daro fragment is one of a series of male figures, either seated or kneeling, with hair tied in a bun or hanging in a long plaited lock. In some instances the hair is tied in a fillet. It is with this series that the two terracotta pieces from Mundigak (Plate 6) and Chhalgarhi may be compared. Another outlier of the same group is a stone head discovered by Stein at Dabarkot among Harappan remains. A further piece which suggests more remote Harappan affinities is the limestone male head from Mundigak IV.3 (Plate 6, No 3). In some of these cases there are indications that an inlay was used for decoration and for the eyes. At best the modelling of these pieces is convincing, but the inferior examples are distorted and improbable. Stone carvings of animals are even more rare than those of human beings, but from Mohenjo-daro come two reclining animals, evidently either bulls or rams, in each case carved from a block of limestone of which a solid part remains as the base. One has an elephant's trunk recalling the composite beasts of the seals. The head in both instances is missing. The modelling of the larger of the two, which incidentally was finished by polishing, is surprisingly sensitive, and bears somewhat the same relation to the human figures as many of the terracotta animals do to their human counterparts.

The two examples of stone sculpture from Harappa have sometimes been held to belong to a much later period, but there are several cogent arguments to favour their Harappan date. First of all no comparable sculptures are known from north India of the Early Historic period, and secondly both have drilled sockets to take dowel pins to attach head or limbs, a technique not found in later sculptures. The first figure is a tiny nude male torso of red sandstone, less than 4 inches in height, with a pendulous belly. As Sir John Marshall pointed out its chief quality lies in the 'refined and wonderfully truthful modelling of the fleshy parts' (Plate 16 A). Indeed it is far finer than any other Harappan stone sculpture. The two tubular drill holes on the front of the shoulders may have been intended to take an inlay. The second figure is no larger, made of a grey stone. It is a nude dancing figure, also male, with twisting shoulders and one raised leg. A dowel pin was used to attach the now missing head (Plate 16 c). It is quite unwarranted to suggest an association of this figure with the much later icon of Śiva as Naṭarāja, Lord of the Dance, and yet it is as convincing and tempting an ascription today as when Marshall proposed it thirty years ago.

Even less plentiful than the remains of stone sculpture are those of cast bronze, mainly from Mohenjo-daro. The most significant specimen is a little figure of a dancing girl about 4½ inches in height (Plate 16 B). The head is inclined back, giving the eyes a characteristically drooping quality, the right arm rests on the hip, and the left, which is heavily bangled, hangs down. She is naked, except for a necklace and her hair is plaited in an elaborate manner. A second figure of comparable size also comes from Mohenjo-daro, as do one or two cast-bronze feet from figures of about the same size. Among animals of bronze one may mention a fine buffalo and a ram. Finally, even if only toys, the little models of bullock-carts and 'ikkas' from Chanhu-daro and Harappa are interesting examples of the skill in casting. Incidentally, the two ikkas, though discovered over 400 miles apart, are virtually identical in all details. Although so few, these specimens testify to a remarkable degree of skill in bronze-working and suggest that this art was well developed in the Harappan cities.

We have already mentioned the seals of the Indus civilization in terms of their role in economic life, and discussed their techniques of manufacture. They form further an impressive part of the surviving examples of Harappan art (Plates 13 and 14). The number so far discovered in excavation must be around 2,000. Of these the great majority have an animal engraved on them, and a short inscription. The animal most frequently encountered is a humpless bull, shown in profile with its horns superimposed on each other and pointing forward. From this feature it has sometimes been called a unicorn. In front of the beast stands a short decorated post, variously interpreted as a standard, manger or even an incense-burner. This animal interests us for two reasons: first because, as we have seen, it must be a descendant of *Bos primigenius* and therefore provides an indication that this breed vied with *Bos indicus* here at this time; and more immediately because the schema that is used is one which was a commonplace in Mesopotamia from Uruk times at least to Achaemenid. Its presence in the Indus valley thus suggests a loan from the West. What is at present not clear is whether the loan was merely of the art-form, or whether cattle of *primigenius* type were also present. The proliferation of representations of Indian humped cattle in terracotta might suggest that these were the main breed in the region, but on the other hand there is a clear suggestion that the humpless west Asiatic variety made their appearance in the Indus valley at this time, only to disappear in subsequent periods. Far less common upon Harappan seals is *Bos indicus* itself. Here the whole portrayal of hump, horns, head and dewlap is Indian, and it is drawn according to a different schema, which is also occasionally found in the Middle East, generally being seen there as evidence of contact with India. The *Bos indicus* is never accorded the honour of a 'standard', suggesting that sacred status was given only to the humpless breed.

Other animals on the seals have a standard or mangers, among them the elephant, the bison, the rhinoceros and the tiger. Of special interest is a considerable group of seals with 'cult' motifs, evidently containing material of a religious character. The craftsmanship of these seals is generally excellent and shows at once considerable skill in the depiction of animals, and a tendency to run into accepted schemata or clichés. This is particularly marked with the hundreds of 'unicorn' bulls, which repeat with only minor changes the same motifs again and again. The cult scenes show a refreshing originality, but many of them are so small that they give little scope for artistic expression.

Considering the whole sweep of Indian prehistoric art we may feel somewhat disappointed at the limitations of the materials it provides us. In quantity they cannot compare with the repertoire of either Egypt or Iraq. We find neither the variety of expression, nor the range of exploitation of media which both these countries witnessed. Stone sculpture is very rare and often comparatively undeveloped, however excellent unique pieces may be; terracotta sculpture was not exploited as it was in Mesopotamia. Even metalwork, in spite of the excellence of the unique pieces, did not develop at all widely.

The total absence of any surviving painting on walls too is disappointing. Thus the evidence is paradoxical and perplexing. We are left wondering whether less durable forms of artistic expression have completely vanished, and whether such crafts as textile design – for which India has been justly renowned during the historical period – can have filled this role as in more recent centuries.

RELIGION

Archaeology can still tell us little of the religion of non-literate stages of society, and in a real sense the history of Indian religion only begins with the Rigveda. But religion has none the less a prehistory, and archaeology can and does afford some evidence of its nature. As yet the remains of the earlier stages of the Stone Age are too shadowy to yield any information, but with the Late Stone Age, and the very clear evidence of its persistence among isolated hunting tribes into comparatively recent times, the first traces of both archaeological and ethnographic information become available. We find, for instance, inhabited caves in which the dead are buried, such as Lekhania in Central India. Other caves which were either inhabited or frequented by Stone Age man, are today associated with cults of folk deities, gods or goddesses. Discussing the rock art of Central India W. S. Wakankar writes, 'At the top of one of the hills stands a temple dedicated to the goddess Kankali. This is actually built over a huge rock shelter which has beautiful drawings of hunted deer.' Gudiyam cave near Madras, which we have already mentioned, contains the shrine of a local goddess, and recent excavations showed that it had been frequented if not actually inhabited by man throughout the Stone Age. Another clue is afforded by Stone Age factory sites which coincide with modern cult spots: the late D. D. Kosambi reported instances of this kind in Maharashtra. Many other examples could be cited and while singly they may not carry conviction, taken together they suggest a definite pattern. All these associations, however, need further and more extensive examination before we can estimate their significance; they are merely suggestive. Ethnographic survivals among hunting groups also require very careful consideration, as their religious concepts have been invaded by, and become closely integrated with, those of neighbouring peoples at many different levels. Accounts of hunting peoples however indicate that their own deities are those to whom they turn for success in hunting, and for the continuance and abundance of fruit, flowers, honey and other forest produce. These, in the case of both the Chenchu and the Veddas, for whom there are fairly comprehensive accounts, include both male and female elements. They may either take the form of separate personalities, or be combined in one personality, such as the Chenchu Garelamaisama. In either case other deities are also worshipped, some of whom may contain further indigenous elements. The Veddas attach great importance to the spirits of ancestors, who merge with benevolent local deities. Both peoples bury their dead in the open with little ceremony, and the Veddas are also recorded as abandoning corpses in rock shelters which they avoid for some years thereafter.

When man started to cultivate crops and to herd his own domesticated animals, an increased interest in fertility and in magical means of promoting it appears to have become an almost universal aspect of culture. It may well be that this interest gave rise to some of the most important new concepts in the whole of religion, namely belief in an afterlife and in resurrection after death, and belief in the transmigration of souls and the cycle of rebirth. Throughout the length and breadth of India there are found today, at the folk level, rites and festivals which are intimately associated with the changing seasons, the sowing and harvesting of crops and the breeding of cattle and other livestock. There is also a whole pantheon of local gods and goddesses, some of whom remain unassimilated while others have been assimilated at different levels into the sanskritized hierarchy of gods of the 'great' classical Indian tradition. There can be no doubt that a very large part of this modern folk religion is extremely ancient and contains traits which originated during the earliest periods of Neolithic–Chalcolithic settlement and expansion.

There is still not much evidence from the first settlements of Baluchistan and Sind. How far the earliest terracotta figurines, both human and animal, were cult objects it is impossible to say; but in later pre-Harappan times the increasing numbers of distinctive female figures, heavily ornamented and with exaggerated features, have been generally seen as mother goddesses, or representations of the Great Mother. So too the increasingly well modelled and often painted figures of bulls may have had some cult significance.

During this period there is already evidence of different burial practices. In the cemetery in mound C at Mundigak, situated outside the main living area, simple inhumations with the body slightly flexed, and generally without grave goods, belong to a date anterior to period III.6. A second group of graves, with communal ossuaries as the common type also dates from this period. The bones had evidently been exposed, or otherwise excarnated, before deposition. In some cases single pots were added as grave goods. A very different picture is provided by the slight evidence from the Kashmir Neolithic settlement at Burzahom. Here burials were among the houses, and in some cases the body had been sprinkled with red ochre. No grave goods were found in the pits, but the skeletons of dogs were buried in the graves with those of people. Another curious feature is the apparently ritual burials of dogs, wolves and ibex. Altogether these graves are most unusual in the Indian context, and seem to belong to a different culture region, with affinities in the Mongolian Neolithic.

In the Neolithic of Karnataka the indications are that stock-raising was the mainstay of the economy, and cattle are found drawn on the rocks around settlements, and as terracotta figurines. Human figures, either depicted on the rocks or in terracotta, are rare, and such examples as are known are male, and often carry a long staff. At some settlements, paintings are found in secluded spots at a discreet distance from the houses, and this led us, at Piklihal, to postulate that such rock shelters must have been cult spots. In one instance the shrine of a mother goddess is still in worship immediately in front of such a cave; and other sites present many comparable indications. We have also suggested that the ash-mounds of this culture, which have been shown to derive from periodical burnings of accumulated cow-dung within cattle-pens, may have been fired in connexion with seasonal festivals, marking such events as the beginning or end of the annual migrations to the forest grazing grounds. Among modern pastoralists in peninsular India bonfires are still lit at festivals at such times. Cattle are also driven through fires as prophylaxis against disease, just as in the need-fires of western Europe.

The burials of this period in the Deccan were scattered among the houses: adults were laid on their backs in pits, in extended posture, frequently with grave goods. These included stone axes, blades and pottery. In the southern Karnataka pottery headrests are occasionally found in the graves (Figure 37). Infants were buried in many cases in urns, probably beneath the house floors. During the course of the second millennium B.C. a new custom with multiple urns forming a sort of sarcophagus for the collected bones, and other grave goods, makes its appearance. This type of burial is paralleled in Maharashtra (Figure 52).

In spite of the mystery of its undeciphered inscriptions, there is still a considerable body of information concerning the religion of the Indus civilization. As we have seen, a number of buildings both on the citadel and in the lower town at Mohenjo-daro have been tentatively identified as temples. It is from these that a part of the small repertoire of stone sculptures, almost certainly all cult icons, derive. But our information goes far beyond this. Thirty years ago Sir John Marshall, in his brilliant chapter upon the religion of the Indus civilization, was able to propose certain basic elements. He concluded that the great numbers of female terracotta figurines were popular representations of the Great Mother Goddess; and he rightly drew parallels between this evidence and the ubiquitous cult of goddesses both throughout modern India and in literature. He further postulated the presence of a great male God, whom he identified with the later Śiva, and who shared many of his epithets. We are of the opinion that the stone cult icons, and therefore probably also the temples, were dedicated to this same deity. One of the most significant representations is to be found on a series of seals. These show him seated in a Yogic posture, upon a low throne flanked by antelopes, and wearing a great horned head-dress; he is ithyphallic, he has perhaps three faces, and he is surrounded by jungle creatures (Plate 14, No 2). Every one of these features can be found in the descriptions of Śiva of later times. Moreover, stones identical in form to the *lingam*, the phallic emblem of Śiva, were found in the cities.

Another group of human figures on seals and amulets, whether male or female, have horns on the head and long tails; they sometimes also have the hind legs and hoofs of cattle.

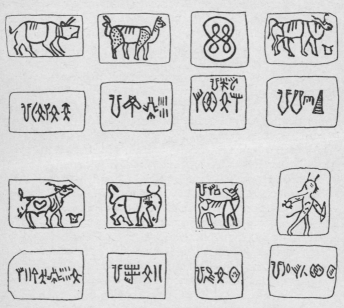

Figure 74. Mohenjo-daro, Harappan copper tablets. 1:2

From the seals, seal impressions, amulets and copper tablets, we may derive a series of items which must belong to the religious ideology of the Harappans. On one seal rearing cobras accompany the Yogi figure. A recurrent theme is of a tree-spirit, of indeterminate sex, shown in a tree, with a tiger or other animal standing before it (Plate 14, No 5). This motif is occasionally combined with a pair of worshippers bearing rooted plants or saplings. Another theme shows a row of seven figures, also of uncertain sex, with long hair plaits, standing before a tree, or tree with spirit. The seven have been variously identified with the seven Rishis (or seers), and with the seven Mothers of later times. Some scenes are strongly suggestive of Mesopotamian mythology: for example, a man grappling with a pair of tigers recalls the Gilgamesh motif, and the horned god, with the legs and tail of a bull, recalls the Bull-man Enkidu of the same epic. Wild and domestic animals are also commonly depicted. Many of these are naturalistic representations, and the extent of their religious significance is not clear, although the bull and cow may be expected to have had a special role comparable with that of later times. We need have no doubt in assigning such a role to the composite animals, such as the creature with the forepart of a human and the hindquarters of a tiger – perhaps the ancestor of the Tiger Mother (Huligammā) of modern south India – or the composite Bull-elephant, the Ram-bull-elephant, and so on. The last has been compared by Mode and Kosambi with a similar beast from Jemdet-Nasr. It also demands comparison with compound creatures, such as the Lion-elephant (*Gajasimha*) of folk-tales and medieval iconography. Even abstract symbols and motifs seem to anticipate later Indian religion. Among these we may note the maze-like closed patterns which recall the auspicious rice-flour designs made by housewives upon thresholds or in courtyards; the *svastika* in several variant forms; and the *pīpal* leaf.

We have already discussed the burial customs of the Harappans in Chapter 6. There is a definite division between grave-yard and city, although it is not clear whether burials were discovered within the city in the earlier excavations. The dominant mode of disposal was extended inhumation, and only in Cemetery H at Harappa was a new practice, the placing of collected, disarticulated bones in large urns, in evidence.

The burials of Cemetery H at Harappa are of importance for more than one reason. In the lower of the two strata (II) they were predominantly inhumations with grave goods. The pottery of some (which we may suppose to have been the earliest in time) is reported to resemble that 'of the mounds', that is to say of the main Harappan occupation. In other cases the pottery introduces both new forms and new painted patterns, which as we have already noticed recall those of sites in Iran. In the upper Stratum (I) we find the new, and probably intrusive rite of burying bones with other goods in large urns. The painted urns tell us all that is so far known of the beliefs of their makers (Figures 29 and 75). On their shoulders these urns bear registers bounded by straight or wavy lines. Common motifs are peacocks, with long streaming feathers on the head. In one case their bodies are hollow and contain small horizontal human forms. A second motif is of bulls or cows, some with curious plant-like forms springing from their horns, one with a *pipal* leaf appearing from the hump. Another shows two beasts facing each other, held by a man with long wavy hair, while a hound stands menacingly behind one of them; in yet another a little man of similar form stands on the back of a creature which shares the features of a centaur with the Harappan Bull-man. Other painted designs are mainly natural: stars, leaves, trees, etc. Vats suggested that the tiny human forms within the peacock are the souls of the dead; that the broad registers represent the river across which they must be carried, and that the peacocks, bulls and so forth are other aids to their crossing. In support of this he quoted possibly related extracts from the Rigveda. Perhaps the most convincing detail is the hound, which he compares with the hound of Yama, the god of death. Thus in this pottery we may find a striking combination of Harappan elements, such as the *pipal* leaf, the bull, and perhaps the peacock, with a use and conception which seem foreign. It is indeed tempting to see in this material evidence of an intrusion of an early wave of Indo-Iranians, perhaps related to the authors of the Rigveda.

There is still regrettably little information about the religion of the Chalcolithic culture of the Deccan. The burial rites here seem to have been largely similar to those of Karnataka, with infant urn burials and adult inhumations among the occupation areas. The multiple urn burials which are found in both these regions are noteworthy (Figure 52). From the Jorwe phase at Nevasa come two terracotta mother goddesses of crude form, with oblong tabular bodies and crudely modelled heads. These are the first indications of a type which becomes fairly widespread in the Iron Age. During the final centuries of the second millennium B.C., in a period in which there are many indi-

Figure 75. Harappa, painted decorations on Cemetery
H pottery

cations of intrusive elements from the north and west, a significant change is seen in the burial customs, with the appearance
of pits lined with stone slabs, in graveyards remote from the
settlements. This new practice may be regarded as the herald
of the Iron Age burial rites of the peninsula. Meanwhile the
evidence at present available suggests that customs in Maharashtra and the peninsula began to differ from those of west and
Central India. In the post-Harappan centuries in these latter
regions no burials are encountered within the settlements themselves, and no separate burial grounds have so far been encountered. It is always dangerous to argue from the negative
and there may be some explanation of this, but the most likely
reason is that already in these regions the Aryan rite of cremation was becoming established, and hence that this is the
beginning of a profound change which was to dominate growing areas of north India, and to be reversed only after the advent
of Muslim burial rites some two millennia later.

With the arrival of iron two broad geographical divisions
demand separate consideration. In the north we enter the growing area referable to the Aryan settlements and the Vedic texts,
and religion may be said to enter its historic phase. The archaeological evidence is so far negligible, although it may be hoped
that more will be forthcoming in the near future. Hencefoward
burials are not found, presumably because of the growing
fashion of cremation; and at best smaller urns containing cremated ashes are discovered. There is so far no trace of religious
structures, nor of icons or cult objects. But during this period,
perhaps towards its close, terracotta, bone or ivory representations of mother goddesses, which one writer has understandably
compared in form to the Eye goddesses of Mesopotamia, occur
at sites in west and north-west India and the Ganges valley.
These may be regarded historically as the forerunners of the
terracotta art which developed in the final centuries of the first
millennium B.C. It is only with the rise of Buddhism in the
centuries after the close of our period that religious architecture
begins to appear, leading through to the splendid monuments
of the turn of the Christian era. The stone cist graves of the
north-west, from the valleys of Swat, Chitral and Dir form a
notable exception to the rule. It is still not clear how often the

cists contain cremated bones, but certainly in many instances the body was placed in the cist without cremation. The fact that the modern Muslim population here still bury their dead in coffin shaped dry stone cists in graveyards contiguous with the ancient, provides a suggestion that this practice has continued in vogue since its first introduction in antiquity.

For the religion of the southern Iron Age our knowledge is derived almost entirely from graves (Plate 32). We have already described their several varieties and main features in Chapter 8. The many excavations show a baffling assortment of burial practices. In some instances simple inhumation is found; in others the unburnt bones were collected after they had been excarnated and placed in an urn or in a stone cist; in others again only fragments of bone were deposited, and often fragments of many individuals are found in a single grave; cremated bones are encountered in rare cases. It may be remarked that in modern practice burial rites vary from caste to caste, and ethnographic reports from south India can show just as great a variety as the Iron Age graves. Through the whole series runs the idea, present in the earliest Tamil literature and in modern practice, of a dual ceremony. The initial funeral leading to the exposure, burial or cremation of the corpse, is followed by a second ceremony, perhaps taking place only after many months, when the collected bones are deposited in their final resting place. Another detail which links some of the graves with modern practice is the use of lime in the infilling. The orientation of portholes and entrances on the cist graves is frequently towards the south, although in some burial grounds it is towards another quarter, and the grounds themselves are most frequently found to be to the south of the settlements. This demands comparison with later Indian tradition where south is the quarter of Yama. Among the grave goods iron is almost universal, and the occasional iron spears and tridents (*triśūlas*) suggest an association with the god Śiva (Figure 64). The discovery in one grave of a trident with a wrought-iron buffalo fixed to the shaft is likewise suggestive, for the buffalo is also associated with Yama; and the buffalo demon was slain by the goddess Durgā, consort of Śiva, with a trident. A number of remains of structures associated with the graveyards have been reported, but none has so far been excavated. In some cases these appear to have been stone enclosures, in others more probably actual buildings or temples. So too may we mention in this connexion the alignments of standing stones oriented on the cardinal points which are usually found in close association with burial grounds. What their purpose may have been, and how they relate to religious or funerary practice, is still mysterious. The picture which we obtain from this evidence, slight as it is, is suggestive of some form of worship of Śiva, but it is too early to say more.

CHAPTER 13

CONCLUSION

AT the beginning of this book we emphasized the importance of a geographical approach to our subject, and we described the principal regions into which the subcontinent could be divided from a basic geographical point of view. We also indicated how in many – but by no means all – cases, modern cultural and linguistic divisions correspond with those of geography. In discussing the early cultures of the subcontinent we have again and again been drawn to notice how closely they too relate to their physical background, and we have seen how changing emphases at different periods have caused fluctuations in the regional pattern. In retrospect the regions we have discussed fall into certain major groups which have tended to remain constant in spite of these fluctuations. The cultural patterns which emerged during the course of the period of Neolithic and Chalcolithic settlement have in many cases continued into modern times and contribute profoundly to the modern cultural and linguistic (not to say national) entities which we outlined in Chapter 2. If any single set of factors may be said to define the complex character of the Indian subcontinent, they are probably the geographical, archaeological and cultural relationships of its major regions.

Viewing the subcontinent in most general terms the regions fall into two classes: those on the frontiers which form contact zones with the outside world and which may therefore be regarded as transitional zones; and those which lie within and whose principal contacts are with one another. In the former class are Baluchistan and the North West Frontier, the Himalayan zone, and the hilly country of Assam and Bengal. In the latter there are three major regions, a western centring upon the Indus system, a northern and eastern centring upon the Ganges system, and a southern or peninsular region. Between these three is the central hill and forest zone which forms something of an internal frontier province. The three major regions have in every sense – archaeological, cultural and political – played leading roles in the history of Indian civilization.

What part the people of the Early and Middle Stone Age played in forming the character of subsequent cultures we are not in a position to estimate. But there can be little doubt that their descendants formed a considerable element in the Late Stone Age population of the subcontinent as a whole, and of southern India in particular. With the Late Stone Age we find ourselves dealing with a body of material which can be interpreted in cultural terms and considered in apposition to surviving entities of society. Among these people we can assume there to have been an important element of the Proto-Australoid or Veddoid type which is still predominant among tribal peoples, and is represented to a greater or lesser degree at all levels of Indian society. Both biologically and culturally the Late Stone Age population, which may have been of no mean proportions, must have contributed some of the most deepseated and – one might almost say – the most Indian elements of the culture of later times. Certain attitudes and assumptions which are now regarded as typically Indian must have their origin in the culture of these people. The complex character of modern society, and the manner in which groups at widely different social and economic levels coexist, often in close proximity to one another, are features to which we have had several times to allude. During the past five millennia, or more, there have been repeated arrivals of new and more advanced elements, from both east and west; and this continuing process has through the years built upon the aboriginal foundation the complicated structure and hierarchy of Indian society. Many of these arrivals constituted new groups within the total body, all more or less self-contained, and many incapsulating features of the culture they had brought with them, together with much that they absorbed from their surroundings. Thus, throughout her prehistory and history, India has presented an increasingly rich and varied fabric, woven of many strands.

Of the frontier provinces Baluchistan is, historically at least, the most important. Through it wave after wave of immigrants and merchants have passed travelling both to and from India proper. Baluchistan may be regarded as essentially a part of the Iranian plateau. Her valleys provided homes for the earliest Neolithic settlers so far known in any part of India or Pakistan, and from the first half of the fourth millennium, if not earlier, there is evidence of an enduring pattern of villages in an arid landscape, their size and growth limited by water supplies and the quantity of land fit for cultivation. The domestic animals and crops seem to have changed little since their introduction in the fourth millennium. Probably the severe restrictions of the environment were responsible for the absence of any development of city life here. The archaeological record shows that throughout her history Baluchistan has remained culturally speaking an Iranian border region, as closely connected with the territories which lie to the north and west as with the east. It is not then surprising that the modern population still speaks Baluchi, a language of the Iranian branch of the Indo-Iranian family. Nevertheless, from the earliest settlements of which we have evidence domestic cattle appear to have been of the humped zebu variety, and this suggests that elements of the culture were of Indian rather than Iranian origin. The impression is strengthened by the appearance in the third millennium of such distinctly Indian motifs as the *pīpal* leaf among the predominantly abstract repertoire of Baluchi painted pottery designs.

Somewhat different is the pattern in the North West Frontier region, where the valleys penetrating deep into the northern mountain mass offer more attractive, and generally more sheltered and secure territories. These valleys seem to have been settled by invading tribes during the second millennium, and since that time they have served as largely refuge areas, in which Dardic languages have survived, preserving many very early Indo-Iranian forms. They served as routes to China and Central Asia, and hence they were to some extent resettled during the Early Historic period by peoples moving up from the plains and bringing with them more specifically Indian culture traits. Thus, although they are archaeologically more or less blank during the Neolithic–Chalcolithic period, their subsequent cultural history is distinct from that of Baluchistan.

As soon as one leaves the valleys of Baluchistan and the North West Frontier, one enters one of the major cultural regions of the Indian subcontinent. The Indus plains, as we have seen, were the home of the earliest Indian civilization; and the name of the river Indus (*Sindhu*) has been extended to the subcontinent as a whole (India) and to the predominant religion of its peoples (Hinduism). The proximity of the outlying provinces of Iranian culture on the one hand and probable presence of as yet almost unknown settlements of a distinctive Indian character to the east, provide two sources for this civilization. Its more immediate ancestors are clearly the towns and villages now coming to light beneath the Harappan culture proper on the Indus plains. On present showing the earliest settlements in this region are in the south, around Amri. These probably date back to the very opening of the third millennium, if not to the close of the fourth. Farther north, in the vicinity of Mohenjo-daro and Kot Diji, they appear to begin some five centuries later, *c.* 2600 B.C.; and farther east, at Kalibangan, the earliest dates so far recorded are some two centuries later still. Radiocarbon dates show with surprising regularity that this phase came to an end around 2100 B.C. when the full-fledged Harappan civilization burst into being. The further investigation of this formative stage, which leads us from the village to the first Indian cities, and which evidently spans somewhat more than five centuries, is an exciting prospect. If, as we are inclined to believe, the Mesopotamian contacts with Meluhha, reported in the time of Sargon of Agade (2371–2316 B.C.), were indeed with the Indus region, then they may well have complemented the internal developments already taking place there. Radiocarbon dates now suggest that the Indus civilization itself flourished for little more than three and a half centuries, until around 1750 B.C., and this period too corresponds remarkably with the principal body of Mesopotamian textual references to trade with Meluhha.

The extent of our knowledge of the Indus civilization is limited, because although a number of excavations have been carried out the range of objects which have survived is considerably more restricted than in either Egypt or Mesopotamia; there is a total absence of pictorial representations of the life of the people, and such short inscriptions as survive, mainly on seals, are still unread. Technically however the Harappan civilization was not backward. As Gordon Childe so rightly pointed out, India produced a 'thoroughly individual and independent civilization of her own, technically the peer of the rest', although resting upon the same fundamental ideas, discoveries and inventions as those of Egypt and Mesopotamia. We are now in a position to add to his statement that the extent and uniformity in terms of town-planning, crafts and industries, of the Harappan culture, far exceeded either. The most important single discovery must have been the exploitation of the Indus flood-plains for agriculture, offering a vast potential production of wheat and barley. Many pieces of equipment, such as the bullock carts, provided prototypes for subsequent generations of Indian craftsmen, to spread through the whole subcontinent and survive into the twentieth century.

The second quarter of the second millennium B.C. witnessed a series of intrusions of peoples from the west: Mohenjo-daro was abandoned, perhaps as a result of natural calamity, but sites in Sind and in the country immediately to the east, in South Rajputana and Saurashtra, testify to no profound break in the record of settled life. In the Punjab at Harappa too, the Cemetery H culture shows evidence of a remarkable fusion of Harappan traits and new traits of Iranian origin. There were, it seems, two separate lines of advance, one passing to the north of the Rajasthan desert and the other to the south. In the south there are suggestions of several distinct waves. The earliest may be associated with the intrusive objects found even during the Harappan period; a second, less clearly defined, with the post-Harappan Jhukar phase in Sind, Rangpur IIB in Saurashtra, and the settlements of the Banas culture at such sites as Ahar in Rajputana. A third wave witnessed a much deeper thrust between *c.* 1300 and 1000 B.C., penetrating deep into the interior of the peninsula and bringing foreign bronze types and eventually iron. To the north there are also several waves, different, but perhaps not entirely unrelated. The first seems to have produced the Cemetery H culture and lasted until *c.* 1500 B.C. A second wave may be detected in the eastern expansion of the culture associated with the copper hoards and the Ochre coloured pottery, probably lasting from around 1500 to 1100 B.C.; and a third, also more clearly defined and powerful, culminating in the arrival of the 'Painted Grey ware' and of iron. There can be little doubt that all these waves originated from the direction of Iran, and that all were of Indo-Iranian speaking peoples.

As new discoveries are made it should become increasingly possible to relate our evidence to that of literature and tradition. A prime question must be to identify the cultural remains of the authors of the Rigveda. As we have seen the Rigveda belongs without question to the northern area, and is undoubtedly a compound work accumulated over several centuries. But it is most unlikely that anything in it reflects directly the earliest, or Cemetery H, phase. More probably some of its earliest parts may be associated with the second or third waves. The interesting thesis advanced by Hoernle and Grierson, of an earlier 'outer band' of Indo-Iranian languages, and a later arrival – the language of the 'Midland' – may supply a clue, since the latter language appears to be the direct descendant of that of the Rigveda. Thus the Vedic Aryans should be associated with a later wave, most probably with the third 'Painted Grey ware' thrust into the Punjab. As we shall see below, the earlier waves may then be associated with the ancestors of dialects of the 'outer band' languages to the east, notably with Bengali. We may expect a somewhat similar situation to the south of the Rajasthan desert. There the Banas culture would appear to represent a nucleus of speakers of one of the 'outer band' dialects, who in their turn expanded to the north-east, towards the Doab; the east into Malwa and Central India; and the south-east into the Deccan. But in any case, both in the north and in the south, the distinction between the several waves is not clearly defined, and there must have been considerable overlapping between provinces.

The developments of these centuries in both areas are of profound significance for subsequent Indian civilization, because only by discovering just what traits survived from the indigenous cultures, or were accepted from the new arrivals, can we understand how they both contributed to the subsequent united culture. But one thing cannot be denied, that there is sufficient evidence of survivals from the Harappan civilization at all levels to warrant our regarding it as a major source.

Beyond the natural frontiers of the Indus system one enters regions which have – in most general terms – an internal uniformity of their own. This uniformity coincides with a comparative absence of western, Iranian components in the culture sequence, and also a preponderance of indigenous, Indian traits. In some ways the whole of this great area appears to have been somewhat conservative, and the southern part in particular is characterized by an innate conservatism in material culture. This is already evident in the Late Stone Age, when the southern peninsula shows a remarkable series of evolved Middle Stone Age elements in contrast to the more advanced industries of western and central India. As it appears in 1967 the earliest settled communities in the Indian peninsula cannot be dated to before 2300 B.C., but it seems likely that further research may necessitate considerable revision of this date.

What is striking about the culture of the Neolithic–Chalcolithic sites of the Deccan is their apparently independent ancestry. Although they share many traits with the Baluchi and Indus cultures, they also have features which at present must be seen as purely Indian. There is an extraordinary continuity linking even the earliest settlements with the whole subsequent pattern of life. It is still not possible to decide whether this culture arose without external stimuli. If outside influences played a part, we still do not know whether they came from the west, as affinities with the far earlier Neolithic cultures of the Middle East and the subsequent grey ware cultures of Iran make most plausible; or from the north, as the central Asiatic and even Chinese elements at Burzahom might indicate; or even – though least probably – from the east. Indeed all these may have made their contributions, but the indications are that there was a strongly indigenous flavour from the start. It has been suggested that the Indian humped cattle were first domesticated in the peninsula, and certainly they had already achieved a dominant economic position in the earliest settlements of the Deccan. A range of food grains was cultivated, some of them almost certainly native to the region. It is interesting to note that local variations in grain utilization at the present day are already reflected during the Neolithic–Chalcolithic period. The house patterns of the earliest settlements, and the general layout of villages can also be found as living elements in the countryside today. Of special importance will be the investigation of the relationship of these cultures to the still almost hypothetical indigenous element which contributes to the pre-Harappan culture of Kalibangan and the Indus valley. The extreme conservatism of the material culture continues to exert itself through long periods: thus the appearance of iron, which in the north is inferred to have coincided with the introduction of western tool types, such as the shaft-hole axe, in the peninsula witnessed the adaptation of a flat rectangular axe of a type already current in copper and bronze in the Harappan and post-Harappan periods. This type survived in the south until the opening of the Christian era.

The southern part of the peninsula is today the homeland of the Dravidian languages, and we may well inquire what – speaking in broadest terms – is likely to have been their history. It has sometimes been claimed, though on no very solid grounds, that the earliest speakers of these languages brought with them into peninsular India both iron and the custom of making megalithic graves. In the light of archaeological evidence this appears to be extremely improbable. There seems to be every reason to associate the primary introduction of iron, though not necessarily its secondary diffusion throughout south India, with the later waves of Indo-Iranian speaking invaders around 1000 B.C. Moreover, the megalithic burial customs developed only after that date. We now know that for at least a millennium prior to the arrival of iron there were established settlements in Karnataka, and probably also in other parts of the peninsula, and these settlements show evidence of a remarkable continuity of culture. Many modern culture traits appear to derive from them, and a substantial part of the population shows physical affinities to the Neolithic people. In the light of all this it is difficult to believe that the Dravidian languages do not owe their origin to the same people who produced the Neolithic cultures there. This view was advanced by one of us in 1960, and discoveries since that time have all tended to reinforce it.

The position in the north-western part of the peninsula, in Maharashtra, is rather different. Archaeologically an important new series of traits appears here during the second millennium B.C., having its affinities with western India, and characterized by the Jorwe culture. These traits may well be associated with the infiltration into the region of Indo-Iranian speaking peoples probably belonging to the earlier 'outer band' group, and speaking the ancestor of modern Marathi. It has been suggested that the place-names of Maharashtra show a substratum of Dravidian elements, and these we may expect to relate to an earlier culture phase, such as that represented by the Malwa ware or an as yet little known pre-Malwa Neolithic phase, akin to that of the south.

Evidence that is now coming to light shows that iron working probably entered India around 1000 B.C., and that it diffused rapidly in both north and south. There is some reason to associate this diffusion with horses, and it is probable that the initial process, though not its secondary parts, may have been closely associated with one of the later waves of Indo-Iranian speaking peoples. However, it seems clear that the continuing progress of the diffusion may have been largely in indigenous hands. Be this as it may the south, and particularly the eastern coastal plains, formed the setting for one of the most important centres of later Indian civilization, that of the Tamilnad.

To the north and east of these regions lies the central belt of hills and forests, still to this day relatively sparsely populated. Here tribal peoples, preserving a hunting and gathering economy, lingered on into the present century. Neolithic–Chalcolithic settlements, some dating back to the beginning of the second millennium, are relatively few and appear as islands in a sea of unsettled forests. This whole central region has formed a target for small scale colonization from very early times, and in Historic times, favourable areas have been settled by means of land gifts to groups of Brahmans, etc. Otherwise, it forms a nucleus around which the more important centres of civilization lie, and the cities and towns which grew up there at such places as Eran, or Tripuri, were probably staging points upon the caravan routes which linked the outer regions.

In the preceding pages we have been looking at India mainly from a western point of view. It is also possible to view it from the east. The eastern border regions, represented by the hills of Assam and Bengal, show many profound influences from Burma and south China, and it is not surprising that the Neolithic culture known from surface collections of stone implements and from the solitary excavation of Daojali Hading should reflect cultural traits deriving from the same direction. These traits are also to be found, though mixed with those of India, in the surface collections of Neolithic tools from the eastern parts of the central region. It is noteworthy that their distribution in India is approximately limited to the areas in which Tibeto-Burman or Munda languages are spoken. Perhaps partly because of the difficulties of communication through the thickly forested mountains of Burma and south China, and partly because of other factors, these eastern influences do not seem to have played nearly so important a role as do the western in the making up of Indian civilization. In this context one may note that Indian contacts with China, when they developed in the first millennium A.D., did so primarily via the western routes across Afghanistan and Central Asia.

Our survey leaves only one major region for consideration, the Ganges valley, stretching from the frontiers of the Punjab and Rajasthan in the west to the deltas of the Ganges and the Brahmaputra in the east. This region may rightly claim to be the principal seat of classical Indian civilization and therefore it is of peculiar interest to discover what archaeology can tell us of the stages of its development. Perhaps because of their largely alluvial character the Ganges plains offer little evidence of human occupation during the Stone Age. The beginnings of settlement there are still largely hypothetical. If for example there is a relationship between the first Neolithic cultures of the Karnataka region and Kashmir, then it may be expected that generically related cultures may also be found in the intervening areas, including the eastern Punjab and Rajasthan. The

Sothi culture may well prove to be such an entity, and could be responsible for the distinctive character of the pre-Harappan culture of Kalibangan. There is more concrete, though still very slight, evidence that during the Harappan period the area of influence or control of that civilization extended eastwards into the Ganges–Jamuna Doab, to such sites as Alamgirpur; and there is also beginning to emerge evidence – though still shadowy – of a post-Harappan sequence in the same area.

It is against this background that we must see the arrival in India of Indo-Iranian speakers, and the Aryans. From the time of Cemetery H at Harappa to the end of the second millennium there are signs of intrusive elements in many parts of the subcontinent, but the geography of the Rigveda concentrates our focus upon the Punjab and territories to the east. If, as we have supposed, the Rigveda is to be associated with one of the later waves of Indo-Iranian speaking invaders, then the earlier waves of 'outer band' speakers, already settled in the Punjab and Doab, far from vanishing into the jungles, as Herzfeld suggested, must have been at least in part displaced by their arrival, and would have moved off eastwards. This movement is no doubt represented by the black-and-red ware now coming to light in the Doab and in the Middle Ganges, and there can be no reason to doubt that it was responsible for the arrival in the lower Ganges valley of the ancestors of the Magadhi–Bengali languages of more recent times.

With the introduction of iron we find an increasing number of settlements in the Doab and these may be fairly certainly associated with the later Vedic literature, from the *Atharva Veda* to the *Brāhmanas*. Before the end of the first quarter of the first millennium there is a further eastward shift into the Central Ganges valley, between Allahabad and Patna, and this too is reflected in the later *Brāhmanas* and first *Upaniṣads*. By the time of the Buddha this central region was emerging as a focus of Indian civilization. The further eastward expansion into the deltaic region doubtless followed as a continuing process, although the earliest evidence of occupation as yet available from such sites as Mahasthan probably dates to the second half of the millennium. Only on the south-western extremities of the delta are there indications at Pandu Rajar Dhibi, Mahisadal and Tamluk of settlements predating the arrival of iron. It is interesting to note that rice seems to have played an important part in this growth of population and expansion during the first half of the millennium and the wide alluvial plains of the Ganges offered a most favourable environment for its cultivation.

While the present evidence suggests that city life was more or less extinguished with the downfall of the Harappan state, it is becoming increasingly clear that a great deal survived, both in Sind and western India, and in the Punjab and the Doab. The hitherto unprovable speculations regarding the presence of Harappan elements in later Indian civilization may shortly be amenable to testing against the growing body of archaeological data. The text-based assessment of early Indian history has necessarily severe limitations, both because of its want of absolute chronology, and because of the restricted area to which any text may truthfully be said to have applied. As archaeological research advances it seems probable that the texts will begin to acquire a quite new significance, and when read in conjunction with the archaeological record will be able to be used with far greater confidence than hitherto. Thus a new and exciting branch of early Indian history is being born.

It is already clear that during the first half of the first millennium B.C. cities began to develop in the Ganges Doab, and in parts of western Central India. Doubtless cities also developed in the Punjab and North-West Frontier region during the period of Achaemenid influence there. The outward mark of these cities is their great defensive ditches and ramparts, often enclosing very considerable areas. The social context in which they arose must have included an expansion of the population, and the spread of settlements which coincided with a period of internecine strife between the growing states of north India. The economic implications of this are reflected in the regulation of weights and measures, and the development of regular means of exchange, leading by the middle of the first millennium B.C. to systems of punch-marked silver coinage. The intellectual expression of this process includes the growing body of late Vedic literature with its advancing speculations upon the sacrifice, eschatology and creation, and culminating in the *Upaniṣads*; the ancillary Vedic studies (*Vedāngas*), including grammar, phonetics, etymology and astronomy; and, at an as yet completely hypothetical date before the third century B.C., the invention of the *Brāhmī* script with all that it entailed.

With the rise of city life in the Ganges valley, a new pattern developed in the subcontinent: the cultural dominance of the Ganges region – the Hindustan of later centuries – exerted itself over all the other regions. A somewhat similar dominance had been exerted by the civilization of the Indus valley a thousand years earlier; but the new Gangetic influence was longer lived and much more widely felt. Doubtless its progress was facilitated by the growing dominance of Sanskrit as an interregional culture language, and of Brahmanical rites as an all-Indian cultural ideal. The subsequent centuries must have witnessed the welding together of the subcontinent into the cultural unity it has retained ever since: a unity with multifarious regional diversity.

From many points of view India has changed little from the time of the *Upaniṣads* onwards. And yet from others she has never ceased to change and to develop. The profound effects of belief in transmigration, and in *Karma* (actions) in directing the course a soul will take after death, beliefs which were already firmly established before 500 B.C., and the equally profound effects of the Indian caste system, have become so deeply ingrained into the Indian outlook that their influence may be seen in almost every aspect of society, even among Muslims and Christians. At the same time the innate conservatism, in material culture, of which we have seen many examples, became a dominant factor. For instance, the potter's foot-wheel may be inferred to have been in use in the Indus valley at least since Harappan times; but throughout the remaining parts of the subcontinent its place has been taken by the less efficient Indian spun-wheel, and by a variety of beating and moulding techniques. In region after region the settlement pattern and house types have continued through the centuries with little change; and agricultural and industrial techniques with little alteration. This leads us to conclude that the way of life which developed in the Indus valley during the Harappan period, and which was subsequently modified and extended during the Iron Age to almost all parts of the subcontinent, and particularly flourished in the alluvial rice-growing plains, to become the source of the common elements in the culture of the different regions, must have been peculiarly well suited to the environment, that it could have demanded so little modification over so long a period, and yet have supported so vast a population: its very success sowing through the centuries the seeds of modern dilemmas.

SELECT LIST OF RADIOCARBON DATES
FOR INDIA AND PAKISTAN

This select list contains primarily dates obtained from samples from India and Pakistan, of more than 2,450 years before present. The series from Mundigak in Afghanistan are also included, although they appear rather erratic. Certain dates from series, or for separate sites, which appear to be wildly aberrant are excluded. Sites are arranged in alphabetical order, and runs are given in ascending order of age. Exceptions to this rule are Ahar, where two series, from different laboratories, are quoted separately, because of their wide divergencies; and Kalibangan where the pre-Harappan and Harappan series are listed separately. In the case of Ahar we have followed in the text the Tata laboratory dates, as these appear more reliable. Dates marked with an asterisk * are quoted from G. Dales, 'Suggested chronology for Afghanistan, Baluchistan and the Indus valley' (*Chronologies in Old World Archaeology, 1966*), being old solid carbon samples increased by a factor of 200-years for the Suess effect. The sample from Pandu Rajar Dhibi does not appear to have been published so far, and is extrapolated from P. C. Dasgupta's *Excavations at Pandu Rajar Dhibi* (1964). The list gives the following data: index number of sample; cultural information, such as period or relevant detail; date before present according to the half-life of radiocarbon of 5568±30 years; date (in brackets) according to the half-life of radiocarbon of 5730±40 years. The B.C. dates used in the text are obtained by subtracting 1950 years from the 'before present' date of the latter. For the cultural information we have followed wherever possible the period names or numbers used by the excavator, but in a few cases we have tried to clarify conflicting statements in different reports, or interpolated information when not expressly given. The laboratories from which the samples are derived include: BM, British Museum, London; GSY, Gif-sur-Yvette, France; P, University of Pennsylvania, U.S.A.; R, Rome, Italy; TF, Tata Institute of Fundamental Research, Bombay, India; UW, University of Washington, Seattle, U.S.A.; UCLA, University of California, Los Angeles, U.S.A.; V, University of Victoria, Australia.

Adamgarh, Madhya Pradesh

TF-120   Late Stone Age (microlithic)   7240±125 (7450±130)

Ahar, Rajasthan

TF-31	Chalcolithic	3130±105	(3223±108)
TF-37	Chalcolithic	3165±110	(3260±113)
TF-32	Chalcolithic	3400±105	(3502±108)
TF-34	Chalcolithic	3570±135	(3677±140)
V-56	Chalcolithic	3715±95	(3826±98)
V-55	Chalcolithic	3825±120	(3940±124)
V-54	Chalcolithic	3835±95	(3960±98)
V-58	Chalcolithic	3890±100	(4007±104)
V-57	Chalcolithic	3975±95	(4094±98)

Atranjikhera, Uttar Pradesh

TF-291	II Painted grey ware period	2415±100	(2487±103)
TF-289	IB Black-and-red ware period	2550±105	(2626±108)
TF-191	II Painted grey ware period	2890±105	(2975±110)

Barama I, Swat

R-195	Grave	2320±45	(2390±46)
R-196	Grave	2585±80	(2662±83)

Burzahom, Kashmir

TF-10	Neolithic	2580±100	(2657±103)
TF-15	Neolithic	3390±105	(3492±108)
TF-129	Neolithic	3670±90	(3775±100)
TF-13	Neolithic	3690±125	(3800±128)
TF-14	Neolithic	3860±340	(3975±350)
TF-127	Neolithic	3935±110	(4050±115)
TF-123	Neolithic	4055±110	(4175±115)
TF-128	Neolithic	4205±115	(4325±120)

Butkara, Swat

R-194   Grave   2425±40   (2498±41)

Chandoli, Maharashtra

TF-43	Chalcolithic	2905±100	(2992±103)
TF-42	Chalcolithic	3035±115	(3126±118)
P-474	Chalcolithic	3099±185	(3192±200)
P-472	Chalcolithic	3157±68	(3251±70)
P-473	Chalcolithic	3184±68	(3280±70)

Chirand, Bihar

TF-336	Black-and-red ware period	2640±95	(2719±98)
TF-334	Black-and-red ware period	2715±120	(2796±123)

Damb Sadaat, Baluchistan

P–523	Period II	4029±74 (4150±76)
UW–60	Period III	4030±160 (4151±165)
UW–59	Period I	4330±70 (4460±73)
L–180B	Period I	4348±350 (4478±361)*
L–180C	Period II	4375±412*
L–180E	Period II	4375±361*
P–522	Period II	4378±196 (4505±202)

Eran, Central India

P–527	Chalcolithic	2515±58 (2590±60)
P–528	Chalcolithic	2878±65 (2964±67)
TF–326	Period IIA	2905±105 (2990±110)
TF–324	Period IIA	3130±105 (3220±110)
P–526	Chalcolithic	3136±68 (3230±70)
P–525	Period II	3193±69 (3289±71)
TF–330	Period I	3220±100 (3315±105)
TF–327	Period I	3280±100 (3375±105)
TF–329	Period I	3300±105 (3395±110)
TF–331	Period I	3355±90 (3450±95)
P–529	Chalcolithic	3869±72 (4023±74)

Hallur, Mysore

TF–573	Early Iron Age, layer 5	2820±100 (2905±103)
TF–575	Chalcolithic, layer 7	2895±100 (2980±103)
TF–570	Early Iron Age, layer 4	2970±105 (3055±108)
TF–580	Neolithic, layer 14	3560±105 (3660±105)

Hastinapur, Uttar Pradesh

| TF–85 | Period II | 2385+125 (2456±129) |
| TF–91 | Period II | 2450±120 (2523±123) |

Kalibangan, Rajasthan

TF–138	Harappan culture	3075±100 (3167±103)
TF–244	Harappan culture	3250±90 (3347±93)
TF–143	Harappan culture	3510±110 (3615±113)
TF–152	Harappan culture	3615±85 (3723±88)
TF–142	Harappan culture	3635±100 (3744±103)
TF–149	Harappan culture	3675±140 (3785±145)
TF–141	Harappan culture	3705±110 (3816±113)
TF–150	Harappan culture	3740±100 (3850±105)
TF–139	Harappan culture	3775±100 (3880±105)
TF–151	Harappan culture	3800±100 (3910±103)
TF–147	Harappan culture	3865±100 (3980±105)
P–481	Harappan culture	3879±72 (3993±74)
TF–145	Harappan culture	3895±100 (4010±105)

TF-153	Harappan culture	3910±110 (4027±115)
TF-163	Harappan culture	3910±100 (4027±103)
TF-25	Harappan culture	3930±110 (4047±103)
TF-160	Harappan culture	4060±100 (4186±103)
TF-240	Pre-Harappan period	3610±110 (3718±113)
TF-154	Pre-Harappan period	3665±110 (3775±113)
TF-156	Pre-Harappan period	3740±105 (3852±108)
TF-165	Pre-Harappan period	3800±100 (3914±103)
TF-161	Pre-Harappan period	3930±100 (4048±103)
TF-162	Pre-Harappan period	3940±100 (4058±103)
TF-241	Pre-Harappan period	4090±90 (4213±93)
TF-157	Pre-Harappan period	4120±100 (4233±103)
TF-155	Pre-Harappan period	4195±115 (4321±118)

Kausambi, Uttar Pradesh

| TF-225 | Period III (NBP) | 2285±105 (2350±110) |
| TF-221 | Period III (NBP) | 2385±100 (2450±105) |

Kayatha, Madhya Pradesh

TF-674	Early Historic period IV	2350±95 (2420±100)
TF-402	Chalcolithic period III	3240±100 (3330±100)
TF-397	Chalcolithic period III	3350±100 (3450±100)
TF-398	Chalcolithic period III	3520±100 (3625±100)
TF-399	Chalcolithic period II	3525±100 (3625±100)
TF-396	Chalcolithic period III	3575±105 (3680±110)
TF-400	Chalcolithic period II	3800±105 (3915±110)
TF-680	Chalcolithic period I	3850±95 (3965±110)

Kili Ghul Mohammad, Baluchistan

UW-61	Period I	5260±80 (5418±83)
P-524	Period I	5474±83 (5638±85)
L-180A	Period I	5497±500 (5662±515)*

Kot Diji, Sind

P-195	Pre-Harappan, late period	3925±134 (4040±138)
P-180	Pre-Harappan, late period	4083±137 (4205±140)
P-179	Pre-Harappan, late period	4161±151 (4285±156)
P-196	Pre-Harappan, early period	4421±141 (4555±145)

Lekhania, Uttar Pradesh

| TF-417 | Burial in rock shelter | 3560±105 (3660±110) |

Lothal, Gujarat

TF-135	Harappan, period IIA	3405±125 (3505±130)
TF-19	Harappan, period II, VA	3650±135 (3759±140)
TF-23	Harappan, period II, VA	3705±105 (3816±108)
TF-133	Harappan, period IIA	3740±110 (3845±113)
TF-29	Harappan, period I, IVA	3740±110 (3845±113)

TF–26	Harappan, period I, IIIB	3830±120	(3944±123)
TF–27	Harappan, period I, IIIB	3840±110	(3955±113)
TF–22	Harappan, period I, IIIB	3845±110	(3960±113)
TF–136	Harappan, period IA	3915±130	(4030±135)

Mahisadal, West Bengal

TF–389	II, Early Iron Age	2565±105	(2640±105)
TF–390	I, Chalcolithic	2725±100	(2805±100)
TF–392	I, Chalcolithic	2950±105	(3035±110)
TF–391	I, Chalcolithic	3235±105	(3330±105)

Mohenjo-daro, Sind

TF–75	Harappan, late level	3600±110	(3710±115)
P–1182A	Mature Harappan	3702±63	(3814±64)
P–1176	Mature Harappan	3801±59	(3916±60)
P–1178A	Mature Harappan	3802±59	(3917±60)
P–1180	Mature Harappan	3828±61	(3943±61)
P–1177	Mature Harappan	3895±64	(4012±66)
P–1179	Mature Harappan	3913±64	(4033±66)

Mundigak, Afghanistan

GSY–51	Period III,1	2995±110	(3085±113)
GSY–52	Period II,1	3480±115	(3584±118)
GSY–50	Period I,5	3945±150	(4063±155)
GSY–53	Period III,5	4185±150	(4310±155)

Navdatoli, Narbada Valley

P–205	Chalcolithic, phase IIID	3294±125	(3393±128)
TF–59	Chalcolithic, phase IIIA	3380±105	(3481±108)
P–204	Chalcolithic, phase IIIC	3449±127	(3552±130)
P–475	Chalcolithic, phase IIIA	3455±70	(3559±73)
P–200	Chalcolithic, phase IIIA	3457+127	(3560±130)
P–201	Chalcolithic, phase IIIA	3492±128	(3607±131)
P–202	Chalcolithic, phase IIIB	3503±128	(3608+131)
P–476	Chalcolithic, phase IIIB	4125±69	(4249±72)

Nevasa, Maharashtra

| P–181 | Chalcolithic, Jorwe phase | 3106±122 | (3199±125) |
| F–40 | Chalcolithic, Jorwe phase | 3110±110 | (3203±113) |

Niai Buthi, Baluchistan

| P–478 | Kulli associations | 3740±64 | (3850±65) |

Noh, Rajasthan

| UCLA–703A | Painted grey ware series | 2480±250 | (2554±258) |
| UCLA–703B | Painted grey ware series | 2690±220 | (2771±226) |

Paiyampalli, Madras

| TF–350 | Iron Age | 2265±100 (2330±105) |
| TF–349 | Neolithic | 3340±100 (3435±100) |

Pandu Rajar Dhibi, West Bengal

Period II (Chalcolithic)   1012±120†

Rojdi, Saurashtra

| TF–199 | Harappan, IB | 3590±100 (3695±105) |
| TF–200 | Harappan, IB | 3810±110 (3920±115) |

Rupar, Punjab

TF–209   Period III, NBP   2365±100 (2435±100)

Sanganakallu, Mysore

| TF–359 | Neolithic | 3400±100 (3500±105) |
| TF–354 | Neolithic | 3440±105 (3540±110) |

Sonegaon, Maharashtra

| TF–379 | Chalcolithic, Jorwe phase | 3150±90 (3240±95) |
| TF–380 | Chalcolithic, Jorwe phase | 3230±105 (3325±110) |

Sonpur, Bihar

TF–376   Pre-NBP period   2510±105 (2587±108)

T. Narsipur, Mysore

| TF–413 | Neolithic | 3345±105 (3445±110) |
| TF–412 | Neolithic | 3645±105 (3755±110) |

Tekkalakota, Mysore

TF–277	Ash pit (Iron Age)	2220±105 (2285±110)
TF–236	Neolithic, period I	3395±105 (3490±105)
TF–237	Neolithic, period I	3465±105 (3565±105)
TF–262	Neolithic, period II	3460±135 (3560±140)
TF–266	Neolithic, period I	3625±100 (3730±105)

Utnur, Andhra Pradesh

TF–168	Neolithic, period IIIA	3875±110 (3990±110)
TF–167	Neolithic, period IIA	3890±110 (4000±115)
BM–54	Neolithic, period IB	4120±150 (4245±155)

† University of Yadavpur; this date is given 'before Christ'.

SELECT BIBLIOGRAPHY

Banerjee, N. R., *The Iron Age in India*, Munshiram Manoharlal, Delhi, 1965.

Basham, A. L., *The Wonder That Was India*, Sidgwick & Jackson, 3rd ed. 1967

Ghosh, A., (ed.) *Archaeological Remains, Monuments and Museums*, Archaeological Survey of India, 2 vols. New Delhi, 1964.

Gordon, D. H., *The Prehistoric Background of Indian Culture*, Madhuri Dhirajlal Desai, Bombay, 1958.

Kosambi, D. D., *An Introduction to the Study of Indian History*, Popular Book Depot, Bombay, 1956.

The Culture and Civilization of Ancient India in Historical Outline, Routledge Kegan Paul, 1965.

Lal, B. B., *Indian Archaeology Since Independence*, Motilal Banarsidass, Delhi, 1964.

Masson, V. M., *Srednyaya Aziya i Drevnii Vostok*, Akademiya Nauk SSSR, Institut Arkheologii Leningradskoe Otdelenie, Moscow, 1964.

Misra, V. N. and Mate, M. S., *Indian Prehistory: 1964*, Deccan College Building Centenary and Silver Jubilee Series, No. 32, Deccan College, Poona, 1965.

Piggott, S., *Prehistoric India*, Penguin Books, 1950.

Roy, S., *The Story of Indian Archaeology (1784–1947)*, Archaeological Survey of India, New Delhi, 1961.

Sankalia, H. D., *Indian Archaeology Today*, Heras Memorial Lectures, 1960, Asia Publishing House, Bombay, 1962.

Prehistory and Protohistory in India and Pakistan, University of Bombay, 1963.

Subbarao, B., *The Personality of India*, M. S. University Archaeological Series, No. 3, 2nd edn, University of Baroda, 1958.

Wheeler, Sir R. E. M., *Early India and Pakistan* (Ancient Peoples and Places), Thames & Hudson, 1959.

The Indus Civilization, supplementary volume to the *Cambridge History of India*, 3rd edn, Cambridge University Press, 1968.

Civilizations of the Indus Valley and Beyond, Thames & Hudson, 1966.

REFERENCES

CHAPTER I

1. History of Archaeological Research in India

The fullest account of the subject is in Sourindranath Roy, *The Story of Indian Archaeology (1784–1947)*, New Delhi, 1961. See also S. Roy, 'Indian archaeology from Jones to Marshall (1784–1902)', and A. Ghosh, 'Fifty years of the Archaeological Survey of India', both in *Ancient India*, 9, 1953; J. Cumming, *Revealing India's Past*, London, 1939; F. R. Allchin, 'Ideas of history in Indian archaeological writing', *Historians of India, Pakistan and Ceylon*, ed. C. H. Philips, London, 1961.

CHAPTER 2

1. General

The introductory volume of the *Imperial Gazetteer of India*, vol. 1, 1908, contains excellent, if now somewhat out-of-date, discussions of the geography, geology, meteorology, botany, ethnology, languages and population of the subcontinent. For general archaeological bibliography the *Annual Bibliography of Indian Archaeology*, vols. 1–20, published by the Kern Institute, Leiden, is most valuable.

2. Geographical

O. H. K. Spate, *India and Pakistan – a regional geography*, 2nd edn, Methuen, 1957, provides a mass of information; L. Dudley Stamp's *Asia, a Regional and Economic Geography*, 11th edn, London, 1962, gives a shorter, less detailed account. For the more narrowly archaeological aspects of geography, see F. J. Richards, 'Geographical factors in Indian archaeology', *Indian Antiquary*, 62, 1933; and B. Subbarao, *The Personality of India*, 2nd edn, Baroda, 1958. See also K. M. Panikkar's *Geographical Factors in Indian History*, Bombay, 1955.

3. Physical and cultural anthropology

The late Professor D. N. Majumdar's *Races and Cultures of India*, 4th edn, London, 1961, gives a useful survey of the physical and cultural anthropology of India, together with an excellent bibliography. B. S. Guha contributed a study of the physical anthropology to the *Census of India, 1931 Report*, vol. 1, part 3, 1953. For ancient skeletal materials, see S. S. Sarkar, *Ancient Races of Baluchistan, Punjab and Sind*, Calcutta, 1964. See also the same author's *Aboriginal Races of India*, Calcutta, 1954. For a recent survey of methods and problems in India, see D. K. Sen, 'Ancient races of India and Pakistan', *Ancient India* 20–21, pp. 178–205. For other references, see under separate chapter headings. For cultural anthropology there are many monographs dealing with specific tribes and communities. For example, see C. G. Seligman, *The Veddas of Ceylon*, Cambridge University Press, 1911; W. H. R. Rivers, *The Todas*, London, 1906; C. von Fürer-Haimendorf, *The Chenchus*, Macmillan, 1943, and *The Raj-Gonds of Adilabad*, Macmillan, 1948; V. Elwin, *The Baiga*, London, 1939, etc. For anthropological studies of Indian village communities, etc., see J. H. Hutton, *Caste in India*, Cambridge University Press, 1946; G. M. Carstairs, *The Twice-Born*, Hogarth Press, 1957; S. C. Dube, *Indian Village*, Routledge, 1955, and many others. A veritable mine of references to all kinds of anthropological and prehistoric writing is to be found in E. von Fürer-Haimendorf's monumental *Anthropological Bibliography of South Asia*, vols 1 and 2, The Hague, 1958, 1964.

CHAPTERS 3 AND 4

1. *General*

The following general accounts of the Indian Stone Age each provide a summary from a different viewpoint, and at a different point in time:

Krishnaswami, V. D., 'Stone Age India', *Ancient India*, 3, 1947.

Subbarao, B., *The Personality of India*, 2nd edn, Baroda, 1958.

Allchin, B., 'The Indian Stone Age Sequence', *Journal of the Royal Anthropological Institute*, vol. 93, part 2, 1963.

Sankalia, H. D., *Prehistory and Protohistory in India and Pakistan* (with further extensive bibliography), Bombay, 1962.

2. *Pleistocene chronology*

A general discussion of problems of Indian Pleistocene chronology and dating will be found together with other papers on prehistory in *Indian Prehistory: 1964*, ed. V. N. Misra and M. S.

Mate, Deccan College Building Centenary and Silver Jubilee Series, No. 2, Poona, 1965.

3. *Regional studies*

Much of the writing on the Indian Stone Age has been in the form of regional studies covering more than one cultural phase. A number of the more important papers are listed below. The list is far from exhaustive, but the majority contain further bibliographies.

PUNJAB: Graziosi, P., *Prehistoric Research in Northwestern Punjab* (Italian Expeditions to the Karakorum (K2) and Hindu Kush, V – Prehistory – Anthropology, vol. 1), Leiden, 1964.

de Terra, H. and Paterson, T. T., *Studies on the Ice Age in India and Associated Human Cultures*, Washington, 1939.

RAJPUTANA: Misra, V. N., 'Palaeolithic Culture of Western Rajputana', *Bulletin of the Deccan College Research Institute*, 21, 1961.

GUJARAT: Wainwright, G. J., *The Pleistocene Deposits of the Lower Narbada River*, M. S. University Archaeology and Ancient History Series, No. 7, Baroda, 1964.

Zeuner, F. E., *Stone Age and Pleistocene Chronology in Gujarat*, Deccan College Monograph Series, No. 6, Poona, 1960.

BOMBAY AND MAHARASHTRA: Malik, S. C., *Stone Age Industries in Bombay and Satara Districts*, M. S. University Archaeology and Ancient History Series No. 4, Baroda; Sankalia, H. D., 'Animal Fossils and Palaeolithic Industries from the Pravara Basin at Nevasa, District Ahmednagar', *Ancient India*, 12, 1956.

Todd, K. R. U., 'Palaeolithic Industries of Bombay', *Journal of the Royal Anthropological Institute*, 69, 1939.

CENTRAL INDIA: Joshi, R. V., 'Narmada Pleistocene Deposits at Maheshwar', *Journal of the Palaeontological Society of India*, 2, 1958.

Joshi, R. V., 'Stone Industries of the Damoh Area, Madhya Pradesh', *Ancient India*, 12, 1961.

Joshi, R. V., 'Acheulian Succession in Central India', *Asian Perspectives*, vol. 8, 1, 1964.

Sen, D. and Ghosh, A. K., 'Lithic Culture Complex in the

Pleistocene Sequence of the Narbada Valley, Central India', *Rivista di Scienze Preistoriche*, 18, fasc. 1–4, 1963.

de Terra, H. and Paterson, T. T., 1939, op. cit.

EASTERN INDIA: Mohapatra, G. C., *The Stone Age Cultures of Orissa*, Deccan College Research Series, Poona, 1962.

SOUTHERN INDIA: Burkitt, M. C. and Cammiade, L. A., 'Fresh Light on the Stone Age of Eastern India', *Antiquity*, vol. 4, 15, 1930.

Krishnaswami, V. D., 'Environmental and Cultural Changes of Prehistoric Man near Madras', *Journal of the Madras Geographical Association*, 13, 1938.

Soundara Rajan, K. V., 'Stone Age Industries near Giddalur District Kurnool', *Ancient India*, 8, 1952.

Soundara Rajan, K. V., 'Studies in the Stone Age of Nagarjunakonda and its Neighbourhood', *Ancient India*, 14, 1958.

CEYLON: Allchin, B., 'The Late Stone Age of Ceylon', *Journal of the Royal Anthropological Institute*, 88, 1958.

Hartley, C., 'The stone implements of Ceylon', *Spolia Zeylanica*, 9, 1913.

Hartley, C., 'On the occurrence of pigmy implements in Ceylon', *Spolia Zeylanica*, 10, 1914.

4. *Special topics*

Specific problems or phases of the Stone Age are dealt with in the following books and papers:

Lal, B. B., 'Palaeoliths from the Beas and Banganga Valleys, Panjab', *Ancient India*, 12, 1956. This paper discusses the relationship of the hand-axe and chopping-tool traditions throughout the subcontinent.

Allchin, B., 'The Indian Middle Stone Age', *Bulletin of the Institute of Archaeology*, (London), 2, 1959.

Sankalia, H. D., 'Middle Stone Age Culture in India and Pakistan', *Science*, vol. 146, 3642, 1964.

Allchin, B., *The Stone Tipped Arrow*, London, 1966; chapters 4, 5 and 6 deal with the Late Stone Age of northern and southern India and Ceylon respectively.

Lal, B. B., 'Birbhanpur, a Microlithic Site in the Damodar Valley', *Ancient India*, 14, 1958.

Todd, K. R. U., 'A Microlithic Industry in Eastern Mysore', *Man*, 27, 1948.

Todd, K. R. U., 'The Microlithic Industries of Bombay', *Ancient India*, 6, 1950.

Zeuner, F. E. and Allchin, B., 'The Microlithic Sites of the Tinnevelly District, Madras State', *Ancient India*, 12, 1956.

Dani, A. H., 'Sanghao excavation: the first season, 1963', *Ancient Pakistan*, 1, 1964.

Joshi, R. V., (in press), 'Late Mesolithic Culture in Central India'.

CHAPTER 5

1. *Introduction*

A useful summary of contemporary evidence on the first settled communities in North Syria and Mesopotamia, Anatolia, etc., is to be found in R. W. Ehrich's *Chronologies in Old World Archaeology*, 2nd edn, Chicago, 1965. The same book has a section on Iran and an excellent summary of the evidence from Baluchistan and Afghanistan by G. F. Dales (in each case with further bibliography). For general discussion of cultural matters relating to the transformation to food production, see R. J. Braidwood and B. Howe, *Prehistoric Investigations in Iraqi Kurdistan*, Chicago, 1960.

2. *Earliest settlements in Baluchistan*

MUNDIGAK: Casal, J.-M., *Fouilles de Mundigak*, 2 vols, Paris, 1961.

KILI GHUL MOHAMMAD AND DAMB SADAAT: Fairservis, W. A., *Excavations in the Quetta Valley*, New York, 1956.

RANA GHUNDAI: Ross, E. J., 'A Chalcolithic Site in North Baluchistan', *Journal of Near Eastern Studies*, vol. 5, 1946.
Piggott, S., *Prehistoric India*, London, 1950.
Fairservis, W. A., *Archaeological surveys in the Zhob and Loralai districts*, New York, 1959.

ANJIRA AND SIAH DAMB: de Cardi, B., *Pakistan Archaeology*, 2, 1965, pp. 86–182.

OTHER SITES: Piggott, op. cit. 1950, and D. H. Gordon, *Prehistoric Background of Indian Culture*, Bombay, 1958.

For the Pirak ware and its possible significance, see R. L. Raikes, 'New prehistoric bichrome ware from the plains of Baluchistan', *East and West*, 14, 1963, and 'Supplementary note on Pirak Bichrome ware', *East and West*, 15, 1965.
For a study of the human skeletal materials from Mundigak,

see C. Mendrez, 'Étude anthropologique', *Bulletin de l'Ecole Française de l'Extrême Orient*, 53, 1966, pp. 99–118.

3. *Pre-Harappan settlements of Sind, Punjab and North Rajputana*

For the ancient geography of the Indus valley, see H. T. Lambrick's *Sind*, Hyderabad, 1964.

AMRI: Casal, J.-M. *Fouilles d'Amri*, 2 vols, Paris, 1964.

KOT DIJI: Khan, F. A., *Pakistan Archaeology*, 2, 1965, pp. 11–85.

HARAPPA: The pre-defence pottery is published by Sir Mortimer Wheeler in *Ancient India*, 3, Calcutta, 1947, pp. 91–97.

KALIBANGAN: *Indian Archaeology – a Review*, 1961, pp. 30–31; 1961–2, pp. 39–44; 1962–3, pp. 20–31, etc.

OTHER SITES IN SIND: Majumdar, N. G., 'Explorations in Sind', *Memoirs of the Archaeological Survey of India*, 48, Delhi, 1934.

CHAPTER 6

1. *The Indus civilization*

The best general introductions to the Indus civilization are to be found in Professor Piggott's *Prehistoric India*, London, 1950; Gordon Childe's *New Light on the Most Ancient East*, 4th edn, Routledge, 1952, ch. 9; D. H. Gordon, *The Prehistoric Background of Indian Culture*, Bombay, 1958, ch. 4; and particularly Sir Mortimer Wheeler, *The Indus Civilization*, 3rd edn, Cambridge University Press, 1968. These provide further bibliography. See also Professor H. Mode's *Indische Frühkulturen*, Basel, 1944; and *Das Frühe Indien*, Stuttgart, 1959. The original excavation reports are still essential reading: Sir John Marshall, *Mohenjo-daro and the Indus Civilization*, 3 vols, London, 1931; E. J. H. Mackay, *Further Excavations at Mohenjo-daro*, 2 vols, New Delhi, 1938; M. S. Vats, *Excavations at Harappa*, 2 vols, Delhi, 1941; E. J. H. Mackay, *Chanhu-daro Excavations*, New Haven, Connecticut, 1943. More recent excavations are:

AMRI: Casal, J.-M., *Fouilles d'Amri*, 2 vols, Paris, 1964.

ALAMGIRPUR: *Indian Archaeology – a Review*,* 1958–9.

KALIBANGAN: *IAR*, 1960–61, 1961–2, 1962–3, 1963–4, 1964–5.

* For the sake of brevity *Indian Archaeology – A Review* is abbreviated to *IAR* in this and subsequent chapters.

Lal B.B. and Thapar, B.K. 'Excavations at Kalibangan, new light on the Indus civilization', *Cultural Forum*, 34, 1967.

LOTHAL: *IAR*, 1954–5, 1955–6, 1956–7, 1957–8, 1958–9.

RUPAR: *IAR*, 1953–4.

DESALPAR: *IAR*, 1963–4.

ROJDI (ROJADI): *IAR*, 1957–8, 1958–9, 1962–3.

KOT DIJI: *Pakistan Archaeology*, 2, 1965.

SUTKAGEN DOR AND SOTKA KOH: Dales, G. F., 'Harappan Outposts on the Makran Coast', *Antiquity*, 36, 1962. Stein, Sir M. Aurel, 'An Archaeological Tour in Gedrosia', *Memoirs of the Archaeological Survey of India*, No. 43, 1931.

MOHENJO-DARO: Dales, G. F., 'New investigations at Mohenjo-daro', *Archaeology*, 18, 1965.

For western contacts and cross-datings, see C. J. Gadd, 'Seals of Ancient Indian Style found at Ur', *Proceedings of the British Academy*, 1932; A. L. Oppenheim, 'Seafaring merchants of Ur', *Journal of the American Oriental Society*, 74, 1954, pp. 6–17; W. F. Leemans, *Foreign trade in the Old Babylonian Period*, Leiden, 1960. On 'Persian Gulf' seals and allied matters, see E. Porada in *Chronologies in Old World Archaeology*, 1965, p. 171; see also B. Buchanan, 'A dated seal impression connecting Babylonia with ancient India', *Archaeology*, vol. 20, 1967. On radiocarbon datings, D. P. Agrawal, 'Harappan chronology: a re-examination of the evidence', in *Studies in Prehistory*, Calcutta, 1966. On chronology, W. A. Fairservis, 'The chronology of the Harappan civilization and the Aryan invasions', in *Man*, 56, 1956; and R. Heine-Geldern, 'The coming of the Aryans and the end of the Harappa culture', in *Man*, 56, 1956.

For reports on skeletal materials from the excavations, see S. S. Sarkar, *Ancient Races of Baluchistan, Panjab and Sind*, Calcutta, 1964; P. Gupta, P. C. Dutta and A. Basu, *Human Skeletal Remains from Harappa*, Calcutta, 1962; R. B. S. Sewell and B. S. Guha, 'Human Remains' in Marshall, *Mohenjo-daro and the Indus Civilization*.

On the Harappan script, see A. H. Dani, *Indian Palaeography*, Oxford University Press, 1963 (with further bibliography); G. R. Hunter, *The Script of Harappa and Mohenjo-daro*, Kegan Paul, 1934. Recent contributions to this subject include S. K. Ray's *Indus Script*, no date, New Delhi; the same author's *Indus Script* (*Memorandum No. 2*), New Delhi, 1965, and *Indus Script*:

Methods of My Study, New Delhi, 1966; B. B. Lal has proved the direction of writing, see his paper 'The direction of writing in the Harappan Script', *Antiquity*, 40, 1965. For the system of weights, see A. S. Hemmy in Marshall, 1931, ch. 29, pp. 589–98.

On the end of the civilization, see R. L. Raikes, 'The end of the ancient cities of the Indus', *American Anthropology*, 1964; the same author's 'The Mohenjo-daro floods', *Antiquity*, 40, 1965; G. F. Dales, 'New investigations at Mohenjo-daro', *Archaeology*, 18, 1965. See also H. T. Lambrick, 'The Indus flood-plain and the "Indus" civilization', *Geographical Journal*, 133, 1967.

2. *The Aryan invasions*

On the Aryans in general, V. G. Childe's, *The Aryans*, 1926, is still basic. See also E. Herzfeld, *Iran in the Ancient East*, Oxford University Press, 1936. For the domestication of the horse, see F. E. Zeuner, *History of Domestication of Animals*, Hutchinson, 1963. For Caucasian and other evidence, C. Schaeffer's *Stratigraphie comparée*, Oxford University Press, 1948, is most useful. In dating the foreign metal imports, we have generally followed Piggott, op. cit., 1950, although Gordon, op. cit., 1958, makes several useful emendations. See also Piggott's 'Notes on certain metal pins and a mace-head in the Harappa culture', *Ancient India*, pp. 26–40. The Moghul Ghundai cairns are published in Stein's *Archaeological Tour in Waziristan and Northern Baluchistan*, Memoirs of the Archaeological Survey of India, No. 37, Delhi, 1929. For the Gilgit bronzes, see K. Jettmar, 'Bronze axes from the Karakoram', *Proceedings of the American Philosophical Society*, 105, 1961. For the trunnion axe in Iran see R. Maxwell Hyslop, 'Bronze lugged axe or adze-blades from Asia', in *Iraq*, vol. 15, 1953, pp. 69–87. For the Swat cairn graves, see A. H. Dani and F. A. Durrani, 'A new grave complex in W. Pakistan', *Asian Perspectives*, 1964, p. 164, and C. S. Antonini, 'Preliminary note on the excavation of the necropolises found in West Pakistan', *East and West*, 14, 1963, and G. Genna, 'First anthropological investigations of the skeletal remains of the Necropolis of Butkara', *East and West*, 15, 1964. The Khurdi hoard is published in *IAR*, 1960–61, and illustrated in the *Handbook to the Centenary Exhibition*, New Delhi, 1961, Plate 3. For a discussion of the references to *arma*, *armaka* in Vedic literature, see T. Burrow in *Journal of Indian History*, 41, 1963. For a general discussion of the literary evidence, see R. C. Majumdar (ed.), *History and culture of the Indian people*, vol. 1, 'The Vedic Age', London, 1951 (with extensive bibliography).

CHAPTER 7

1. *Neolithic groups and cultures*

General. For general discussion of the occurrence and significance of Neolithic tools in India, see E. C. Worman, 'The Neolithic problem in the prehistory of India', *J. Washington Acad. Sci.*, 30, 1949; V. D. Krishnaswami, 'The Neolithic pattern of India', *Ancient India*, 16, Delhi, 1960; B. K. Thapar, 'Neolithic problem in India', *Indian Prehistory: 1964*, Poona, 1965. For east Indian tools and their relations with those of China and Southeast Asia, see A. H. Dani, *Prehistory and Protohistory of Eastern India*, Calcutta, 1960.

NORTHERN NEOLITHIC: The excavations at Burzahom are so far only in summary reports in *IAR*, 1960–61, 1961–2, 1962–3. For the Chinese parallels, see T. K. Cheng, *Archaeology in China*, vol. 1, Cambridge University Press, 1959, and K. C. Chang, *Archaeology of Ancient China*, New Haven, 1963. For the Siberian parallels, see A. P. Okladnikov, 'The Shilka Cave', translated in H. N. Michael's *Archaeology and Geomorphology of Northern Asia*, Toronto, 1964. The Siberian Neolithic cultures provide much interesting comparative material on northern Neolithic economies. The Mongolian evidence is in J. Maringer's, *Contribution to the Prehistory of Mongolia*, Stockholm, 1950.

SOUTHERN GROUP: The principal excavations are:

Brahmagiri: Sir R. E. M. Wheeler, *Ancient India*, 4, 1947.

Sanganakallu: Subbarao, B., *Stone Age Cultures of Bellary*, Poona, 1948.

Piklihal: Allchin, F. R., *Piklihal Excavations*, Hyderabad, 1960.

Maski: Thapar, B. K., *Ancient India*, 13, 1957.

Tekkalakota: Nagaraja Rao, M. S., *Stone Age Hill Dwellers of Tekkalakota*, Poona, 1965.

Utnur: Allchin, F. R., *Neolithic Cattle-Keepers of South India*, Cambridge University Press, 1963.

T. Narsipur: *IAR*, 1959–60, 1961–2.

Hallur: *IAR*, 1964–5.

EASTERN GROUP: The only excavation so far reported is Daojali Hading, *IAR*, 1963–4. See also T. C. Sharma, 'A note on the neolithic pottery of Assam', *Man* 1967, pp. 126–8. Surface collections have been analysed, with rather unsatisfactory illustrations, by A. H. Dani in his *Pre-history and Protohistory of Eastern India*, Calcutta, 1960, and more recently by Dr T. C. Sharma in his as yet unpublished Ph.D. thesis (London, 1966) on the 'Prehistoric Archaeology of Assam'.

CENTRAL GROUP: Very little is published on this area. See W. Theobald's paper on 'Celts found in Bundelkhand' in *Proceedings of the Asiatic Society of Bengal*, 1862, and H. Rivett-Carnac's 'Stone implements found in the Banda district', *Proceedings of the Asiatic Society of Bengal*, 1882.

EASTERN CENTRAL GROUP: The Kuchai excavation, *IAR*, 1961–2; G. Anderson's paper on 'Notes on prehistoric implements found in Singbhum district', *J. Bihar and Orissa Res. Soc.*, 1917; P. O. Bodding's papers on the Santal collections, in *Journal of the Asiatic Society of Bengal*, 1901, 1904; and F. R. Allchin's paper on 'The Neolithic Industry of the Santal Parganas', *Bulletin of the School of Oriental and African Studies*, 1962.

2. *Expansion of post-Harappan cultures*

Regrettably few of the excavations mentioned in this section have yet been published in full. All those from *Indian Archaeology – A Review*, are short summaries of the season's work. A useful survey of much of this evidence is given by J. P. Joshi, 'Comparative stratigraphy of the protohistoric cultures of the Indo-Pakistan subcontinent', *Eastern Anthropologist*, 15, 1962.

SAURASHTRA: Rangpur: 'Excavation at Rangpur and other explorations in Gujarat', by S. R. Rao, *Ancient India*, 18 and 19, 1963, pp. 5–207.
Somnath (Prabhas Patan): *IAR*, 1955–6, 1956–7.
Rojadi: *IAR*, 1957–8, 1958–9, 1962–3.
Lothal: see references in Chapter 6.

RAJPUTANA (BANAS CULTURE): Ahar: *IAR*, 1954–5, 1955–6, 1961–2.
Gilund: *IAR*, 1959–60.

PUNJAB: Rupar and Bara: *IAR*, 1953–4.

MALWA: Navdatoli: H. D. Sankalia, B. Subbarao and S. B. Deo, *Excavations at Maheshwar and Navdatoli, 1952–53*, Poona, 1958, pp. 1–257; *IAR*, 1957–8.

Nagda: *IAR*, 1955–6.

MAHARASHTRA: Nevasa: H. D. Sankalia *et al.*, *From History to Pre-History at Nevasa (1954–56)*, Poona, 1960, pp. 1–549.

Jorwe: H. D. Sankalia and S. B. Deo, *Excavations at Nasik and Jorwe*, Poona, 1955.

Chandoli: S. B. Deo and Z. D. Ansari, *Chalcolithic Chandoli*, Poona, 1965

Prakash: Thapar, B. K., 'Prakash 1955', *Ancient India* 20 & 21, 1964 and 65, pp. 5–167; *IAR*, 1954–5.

Daimabad: *IAR*, 1958–9; Bahal: *IAR*, 1956–7; Sonegaon; *IAR*, 1964–5; Bahurupa, Sawalda: *IAR*, 1959–60.

CENTRAL INDIA, BENGAL AND EASTERN COASTAL INDIA: Tripuri: M. G. Dikshit, *Tripuri – 1952*, Nagpur, 1955.

Eran: *IAR*, 1960–61, 1963–4. Pandu Rajar Dhibi: *IAR*, 1961–2 and P. C. Das Gupta, *Excavations at Pandu Rajar Dhibi*, *Calcutta*, 1964. Mahisadal: *IAR*, 1963–4.

Patpad: F. R. Allchin, 'Painted pottery from Patpad', *Antiquity*, vol. 36, 143, 1961, pp. 221–4.

Kesarapalli: *IAR*, 1961–2.

GANGES-JAMUNA DOAB: On the copper hoards, see B. B. Lal, 'Further copper hoards from the Gangetic Basin', *Ancient India*, 7, 1951, with extensive bibliography.

Hastinapura: B. B. Lal, 'Excavations at Hastinapura', *Ancient India*, 10 and 11, 1954 and 1955.

Atranjikhera: *IAR*, 1962–3.

CHAPTER 8

1. *General*

For a useful survey of evidence at this time, see N. R. Banerjee's *Iron Age in India*, Delhi, 1965. For iron technology in India, see bibliography for Chapter 11. See also N. R. Banerjee's paper 'The Iron Age in India', *Indian Prehistory: 1964*, Poona, 1965, and subsequent discussion. For general synthesis, see also J. P. Joshi's 'Comparative stratigraphy of protohistoric cultures of the Indo-Pakistan subcontinent', *Eastern Anthropologist*, 15, 1962.

2. *Iron Age settlements*

Many of the sites have already been referred to in the previous chapter.

PUNJAB AND DOAB: In addition to Rupar, Hastinapur, etc.,

the following excavations are noteworthy: Noh, *IAR*, 1963–4, 1964–5; Alamgirpur, *IAR*, 1958–9; Autha, *IAR*, 1964–5; Ahicchatra, *IAR*, 1963–4.

CENTRAL GANGES VALLEY: Sonepur: *IAR*, 1956–7, 1959–60, 1960–61, 1961–2.
Chirand: *IAR*, 1962–3, 1963–4, 1964–5.
Prahladpur: *IAR*, 1962–3.
Buxar: *IAR*, 1963–4.
Rajghat (Banaras): *IAR*, 1960–61, 1961–2, 1962–3.
Kausambi: G. R. Sharma, *Excavations at Kausambi (1957–59)*, Allahabad, 1960; *IAR*, 1959–60, 1960–61, 1961–2.

SAURASHTRA, MALWA, CENTRAL INDIA: sites already quoted in previous chapters. Broach: *IAR*, 1959–60; Nagal: *IAR*, 1961–2; Nagara (Cambay): *IAR*, 1963–4, 1964–5.

MAHARASHTRA: Tekwada: *IAR*, 1956–7.
Ranjala: *IAR*, 1960–61.

KARNATAKA: In addition to sites mentioned in Chapter 6, see also Paiyampalli: *IAR*, 1964–5.

TAMILNAD: Arikamedu: J.-M. Casal, *Fouilles de Virampatnam*, Paris, 1949.
Kunnattur: *IAR*, 1954–5, 1955–6, 1956–7.
Tirukkambuliyur: *IAR*, 1961–2.
Alagarai: *IAR*, 1963–4.

3. *The south Indian Iron Age grave complex*

'A bibliography on Indian megaliths' by K. S. Ramachandran is published in the *Quarterly Journal of the Mythic Society of Bangalore*, vols 52, 1961, and 53, 1962–3. Useful summaries of the evidence are to be found in *Antiquités Nationales et Internationales*, fascs. 3 and 4, September 1960, Paris, Centre d'études pré- et protohistoriques de l'École Pratique des Hautes Études (Sorbonne), section 6, by N. R. Banerjee; and by V. D. Krishnaswami 'Megalithic types of south India', *Ancient India*, 5, 1949. On the stone alignments, see F. R. Allchin, 'The stone alignments of southern Hyderabad', *Man*, 56, 1956. On early literary references in Tamil, see K. R. Srinivasan, 'Megalithic burials and urn fields in south India in the light of Tamil literature and tradition', *Ancient India*, 2, 1946, and 'Megalithic monuments of south India', in *Trans. Arch. Soc. S. India*, 1958–9. For the scratched marks on the black-and-red pottery, see B. B. Lal,

'From the megalithic to the Harappa', *Ancient India*, 16, 1960.
For a note on horse furniture in graves, see K. S. Ramachandran, 'Bridle bits from Indian megaliths', *Quarterly Journal of the Mythic Society of Bangalore*, LI, 1961, pp. 170–2.

Among recent excavations the following are noteworthy:

Wheelcr, Sir R. E. M., 'Brahmagiri and Chandravalli', *Ancient India*, 4, 1947–8.

Thapar, B. K., 'Maski, 1954', *Ancient India*, 13, 1957.

Banerji, N. R. and Soundararajan, K. V., 'Sanur 1950 and 1952', *Ancient India*, 15, 1959.

Thapar, B. K., 'Porkalam 1948', *Ancient India*, 8, 1952.

Arikamedu, etc.: Casal, J.-M. and G., *Site urbain et sites funéraires des environs de Pondichérry*, Paris, 1956.

Jadigenahalli: Seshadri, M., *Report on the Jadigenahalli megalithic excavations*, Mysore, 1960.

CHAPTER 9

1. *Patterns of settlement*

Apart from the works already quoted in previous chapters, there are a number of papers dealing specifically with settlements. Among them we may mention Professor H. D. Sankalia's 'Houses and habitations through the ages', *Bulletin of the Deccan College Research Institute* (S. K. De Felicitation Volume); M. S. Nagaraja Rao, 'Survival of certain Neolithic elements among the Boyas of Tekkalakota', *Anthropos*, vol. 60, 1965, pp. 482–6, and 'New evidence for Neolithic life in India: excavations in the southern Deccan', *Archaeology*, vol. 20, No 1, 1967. W. A. Fairservis has discussed the settlements of Baluchistan and the Indus valley in his paper 'The Harappan civilization – new evidence and more theory', *American Museum Novitates*, 2055, 1961.

CHAPTER 10

1. *Agriculture*

Most of the identifications of flora and fauna are to be found in the excavation reports already listed in Chapters 3–8. There are several monographs dealing with these topics: B. Prasad, 'Animal remains from Harappa', *Memoirs of the Archaeological Survey of India*, 51, 1936; Vishnu Mittre, 'Plant economy in ancient Navdatoli and Maheshwar', *Technical reports on archaeological remains*, Poona, 1961; J. Clutton-Brock, *Excavations at Langhnaj, 1944–63, Part II, The Fauna*, Poona, 1965. For animal remains from Mundigak, see J. B. Poulain, 'Étude de la faune', in *Bulletin de l'Ecole Française de l'Extrême Orient* 1966, 53, pp. 119–35. On the horse in the Indus civilization, see Bholanath, 'Remains of the horse and the Indian elephant from the prehistoric site of Harappa', *Proceedings of the First All-India Congress of Zoology*, 1959. D. D. Kosambi's *Introduction to the Study of Indian History*, Bombay, 1956, has many stimulating ideas on early Indian agriculture. See also H. T. Lambrick's *Sind*, Hyderabad, 1964. On irrigation and climate in Baluchistan, see R. L. Raikes and R. H. Dyson, 'The Prehistoric climate of the Indus and Baluchistan', *American Anthropology*, 1961; and R. L. Raikes, 'The ancient gabarbands of Baluchistan', *East and West*, 15, 1965.

2. *Trade and economy*

Further references on trade include: S. R. Rao, 'Shipping and maritime trade of the Indus people', *Expedition*, 1965, pp. 30–37; W. F. Leemans, *Foreign trade in the Old Babylonian period*, Leiden, 1960; T. G. Bibby, 'The ancient Indian style seals from Bahrain', *Antiquity*, 32, 1958, p. 128; A. L. Oppenheim, 'Seafaring merchants from Ur', *JAOS*, 1954; S. N. Kramer, 'Dilmun, quest for paradise', *Antiquity*, 37, 1963 (where the case for identifying Tilmun with a west Indian location is discussed); B. K. Thapar, 'Relationship of the Indian Chalcolithic Cultures with West Asia', *Indian Prehistory: 1964*, Poona, 1965; F. A. Khan, *The Indus Valley* and *Early Iran*, Karachi, 1964; H. D. Sankalia, 'New light on the Indo-Iranian or western Asiatic relations between 1700 B.C.–1200 B.C.', *Artibus Asiae*, 26, 1963, pp. 312–32; F.R. and B. Allchin, 'The archaeology of a river crossing', *Indian Anthropology*, Bombay, 1962, pp. 52–65.

CHAPTER 11

1. *Stone technology*

The only book which deals specifically with the techniques of manufacturing stone tools in India is H. D. Sankalia, *Stone Tools, Their Techniques, Names and Functions*, Poona, 1964. For an account of the manufacture of blades, see B. Subbarao, 'Chalcolithic blade industry of Maheshwar', *Bulletin of the Deccan College Research Institute*, 17, 1956. Other references are given in Chapters 3 and 4. For a general statement of stoneworking techniques throughout the world, see Kenneth Oakley, *Man the Tool-maker*, British Museum of Natural History, 1958.

2. *Copper and bronze*

No general study of ancient Indian copper and bronze technology has been made since P. Neogi's *Copper in Ancient India*, Calcutta, 1918, and this work is more concerned with literary sources than technology. However, many individual reports, particularly those of Sir John Marshall and others on the Indus valley sites, contain detailed analyses and other data of copper and bronze objects. A recent summary of the data is in C. C. Lamberg-Karlovsky's, 'Archaeology and metallurgical technology in prehistoric Afghanistan, India and Pakistan', *American Anthropologist*, 69, 1967.

3. *Gold-working and mining*

See L. Munn, 'Observations and notes on the method of ancient gold mining in southern India', *Tr. Min. Geol. Inst. India*, 30, 1936; F. R. Allchin, 'Upon the antiquity and methods of gold mining in ancient India', *J. Econ. Social. Hist. Orient*, 5, 1962 (with further bibliography).

4. *Iron*

An old but valuable book is P. Neogi's *Iron in Ancient India*, Calcutta, 1914. Since then most writers have limited themselves to literary references to iron. The most comprehensive account of the introduction of iron to India is in N. R. Banerjee's *Iron Age in India*, Delhi, 1965 (with extensive bibliography). See also L. Gopal, 'Antiquity of iron in India', *Uttar Bharati*, ix, 3, 1962; S. D. Singh, 'Iron in Ancient India', *J. Econ. Social Hist. Orient* 5, 1962. For modern primitive techniques, see V. Elwin, *The Agaria*, London, 1942; and W. Ruben, *Eisenschmiede und Dämonen in Indien*, Leiden, 1939.

5. *Pottery*

No general study of Indian pottery technology has so far appeared; the nearest approach is in Hindi, by Dr Govind Chand, *Ancient Indian Earthenware Vessels*, Banaras, 1960. Many excavation reports contain studies of technical aspects. Among special papers see E. Mackay, 'Painted pottery in modern Sind', *Journal of the Royal Anthropological Institute*, 60, 1930; F. R. Allchin, 'Poor men's thalis, a Deccan potter's technique', *Bulletin of the School of Oriental and African Studies*, 22, 1959.

6. *Other crafts*

P. Ray's *History of Chemistry in Ancient and Medieval India*, Calcutta, 1955, contains much interesting information on many aspects of Indian technology. For bead-making, see E. Mackay, 'Bead-making in ancient Sind', *Journal of the American Oriental Society*, 57, 1937, and M. G. Dikshit, *Etched Carnelian Beads in India*, Poona, 1949. For the early occurrence of glass see M. G. Dikshit's exhaustive *Glass in India*, Bombay, 1967.

CHAPTER 12

1. Cave art

Of the earlier literature the most comprehensive survey was by M. Ghosh, 'Rock paintings and other antiquities of prehistoric and later times', *Memoirs of the Archaeological Survey of India*, 24, 1932. A survey of the whole subject is in Gordon's *Prehistoric Background of Indian Culture*, Bombay, 1958, ch. 6. See also Gordon's papers on 'Indian rock paintings' in *Science and Culture*, 5, Calcutta, 1939. For examples of the South Indian bruisings and paintings, see Allchin, *Piklihal Excavations*, Hyderabad, 1961. In recent years V. S. Wakankar has contributed several useful articles, particularly 'Painted rock shelters of India', *Rivista di scienze preistoriche*, Florence, 1962. For Morhana Pahar chariots, see B. Allchin, 'Morhana Pahar, a rediscovery', *Man*, 58, 1958.

2. Painted pottery and terracottas

Most of the extensive literature on terracottas deals mainly with those of the early historic period, and is therefore not relevant to this book. Other references are to be found in works already quoted.

3. Art of the Indus civilization

The best statement on the various aspects of Harappan art is still to be found in Marshall's *Mohenjo-daro and the Indus Civilization*, particularly chs. 4, 18 and 19. Shorter statements are in works of Wheeler, Piggott, etc., quoted in earlier chapters.

4. Religion

There are few specifically archaeological studies of early Indian religion. On the religion of the Indus civilization, see Marshall's *Mohenjo-daro and the Indus Civilization*, ch. 5. The late Professor D. D. Kosambi has much to say which has bearing on ancient religion, see particularly his *Myth and Reality*, Bombay, 1962, and 'At the crossroads', *Journal of the Royal Asiatic Society*, 1960.

INDEX

Principal references are in **heavy** *type*

*A History of India is
described overleaf*

A HISTORY OF INDIA

VOLUME ONE

Romila Thapar

The first volume of this new history traces the evolution of India before contact with modern Europe was established in the sixteenth century. Romila Thapar is the Reader in History at the University of Delhi: her account of the development of India's social and economic structure is arranged within a framework of the principal political and dynastic events. Her narrative covers some 2,500 years of India's history, from the establishment of Aryan culture in about 1000 B.C. to the coming of the Mughals in A.D. 1526 and the first appearance of European trading companies. In particular she deals interestingly with the many manifestations of Indian culture, as seen in religion, art, and literature, in ideas and institutions.

VOLUME TWO

Percival Spear

Dr Spear, a specialist in Indian history, makes the unusual and illuminating approach to more recent Indian history of dealing with the Mughal and British periods together in one volume, on the principle of continuity. He views the Mughal rule as a preparation and a precondition for the modern age ushered in by the British Raj as a harbinger to India of western civilization, which precipitated the transformation of India that is still in progress.